AI and Expert Systems

Related Titles From McGraw-Hill

ISBN	AUTHOR	TITLE
0-07-852109-2	Thompson, Thompson	*MicroExpert Software for IBM PC*
0-07-024327-1	Greene	*Turning the Tables*
0-07-037495-3	Levine, Drang, Edelson	*AI and Expert Systems: A Comprehensive Guide, Turbo Pascal Version, 2/e*
0-07-037500-3	Levine, Drang, Edelson	*AI and Expert Systems: A Comprehensive Guide, C Language, 2/e*
0-07-044088-3	Murray, Murray	*Expert Systems in Data Processing, 2/e*
0-07-053614-7	Rolston	*Principles of Artificial Intelligence and Expert Systems Development*
0-07-061573-X	Stock	*AI Theory and Applications in the VAX Environment*
0-07-070407-4	Williams	*The Intelligent Micro*
0-07-008600-1	Brulé, Blount	*Knowledge Acquisition*
0-07-031606-6	Hwang, DeGroot	*Parallel Processing for Supercomputing and Artificial Intelligence*
0-07-001404-3	Allerhand (Ranade, Ed.)	*Knowledge-Based Speech Pattern Recognition*
0-07-023437-X	Girard, Jones	*Building Knowledge Systems*
0-07-026909-2	Hart	*Knowledge Acquisition for Expert Systems*
0-07-003350-1	Baker	*Artificial Intelligence with Ada*
0-07-006306-0	Bock	*Artificial Intelligence: An Introduction to Collective Learning Systems*
0-07-005397-9	Birnes	*The Microcomputer Applications Handbook*
0-07-005393-6	Birnes	*McGraw-Hill Personal Computer Programming Encyclopedia*
0-07-005395-2	Birnes	*On-Line Programming Languages and Assemblers*
0-07-005394-4	Birnes	*High-Level Languages and Software Applications Reference*
0-07-005396-0	Birnes	*PC Hardware and Systems Implementations*
0-07-057552-5	Simon	*How to Be a Successful Computer Consultant, 2/e*

For more information about other McGraw-Hill materials, call 1-800-2-MCGRAW in the United States. In other countries, call your nearest McGraw-Hill office.

AI and Expert Systems

A Comprehensive Guide, C Language

Robert I. Levine
Senior Research Engineer, Unisys Corporation

Diane E. Drang
Director of Educational Services, Jewish Board Family & Children's Services

Barry Edelson
Editor and author

Second Edition

McGraw-Hill, Inc.

New York St. Louis San Francisco Auckland Bogotá
Caracas Hamburg Lisbon London Madrid
Mexico Milan Montreal New Delhi Paris
San Juan São Paulo Singapore
Sydney Tokyo Toronto

Library of Congress Cataloging-in-Publication Data

Levine, Robert I.
    AI and expert systems: a comprehensive guide, C language / Robert
I. Levine, Diane E. Drang, Barry Edelson.—2nd ed.

        p.   cm.
    ISBN 0-07-037500-3
    1. Artificial intelligence.   2. Expert systems (Computer science)
I. Drang, Diane E.   II. Edelson, Barry.   III. Title.
Q335.L464   1990
006.3—dc20   90-32788

1234567890   DOC/DOC   9876543210

ISBN   0-07-037500-3

The sponsoring editor for this book was Theron Shreve, the editing
supervisor was Stephen M. Smith, the designer was Naomi
Auerbach, and the production supervisor was Suzanne W. Babeuf.
It was set in Century Schoolbook by Professional Composition, Inc.

Printed and bound by R. R. Donnelley & Sons Company.

For more information about other McGraw-Hill materials,
call 1-800-2-MCGRAW in the United States. In other
countries, call your nearest McGraw-Hill office.

Contents

Preface

Welcome to the inner workings of the brain. Let us take an odyssey into the understanding of how we learn, think, and reason. We will take you into the world of expert systems and neural networks, the second generation of artificial intelligence. Over the next few years, neural network programming techniques will invade many areas presently limited by expert system knowledge. The ability to increase domain knowledge beyond that of experts is necessary for the rapid advancement of artificial intelligence. Neural networks are already showing up in such areas as speech and vision systems. As artificial intelligence which contains expert systems and neural networks reaches more and more areas of daily living, the need to understand and the ability to apply the concepts will become more of a necessity.

This book introduces and explains the concepts of neural networks and advanced artificial intelligence in a language and a set of pictures that everyone can understand. We will take you into a more advanced world of artificial intelligence, showing you how to use many methods (multiple paradigms) for solving problems. Then we will bring all the concepts together by giving you an understanding of object oriented systems. These concepts will enable you to approach the design of both simple and advanced systems.

This book teaches applied concepts. All the programming you will see in these pages can be implemented on a first-generation personal and home computer. Short programs, written in C, are provided in each of the chapters that contain concepts. These programs are easy to use and understand.

This book provides you with a simple uncomplicated view of the first and second generation of artificial intelligence. It has been carefully planned so that each chapter is self-contained. This technique allows you to learn concepts without having to make frequent references to previous chapters. The combination of this technique, a simple approach, and examples that will appeal to a wide range of people makes this book required reading for anyone trying to understand the basic concepts. It is designed to be used by advanced students, corporate managers, and programmers as well as noncomputer people. There are many step-by-step illustrations and more than 50 examples. These are designed to make the subject matter very easy to understand.

Chapter 1 provides the reader with an overview of the concept of intelligence and how this concept can be identified.

Chapter 2 shows how this concept can be transferred to a computer to create artificial intelligence.

Chapter 3 discusses the concept of expert systems and its relationship to artificial intelligence.

Chapter 4 provides a brief and simple overview of natural language processing.

Chapter 5 discusses forward chaining, providing an extensive set of examples and a forward chaining tool written in C. The tool can be used in a limited way to experiment with the concepts; it can also be easily modified into a more powerful structure.

Chapter 6 discusses backward chaining in a way that is similar to Chapter 5. A backward chaining tool is also provided in this chapter.

Chapter 7 discusses bayesian probability and fuzzy conditions as they apply to expert systems. A programming example illustrating how the concepts can be applied to a rule-based system is provided.

Chapter 8 provides a discussion of the design of a truncated expert system for personal finance. This topic applies to anyone who has money dealings.

Chapter 9 provides a discussion of the design of a truncated expert system for optimizing a sales effort with a customer. This topic applies to all corporations and people since everyone is always selling something.

Chapter 10 discusses the design of an expert system that diagnoses learning problems. This is of interest to schools, corporations analyzing employee capabilities, concerned parents, and individuals.

Chapter 11 discusses object-oriented programming as it applies to expert systems. A set of examples which clearly illustrate some of the concepts is provided. An object-oriented system is written in C to allow you to experiment with the concepts.

Chapter 12 discusses an engineering application using object-oriented programming. A worked-out example is provided.

Chapter 13 provides an expert system example that issues flood warnings using object-oriented programming.

Chapters 14, 15, and 16 discuss semantic nets, certainty factors, and automated learning. A program in C is provided for each of these topics.

Chapter 17 discusses how PROLOG can be used as a tool for answering questions about a knowledge base. Examples illustrating the concepts are provided.

Chapter 18 discusses some basic concepts in LISP and provides you with some understanding of the language.

Chapter 19 discusses a conceptual overview of neural networks.

Chapter 20 provides software examples of neural networks.

Also included is a bibliography that provides you with a list of books and articles, which can be used to augment this book, and a short description of the pertinent topics contained in each.

If you're a student, a programmer, a home computer novice, a professional using a personal computer in your business, a person already involved in artificial intelligence, or just curious about it, this book is for you.

A disc containing all the listed programs in the book is available. If you would like to order one, please see the back of this book for further information and instructions.

Robert I. Levine
Diane E. Drang
Barry Edelson

Acknowledgment

We would like to acknowledge Professor Robert Hong of Grumman Corporation and Polytechnic Institute of New York for his thought-provoking seminars in artificial intelligence.

Human and Machine Intelligence

Section 1 introduces artificial intelligence and expert systems, acquainting us with how they work. Artificial intelligence is simply the transfer of intelligence to machines. Expert systems deal with a small area of expertise that can be converted from human to artificial intelligence.

We will take a close look at these concepts, using some common everyday experiences as examples. This will allow us to dissect the pieces of artificial intelligence and see how we can make them work for us. The process is simple, so let's get started.

1

An Overview of Intelligence

What Is Artificial Intelligence?

Artificial intelligence (AI) is simply a way of making a computer think intelligently. This is accomplished by studying how people think when they are trying to make decisions and solve problems, breaking those thought processes down into basic steps, and designing a computer program that solves problems using those same steps. AI thereby provides a simple, structured approach to designing complex decision-making programs.

What Is Programming Like
without Artificial Intelligence?

A standard computer program can only provide answers to problems for which it is specifically programmed. If a standard program needs to be modified in order to accommodate new information, the entire program may have to be scanned until the optimum space is found to insert the modification. This is not only time consuming, but other parts of the program may be adversely affected in the process and errors may result.

Artificial intelligence, as its name implies, really does enable a computer to think. By simplifying the way programs are put together, AI imitates the basic human learning process by which new information is absorbed and made available for future reference. The human mind can incorporate new knowledge without changing the way the mind works or disturbing all the other facts that are already stored in the brain. An AI program works in very much the same way. It will become apparent as you read this book that changes made to AI programs are far simpler to implement than those made to standard programs.

How Does Artificial Intelligence Make Programming Better?

AI techniques allow the construction of a program in which each piece of the program represents a highly independent and identifiable step toward the solution of a problem or set of problems. Let's consider this carefully. Each piece of the program is like a piece of information in a person's mind. If that information is disputed, the mind can automatically adjust its thinking to accommodate a new set of facts. One doesn't have to go about reconsidering every piece of information one has ever learned, only those few pieces that are relevant to the particular change.

A standard program can do everything an artificial intelligence program can do, but it cannot be programmed as easily or as quickly. In both types of programs, all pieces are interdependent in the way they carry out their designed function. But an AI program possesses a notable characteristic which is equivalent to a vital characteristic of human intelligence. Each minute piece can be modified without affecting the structure of the entire program. This flexibility provides greater programming efficiency and understandability—in a word, intelligence.

How Does Human Intelligence Work?

Since AI is a science rooted in human thought processes, an examination of how people think is essential. Of course, no one knows exactly how the mind works. Human intelligence is a complex function that scientists have only begun to understand, but enough is known for us to make certain assumptions about how we think and to apply those assumptions in designing AI programs.

Goals

All thinking helps us accomplish something. When the alarm clock rings in the morning, a thought process must be employed to guide your hand to the button to turn it off. It isn't an automatic reaction; a specific response was sought to solve a particular problem. The final results to which all our thought processes are directed are called "goals."

Once you have reached the goal of turning off the alarm, your mind is immediately confronted with other goals to be reached, such as getting to the bathroom, brushing your teeth, getting dressed, making and eating breakfast, going to the bus stop, and so on. These are all goals which, when accomplished, lead you to the ultimate goal of getting to work and getting there on time. None of the thoughts guiding you to this final result are random or arbitrary. They have been pressed into service because every step of the way you had a specific goal in mind. When engaged in the most simple physical task or the most complex mental activity, the mind is sharply focused on a goal. Without goals, we have no reason to think. Examples of various types of goals are listed below:

1. Mapping the shortest route between New York and Boston
2. Deciding on the best type of wine to drink with certain fish
3. Learning to tie my shoes
4. Deciding how to determine if my child understands the concepts of arithmetic

When designing an AI system, the goal of the system must always be kept in mind. Remember, we don't do things because we think, we think because there are things we have to do.

Now that we understand where our minds are going when they're at work, let's consider just how we arrive at the multitude of goals we must reach every day.

Facts and Rules

We all know that the human mind possesses a vast store of knowledge relating to a countless array of objects and ideas. Survival depends on our ability to apply this knowledge to any situation that arises and to continuously learn from new experiences so that we will be able to respond to similar situations in the future. What is generally considered to be "intelligence" can be broken down into a collection of facts and a means of utilizing these facts to reach goals. This is done, in part, by formulating sets of rules relating to all the facts stored in the brain. An example of the type of facts and related rules we use every day follows:

Fact/rule set 1
   Fact 1: A burning stove is hot.
   Rule 1: If I put my hand on a burning stove, THEN it will hurt.

Fact/rule set 2
    Fact 2: During rush hour, streets are crowded with cars.
    Rule 2: IF I try to cross a major highway on foot during rush hour, THEN I
        may get hit by a car.

Fact/rule set 3
    Fact 3a: Quiet dark streets are dangerous.
    Fact 3b: Old people usually don't commit violent crimes.
    Fact 3c: Police protect people from crime.
    Rule 3a: IF I am on a quiet dark street and I see an old person, THEN I
        should not particularly worry about my safety.
    Rule 3b: IF I am on a quiet dark street and see a police officer, THEN I
        should feel secure.

Fact/rule set 4
    Fact 4: When two digits whose sum is greater than nine are added, a carry-
        ing procedure is called for.
    Rule 4: IF I have to add a column of digits and the sum is greater than nine,
        THEN I must refer to fact 4 to know how to carry out the addition.

Notice that in the example just given all the rules are expressed in
an IF-THEN, or conditional, relationship. That is, IF a certain condition exists, THEN an action or other response will result. Some facts
are obviously more complicated than others, and some rules relate to
more than one fact. In general, human beings have the capacity to
relate very complex sets of rules and facts in the attempt to reach some
very complicated goals.

Pruning

When the human mind sets out to solve even the simplest problem, it
has a vast store of information on which to draw in determining the
proper course of action. Let's go back to the example we used earlier.
You step out of your house on your way to work, and you walk to the
street corner. As you wait to cross the street, your brain is bombarded
with all kinds of data. The speed and volume of the traffic, the distance
to the other curb, the traffic signals at the intersection—all these
factors must be considered before you make a move. In addition, an
enormous number of sensory impressions that are totally irrelevant to
the problem of crossing the street are also being processed at the same
time—weather conditions, the color and models of the passing cars, the
type and height of the trees on the edge of the curb, the appearance of
all the nearby buildings. You are also undoubtedly thinking about
where you are going and how quickly you want to get there, whom you
might see when you arrive, and so on.
    As you can see, if you had to deal with this multitude of directly

related, indirectly related, and totally unrelated facts before you stepped off the curb, you might very well stand there for years. If we do indeed have so many facts and rules to process all the time, how does the mind extract the right set of rules quickly to fit each particular situation? When you want to cross the street, how does the mind know to apply, among others, fact/rule set 2, which pertains to traffic, and not fact/rule set 4, which pertains to arithmetic?

There exists a more sophisticated system which guides the selection of a proper response to a specific situation. This process is known as "pruning." As its name suggests, pruning eliminates pathways of thought that are not relevant to the immediate objective of reaching a goal. Just as one might cut off the lower branches of a tree to help its overall growth, so the pruning mechanism in our brains cuts us off from any facts and rules that won't lead us to the goal. When the mind is confronted with a situation, the pruning mechanism guides the thought processes by focusing only on those rules that are pertinent to solving the immediate problem.

An overview of how pruning helps the brain to distinguish one set of rules from another is shown in Figure 1-1. In this case pruning helps us decide whether to take path A or path B. It does this with an IF-THEN test of a condition. If the condition is A, it takes path A; if B, it takes path B.

Pruning can be likened to the task of an office manager who delegates tasks according to a set of priorities. The secretary, the word processor, the clerk, and everyone else on the staff have their assigned jobs to perform. But when everyone is called upon to help complete a particular project quickly, someone must decide not merely what everyone has to do, but when they must do it. Without such decisions being made, some personnel might sit idle, waiting for others to com-

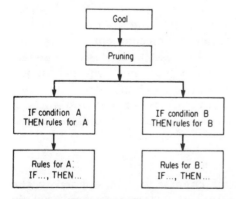

Figure 1-1   Pruning in action.

plete related tasks, while some might waste precious time performing tasks that can wait until later. A lot of work may get done, but all that good energy is wasted if, in the end result, the goal of putting the project together properly isn't met.

Without pruning, our brains would be crippled in much the same way the office would without the manager. We would have to process every rule in our brains for every single problem we had to solve. Everything we need to know to make decisions may be present in our brains all the time—like the capable members of the staff who are all doing what they're supposed to be doing—but unless the right information is pulled out at just the right time, all our knowledge is wasted. Pruning provides a vital order to our thoughts, without which life would not merely be slowed down, as in the office, but would be virtually impossible.

Inference Mechanism

When we reach a goal, we are not only solving an immediate problem but are also acquiring new knowledge at the same time. Consider the following information:

1. Jim's parents are John and Mary.
2. Jane's parents are John and Mary.

The goal is to determine the relationship between John and Jane. Pruning zeroes in on a rule safely tucked away in the brain that instantly ends the mystery: IF a male person and a female person have the same parents, THEN they are brother and sister.

We reach our goal by inferring the answer to the question of Jim and Jane's relationship from the rule we had previously learned. And in the process of reaching the goal, a new fact is derived: Jim and Jane are brother and sister. The portion of the intelligence that helped us arrive at this new fact is called the "inference mechanism." It is central to our ability to learn from experience because it enables us to generate new facts from existing ones by applying already acquired knowledge to new situations. We will see in the next chapter that the inference mechanism also aids in the detection of errors in our thinking and allows us to modify and improve the rules we use in reaching the goals.

Summary

Since the concepts described in this chapter will be applied in the following chapters to artificial intelligence systems, we should briefly review what we've discussed so far.

1. A specific goal sets our thought process in motion.

2. A vast collection of facts and their related rules wait to be called upon to help reach the goal.

3. Pruning helps us carry out a quick efficient search for only those rules that pertain to the immediate goal.

4. The inference mechanism completes the process by drawing inferences from the rules called upon by the pruning mechanism and by generating new facts that instantly become a part of our storehouse of knowledge.

Developing an Artificial Intelligence System

All the elements that comprise the human decision-making process—goals, facts, rules, inference mechanism, and pruning—must be collected in a computer program for it to be properly described as possessing artificial intelligence. All the AI system designs we will discuss in this book have the same basic configuration. Figure 2-1 illustrates the components of a rule-based AI system.

This program structure, which is based on the separate identification of its various components, is the single most important factor in making AI programming superior to ordinary programming. Modifications can be made to one or more of the parts of the design without upsetting the structure of the entire system. This design concept is also revolutionary in another fundamental way. Because we've identified the elements that comprise human thought processes, we can transfer the way we think about any problem into the AI program. If we can determine what our minds do at a given stage of any decision-making process, we can easily find in this program design a section that corresponds to an equivalent aspect of human intelligence.

Defining Goals

Since reaching goals is the aim of any AI system, the first step in designing such a system is to define a set of goals. You must know what sort of problem you want to solve and be able to describe the problem in concrete terms before you can go about creating a program to solve it.

Let's go back to the goal of getting to work, which we talked about in Chapter 1. We will assume that your beautifully designed human intelligence system has guided you safely and quickly across the street. Now you are waiting at the bus stop, and you have only a moment or two to consider which of two buses that pick up passengers on this corner is the best one for you to take this morning. Only a half a block away is the bus that makes all the local stops, and it's approaching fast. Do you want to board the local bus or wait for the express bus? This decision—which bus will be better—is the goal.

There are any number of essential facts to be weighed before the decision can be made, all based on prior experience in traveling on the buses to work. For instance, how long will it be before the express bus arrives? On which bus will I be more likely to get a seat? Certain rules are called into play as well, thanks to pruning, such as "IF I have to wait more than 10 minutes for the express bus, THEN it will take longer for me to get to work than if I'd taken the local bus." Rules are at work all the time, even those within the pruning mechanism which oversee all thought processes by locating the specific rules needed to make the decision at hand. Facts and rules related to the tasks that await you when you arrive at work have no bearing at all on the goal of getting there. Similarly, in an AI program, all facts and rules are irrelevant except those that aid in reaching the stated goal.

Let's now focus on another goal, which is one of the goals we will discuss extensively in Section 3 when we design actual AI programs. The goal is to determine if a child has learning problems in arithmetic. This may seem like a radical departure from the example we have just been using, but that is precisely why we've chosen it: to make it perfectly clear that our basic thought processes are the same when we try to solve similar problems and that the same fundamental AI system design can be utilized to reach a vast range of goals, however diverse

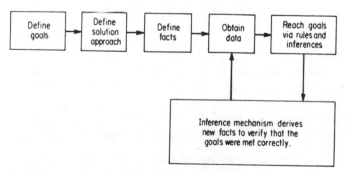

Figure 2-1 Components of a rule-based AI system.

they may appear. Our new goal can be broken down into different areas of arithmetic and can be expressed in several different ways:

Does PERSON have a learning problem in ADDITION?

Does PERSON have a learning problem in SUBTRACTION?

Does PERSON have a learning problem in MULTIPLICATION?

Does PERSON have a learning problem in DIVISION?

The object PERSON is known as a variable because it does not represent a specific individual but *any* individual. We have made PERSON a variable so that we can use the same goals in evaluating many different people, just as we might have made bus a variable in our previous example so that we might be able to consider the route of any bus. The way to represent the variable with an actual person is to substitute a person's name for that variable. The way to represent a variable with a person in a computer is by the following C statements:

```
printf( " ENTER NAME OF PERSON BEING EVALUATED? " );

gets(&PERSON);
```

When this C input statement is executed by the computer, the following will appear on the screen:

```
ENTER NAME OF PERSON BEING EVALUATED?
```

You would then enter the name of the person—let's say, Andrew Jones—in response to the computer's question. Whenever the variable PERSON is now referred to anywhere in the facts, rules, or goals, the name Andrew Jones will be substituted for it. When a variable has been assigned a specific value, it is referred to as "instantiated." We can now say that our goal is to find out if the individual Andrew Jones has a learning problem in any or all areas of arithmetic.

Defining Facts

Facts are an essential ingredient in an AI system. Without them, there would be no way to reach the goals. To reach the goal of deciding which bus to take, some supporting facts specific to that situation were needed. Obviously, as every predicament has its own particular scenario, every goal has its own facts. Let's concentrate on just one of the arithmetic goals to see how the use of facts is implemented:

Does PERSON have a learning problem in subtraction?

Subtraction is a function that requires certain mathematical skills. These skills are the facts that support the goal, some of which follow. In order to subtract, a person must be able to

1. Subtract two numbers without borrowing (2)
2. Subtract two numbers with single column borrowing (1)
3. Subtract two numbers with multiple column borrowing (1)

The numbers in parentheses at the end of the facts represent their relative importance to one another in our evaluation of the individual's learning problem. These numbers are similar to ones we are given on school tests. Some test questions are worth more than others. Each of the facts defines a required skill for mastering subtraction, and the inability to perform any one of these skills indicates a problem in this area. The higher the number assigned to each fact, the more important that fact is in contributing to a learning problem in subtraction. We will see shortly how placing these numerical values on facts is used in reaching goals.

Obtaining Data

Once the facts that we will use to reach the goal have been defined, we must acquire data that is needed to instantiate the variables. That is, we've established what people in general must know to do subtraction, but now we need to find out how much our subject, Andrew Jones, knows. To do this, the facts must first be turned into questions; the answers we receive are the data we can use as we move toward our goal. The list below shows what questions should be asked to obtain data about the facts listed under subtraction.

Can PERSON subtract two numbers without borrowing?

Can PERSON subtract two numbers with single column borrowing?

Can PERSON subtract two numbers with multiple column borrowing?

Just as we replace the variable PERSON with Andrew Jones, we replace the facts, as represented by these questions, with responses. The instantiated facts become the data. In simple terms, the yes and no answers we will receive are the data that we are assigning to the facts. This data is then placed in a database so that it can be analyzed in our evaluation of Andrew Jones' possible learning problem. We need a computer program that will ask these questions and accumulate the necessary data. An example follows:

```
/*the variable PERSON will contain the name of the person being
evaluated*/

printf("ENTER NAME OF PERSON BEING EVALUATED?");

gets(&PERSON);

/*S1 will contain a yes or no answer to the following*/

printf("CAN %S SUBTRACT TWO NUMBERS WITHOUT BORROWING?",PERSON);

gets(&S1);

/*S2 will contain a yes or no answer to the following*/

printf("CAN %S SUBTRACT TWO NUMBERS WITH SINGLE COLUMN
BORROWING?",PERSON);

gets(&S2);

/*S3 will contain a yes or no to the following*/

printf("CAN %S SUBTRACT TWO NUMBERS WITH MULTIPLE COLUMN
BORROWING?",PERSON);

gets(&S3);
```

When this program is run, a dialogue will appear on the personal computer screen that will ask questions that will provide the relevant data concerning an individual's learning problem in subtraction. This dialogue follows. The computer output is in capital letters and the answers that might be given are in lower case.

```
ENTER NAME OF PERSON BEING EVALUATED ? andrew jones

CAN ANDREW JONES SUBTRACT TWO NUMBERS WITHOUT BORROWING ? yes

CAN ANDREW JONES SUBTRACT TWO NUMBERS WITH SINGLE COLUMN
BORROWING ? no

CAN ANDREW JONES SUBTRACT TWO NUMBERS WITH MULTIPLE COLUMN
BORROWING ? no
```

Each of the instantiated variables now becomes part of the database, as shown in Figure 2-2.

What we've done so far is quite simple. We defined some facts necessary to understanding subtraction, we designed a computer program that would ask the relevant questions pertaining to these facts, and then we stored the answers so they can be analyzed. This is the equivalent to what your brain does automatically when trying to decide between the local and express buses. That is, you "ask" yourself all the relevant questions concerning these two buses based on the facts you already know about them and about buses in general. The answers to the questions that are derived from the facts help you make your final decision. The facts and rules, which we will soon discuss, are stored in an area of the computer known as the "knowledge base."

When you are facing the bus dilemma, not all considerations are equal. You may not care as much about getting a seat, for example, as you do about getting to work on time, or vice versa. Colloquially, we say that we "weigh" these considerations in coming to a conclusion, and that is why the numbers in parentheses are referred to as "weighting factors." Some aspects of getting to work are not as important as others, just as some requirements for doing subtraction are more crucial than others in diagnosing a learning problem.

A no answer to any of the questions in Figure 2-2 indicates that Andrew has a problem with the subtraction skill represented by the fact; a yes answer indicates that Andrew possesses that skill. By obtaining the sum of all the weighting factors associated with the no answers, we can get an indication of the severity of Andrew's problem in subtraction, as follows:

S1 (2) yes   0
S2 (1) no   1
S3 (1) no   1
Sum weighting factor = 2

The total number representing the degree of Andrew's learning problem is called simply the "sum weighting factor." As we have said, this number can be used to determine whether Andrew has a problem in subtraction and just how severe that problem is. Sum weighting factors are simply means of quantifying for the computer program a wide range of possibilities. The maximum sum weighting factor in this example—which would indicate a serious problem in doing subtraction—would be obtained if all the answers were no. Here, that number is 4. The equivalent worst-case scenario in our bus example might be that you decided to wait for the express bus and ended up getting to work an hour late and had to stand all the way. You might very well

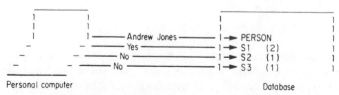

Personal computer   Database

Figure 2-2   Transferring the answers.

want to consider the very worst that could happen as a consequence of your decision.

Rules and Inferences

As we saw in Chapter 1, we need rules in order to apply the facts we know to situations that arise. The rules in our AI system must be designed to help us evaluate the data so that we can reach the goal of finding out if a person has a learning problem in arithmetic. We have singled out subtraction, so let us establish a rule related to the subtraction goal and call it the "subtraction rule." It reads like this:

> IF the sum weighting factor for subtraction is greater than 1, THEN PERSON has a learning problem in subtraction.

Since the sum weighting factor for Andrew Jones is 2, we can use the subtraction rule to infer that Andrew does indeed have a problem in subtraction. The rule has provided a practical application of the data we've accumulated. The value 1 in the rule is called a "threshold" of decision level.

We promised that AI makes programming easier and more flexible, and now you can begin to see how. Instead of establishing the subtraction rule, we could have employed a set of facts which would have covered all the possible ways the sum weighting factor could be greater than 1. The facts we would need to cover all possible contingencies and their weighting factors follow. A learning problem in subtraction exists when

1. (S1 = no) and (S2 = yes) and (S3 = yes)
   sum weighting factor = 2

2. (S1 = no) and (S2 = yes) and (S3 = no)
   sum weighting factor = 3

3. (S1 = no) and (S2 = no) and (S3 = yes)
   sum weighting factor = 3

4. (S1 = no) and (S2 = no) and (S3 = no)
   sum weighting factor = 4

5. (S1 = yes) and (S2 = no) and (S3 = no)
   sum weighting factor = 2

Notice that the sum weighting factor for each set of facts is greater than 1. What we have in this list are really just five different sets of facts. The subtraction rule, however, covers *all* these facts and renders the programming of these facts unnecessary. It is obviously a lot easier to program a single all-encompassing rule than several specialized facts that are much more limited in their application. Without rules, you would still be standing on the corner waiting to cross the street, assaulted by an army of facts and associated data but with no means of processing them. You wouldn't have to worry about the bus because you'd never even make it to the bus stop!

So far the design of our program has included

1. Defining goals
2. Defining facts to support the goals
3. Obtaining data that corresponds to the facts and is specific to a given situation or subject
4. Evaluating the data via rules and inferences

The process of reaching goals in this way is known as "forward chaining," that is, using the data to arrive at a conclusion. It enables us to proceed in a logical fashion from one step to another as outlined in Figure 2-1.

Verification through the Inference Mechanism

Let's take another example to illustrate how inferences are verified. Suppose a murder has been committed: A person is found locked in an apartment, shot three times. The medical examiner rules out the possibility of suicide because of the angle of the wounds (pruning in action), and the police immediately go to work. The first thing they consider is who else besides the victim had a key to the apartment. They question the landlord and several neighbors, who say the murdered person had a friend who frequently came to use the apartment. Further investigation reveals that the couple had recently been quarreling.

The police now have a suspect. They are able to infer from their interviews that the victim's friend is probably the murderer (forward chaining), using the data from the interviews to arrive at the conclusion, but they need some concrete evidence to nail down the case. Their best chance of nabbing the suspect is to find the murder weapon. They obtain a search warrant for the friend's apartment and look through the belongings, but to no avail. Finally, a detective finds a gun in a garbage can in a nearby alley. A fingerprint check verifies that the gun indeed was handled by the friend, and a ballistics test establishes that it is the murder weapon. Case solved. By obtaining a new piece of data and seeing if it was consistent with their original conclusion, the police verified the goal of identifying the murderer. The process of using a conclusion to look for supporting data is known as "backward chain-ing." In this case, the conclusion is the suspect and the data is the weapon.

In an AI program, the goal is also verified by a similar process. Were we correct when we concluded earlier that Andrew Jones has a learn-ing problem in subtraction? The goal has been reached, but to deter-mine if it was reached correctly we must approach the problem again with new data and new rules. A rule that might verify if an individual has a learning problem in subtraction might be

> IF a person achieves a score on a standard arithmetic test in subtraction that is below grade level, THEN the person will achieve a weighting factor in subtraction that is greater than 1 (that is, the person has a problem in subtraction).

All we must do to confirm that we have reached our goal of identify-ing a learning problem in subtraction is to verify that the score achieved on a standardized subtraction test is below grade level. This C program does just that:

```
/*grade level on subtraction test*/

printf( "ENTER GRADE LEVEL ON SUBTRACTION TEST?" );

gets(&GT);

/*student's grade level*/

printf( "ENTER STUDENT'S GRADE LEVEL?" );

gets(&GS);

G=GS-GT;

IF (G>0) VER=1;
```

Taking new data derived by the inference mechanism, which as-sumes the conclusion is correct, and matching it against the origi-nal data for verification is another example of backward chaining. As its name implies, backward chaining moves in the opposite direction from forward chaining. Rather than moving toward a goal by defining facts and obtaining data, backward chaining begins after the goal has initially been reached. An overview of forward and backward chaining as they figure in our original AI program design model is illustrated in Figure 2-3.

If it is determined that Andrew Jones has a problem with subtrac-tion, the inference mechanism will check to see if he also received deficient test scores in subtraction. If he did, it is assumed that the goal was reached correctly. If his test scores are not deficient, there is insufficient data to support reaching the goal, and some new steps must be taken to reverify the goal. That is, we must resolve the conflict that Andrew Jones is deficient in certain subtraction skills, yet he received a passing score on a standardized subtraction test.

Pruning

In the brain, the pruning mechanism guides the search for additional rules to verify a goal until all possible avenues have been exhausted. Since the brain possesses an enormous store of information, there may be many rules that apply to reaching or verifying a single goal, some or all of which may be called upon in any given instant.

Pruning enables the computer to skip or process any portion of the knowledge base according to its relevance to a particular goal. If Andrew Jones scored extremely well on a standardized arithmetic test, the pruning mechanism would skip over the portion of the knowledge base that evaluates data concerning arithmetic skills. On the other hand, if Andrew scored poorly on such a test, the pruning mechanism would guide the program to process that section. This eliminates processing paths that won't help in reaching our goal.

Remember that in Chapter 1 we discussed how pruning can be expressed as a set of rules. The pruning mechanism makes use of its own special rules in order to make decisions. A pruning rule that pertains to the subtraction example would be

> IF the subtraction test score exceeds the student's grade by 2 years or more, THEN skip the portion of the program that inputs subtraction data and evaluates it.

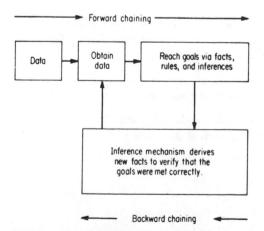

Figure 2-3 Configuration and operation of an AI program.

This rule can be implemented in C as follows:

```
void SUBTRACTION_EVALUATION( );

  void CALCULATION( );
    {

    }
    printf( "SUBTRACTION TEST SCORE?" );
    gets(&SS);
    printf( "STUDENT GRADE LEVEL?" );
    gets(&GL):
/*if subtraction test score is 2 years or more above student's*/
/*grade, skip subtraction learning problem evaluation section*/
    G=SS-(GL+2);
    IF (G<0)
  /*next learning problem*/

    ELSE
    CALCULATION( );

  }
```

Pruning simply overrides unnecessary and irrelevant considerations in both the brain and in artificial intelligence systems. A pruning rule for our getting-to-work example might be

IF it's raining very hard, THEN ignore all information regarding the local and express buses and take the first bus that comes along.

Just how we provide the computer with sufficient information to create an artificial intelligence program is discussed in the next chapter.

3

Defining Expert Systems

We saw in the previous chapter how goals can be reached in an artificial intelligence system via facts, rules, an inference mechanism, and pruning. Specific areas of interest for which we can design an AI system, such as diagnosing learning problems or riding buses, are called "domains." If you're now thinking that you can create AI programs to cover every domain imaginable, you're going to run into some serious problems. In the first place, the facts and rules needed to reach all goals in all domains are virtually infinite. It will be a very long time, if ever, before we can record the vast amount of knowledge required to accomplish such a task. Furthermore, there is no computer yet in existence that can store or process anything even approaching that much information. What we need to do is confine ourselves to those areas that contain just enough information that can be shaped into a computer program.

Even though we must be realistic about the present limits of this new technology, we have just seen in Chapter 2 that there certainly are practical applications for artificial intelligence programs. Working AI systems can be developed for small domains, some examples of which are illustrated in Figure 3-1.

For practical reasons, we must choose to work in domains that contain a manageable amount of information. An artificial intelligence system created to solve problems in a particular domain is called an "expert system." All the knowledge in the expert system is provided by people who are experts in that domain. Remember the weighting factors we assigned to the subtraction skills in Chapter 2? Those numbers were not arrived at arbitrarily; they represent knowledge that comes from research in a field of study. All expert systems are based on up-to-date expert information for a given domain.

Heuristic Rules

Suppose a group of experts is called upon to solve this problem: There is an oil spill in a river, and any one of several factories situated along the river's edge might be the source of the spill. The goal is to determine exactly where oil is coming from so that it can be stopped.

An expert system for solving this type of problem will first of all contain a mechanism for performing calculations. For example, the rate at which oil disperses in water, the direction and velocity of the river's currents, and other such factors can be employed to approximate the location of the spill. Once this information is gathered and a determination of the spill site is made, let's say to within an accuracy of 1 mile, a special set of rules is used to zero in on the precise factory location, as shown in the listing of rule H1 and rule H2 that follows. These rules are called "heuristic rules," and they differ from rules we discussed in the previous chapters in one fundamental way: Heuristic rules are not formulated as a result of ordinary, accepted knowledge but are rules that only an expert would know.

Rule H1:
   IF there is one factory along the river within 1 mile upstream from the spill's calculated location, THEN assume it is that factory that caused the spill.
Rule H2:
   IF there is more than one factory within 1 mile upstream from the spill's calculated location, THEN assume as a first choice that it is the factory that uses the most oil in its operations.

We saw in Chapters 1 and 2 how the pruning mechanism makes our thought processes more efficient by reducing the number of avenues of thought we must consider before getting down to the business of satisfying a goal. In an expert system, a pruning mechanism which utilizes heuristic rules is called the "heuristic search mechanism." The heuristic search mechanism can be represented in much the same way as the pruning mechanism in Chapter 1, as shown in Figure 3-2.

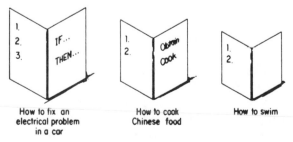

How to fix an
electrical problem
in a car

How to cook
Chinese food

How to swim

Figure 3-1   Some manageable domains.

Once the heuristic search mechanism has focused attention on the factory most likely to be causing the spill, the expert system can then apply another set of rules to verify that factory X is the source. For example, certain vulnerable spots in the factory's oil pipeline system would probably be considered first. Here is a heuristic rule that might be useful in this situation.

> IF the oil pipeline pressure in factory location 1 is less than the surrounding water pressure of the river, THEN examine pipeline location 32.

Only a person experienced with these problems in that factory would know that rule. It is a rule-of-thumb, or a heuristic rule.

Blackboard

It is often the case that a problem may be too complex for one expert system to solve by itself. In our oil slick problem, for example, one expert system was able to find the location of the spill, but if we wanted to contain the spill, another kind of expertise would be needed. The expert system called upon to do the containing would need to have certain information that was included in the expert system that found the spill location. Then the second expert system would bring its specific calculation and heuristic search mechanism to bear upon the problem and might ultimately recommend that a certain chemical is best suited to neutralize oil of that particular grade under these particular circumstances. The communication of information between expert systems is done by a mechanism called a "blackboard." The blackboard is a location within the computer's memory in which information that is stored within an expert system is "posted" so any other expert system can refer to it if it needs the information contained there to reach its goals.

The blackboard is a structure that contains information that can be viewed by cooperating expert systems. What these systems do with

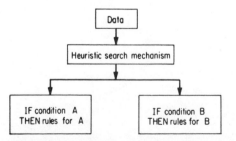

Figure 3-2   How pruning works in an expert system.

this information depends on the application. Have you ever come into a classroom and seen a message on the blackboard saying that the class has been changed to another room? This message may have been written by the school secretary who was informed that the teacher would be absent for the day; therefore, the need arose to combine similar classes under one teacher. The secretary was alertly watching for this situation and reacted accordingly. The concept of the blackboard for posting, modifying, and *watching for changes* is very important for cooperating systems.

You Can Do It

To create an expert system, a team consisting of an expert and a knowledge engineer gathers the facts, rules, and heuristic rules for a domain and organizes them into an AI program. You're probably now thinking, "But I'm not a knowledge engineer; how does all this apply to me?" The understanding you have gained about AI in the first two chapters has already begun to make you one. If you know how to program a computer in this way, you'll be well on your way before you get to the end of this book. If you know how to fix cars, cook Chinese food, or swim, you can be the knowledge engineer who designs an expert system in any of these or comparable domains.

Section 2 will outline some methods for implementing expert systems that can be done on a personal computer. Section 3 will detail the design of some popular topics into expert systems. You will be able to use some of these designs as paradigms for creating other expert systems.

4

Natural Language Processing

Communication between people and computers is an area in which a tremendous amount of research is now being done. The ultimate goal—still some distance away—is to enable the user to "speak" to the computer entirely in a human language such as English and have the computer speak back in that language. A true artificial intelligence must be able to do this. It is hoped that someday, by simply having a conversation, people will be able to explain what task they want performed and the computer will respond in kind.

This may sound like a simple matter, but that's because you've been speaking and hearing human language since you were a small child and you take most of its complex characteristics entirely for granted. If you've worked with C or any other computer language, you know how accurately you must write a program to get the computer to do exactly what you want. Computers are only as smart as the people make them; since they can't "think" for themselves, we have to give them very specific instructions for every minute function they perform. Human beings come into the world "programmed" to learn language; half the job is already done. To make a computer understand language, we not only have to break language down into its basic elements and enter this data into the computer, but we have to design computers and computer programs that can accept this information in the first place.

Creating this kind of communication system between people and computers is called "natural language processing." The purpose of this chapter is to give you some understanding of this vital and exciting aspect of artificial intelligence.

Let's see just how tough this task really is. If you had an artificial intelligence robot that could fix things, you might give it one of the following commands:

1. Fix the car by the house with the flat tire.
2. Fix the car by the house with the red curtains.

Even though sentence 1 is grammatically incorrect, any person can make sense out of it—we all know that a house cannot have a flat tire. We may recognize the error, but more important, we instantly correct it in our minds; that is, it is obviously the car that has the flat tire and not the house. The robot would have to know more than just the meaning of the words and their relationship to one another, or it might very well attempt to find a house with a flat tire on it somewhere. Since both sentences have the identical structure, the robot must not only possess a knowledge of grammar but must also be able to associate descriptions and objects. It is important to keep in mind that *our* rules of language only make sense to *us*; the robot needs its own special rules to understand what we are talking about.

An artificial intelligence, like the robot, must also be able to analyze sentences in relation to other sentences. Take these two sentences, for example:

1. John drank milk.
2. He then put on his coat.

The "He" in sentence 2 naturally refers to "John" in sentence 1. Without sentence 1, sentence 2 would have little meaning. All human languages are referred to as "context sensitive." That is, sentence 2 needed, or was sensitive to, sentence 1 in order to be fully interpreted. A language whose sentence interpretation can be accomplished without knowledge of other sentences is called "context free," that is, free of what took place before or after.

The process employed in getting a computer to understand sentences is made up of programs which together comprise the "natural language analyzer." The three basic functions of language analysis are

1. Lexical analysis (analyzing words)
2. Syntactical analysis (analyzing the placement of words in a sentence, including rules of grammar)
3. Semantic analysis (analyzing the meaning of a sentence by itself and in relation to other sentences)

Lexical Analysis

Dividing sentences into words and punctuation marks (written) or pauses (spoken) is called "lexical analysis." The words themselves can be further divided into roots, prefixes, and suffixes. For example, a very simple word such as "going" can be subdivided as

going (word)

go (root)

ing (suffix)

The word "understand" consists of

under (prefix)

stand (root)

A lexicon or dictionary defines words, but to get the computer to understand them in context is a considerably more difficult task.

Syntax Analysis

Breaking a sentence down into its component parts is a vital step in getting the computer to understand language. We must be able to translate the rules of grammar and syntax into a form that the computer can handle.

A sentence (S) is generally composed of a noun phrase (NP) and a verb phrase (VP) which can be represented as

$S \rightarrow NP, VP$

A noun phrase can usually be further broken down into a determiner (such as an article, conjunction, pronoun, etc.) and a noun, represented as

$NP \rightarrow DET, N$

A verb phrase can also be broken down further into a verb followed by another noun phrase, as

$VP \rightarrow V, NP$

A noun phrase, however, can also be just a simple noun:

$NP \rightarrow N$

A common way of breaking down a sentence is by creating a parse tree, which is a diagrammatic representation of the syntactical structure of a sentence. The sentence

A plane flew home

could have the structure shown in Figure 4-1. The words of the sentence are identified and each word is classified by type. The word "A" is a determiner (DET), "plane" is a noun (N), "flew" is a verb (V), and "home" is a noun (N).

Semantic Analysis

Once the sentence is broken down, it undergoes semantic analysis, the process by which the computer attempts to make meaning out of it. In an artificial intelligence system, we would apply a set of rules to establish the meaning in a way that the computer can use. Let's take the previous sentence as an example:

DET   N   V   N
 A   plane flew   home.

The semantic analyzer might have the following set of rules in its knowledge base for interpreting the sentence:

Rule 1:
    IF a determiner is the first part of a sentence and is followed by a noun, THEN the noun is known as the subject.
Rule 2:
    IF a verb follows a subject, THEN the verb tells us what the subject did.
Rule 3:
    IF a noun follows a subject and a verb in that order, THEN the noun is an object.

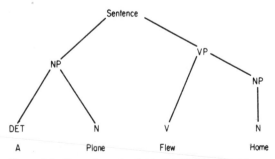

Figure 4-1   Parse tree structure of a sentence.

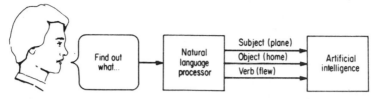

Figure 4-2   Natural language processor.

Rule 4:
>   IF a sentence has the form subject, verb, object, THEN we know what the subject did (verb) in relation to the object.

To make this more comprehensible, let's put this to a practical application. Suppose an artificial intelligence system had to perform the following task: Find out what the plane did and what its objective was. The task caused the sentence "A plane flew home" to trigger rule 1 which identified the plane as the subject. Rule 2 then told us the plane flew. Rules 3 and 4 identified "home" as the objective. This example illustrates how a natural language processor using its knowledge base of lexical, syntactical, and semantic rules processes or "understands" a sentence.

A natural language processor can be used at the front of another artificial intelligence system, allowing data to be passed on verbally, as in Figure 4-2.

Essentially, natural language processing can free the computer user from the limitation of the complexities of computer languages. Once the programs that will enable the computer to understand us and "talk" to us in plain English have been perfected, we will have taken a major step toward achieving a genuinely "intelligent" computer.

Inference Mechanisms:
Tools for Machine Thinking

In Section 2 we will build a more comprehensive understanding of how to plan and use an expert system. We will provide the tools for you to construct your own expert system. By explaining how the tools work, we will put you in a position to design your own.

5

Forward Chaining

Now we are ready to design an actual expert system tool. Remember, a tool is used to help make a task easier. The tool we will create is used for solving a particular type of problem. There are many ways to solve a problem; some methods are better than other methods for solving certain types of problems. The tool we need must be applicable to the kinds of problems found in the expert domain being considered, or it won't be much help in solving problems within that domain. A saw can't help you fix a car, and a wrench can't help you cut down a tree.

Let's consider this problem: What would you do if you were driving and the temperature in your engine started rising? Of course, you'd get nervous. Most of us have encountered this problem when stuck in heavy traffic on a hot day. Let's restate this problem in a more general way. We have a condition (overheating) and we want to know what the result or consequence of this condition will be (Will the car stall?). Stop a minute and consider what happened. We first stated that a condition occurred, which was the overheating of the engine. Then we thought about all the rules we knew that were related to that condition. Some of these rules are

Rule 1
 IF the car overheats, THEN the car will stall.
Rule 2
 IF the car stalls, THEN it will cost me money, AND I will be late getting home.

How do you arrive at the conclusion that this situation will cost money and cause you to be late? Keep in mind, as we describe the course of events, these two words: forward and chaining. The condition that triggered a chain of events is the car overheating. This caused the first part of rule 1, the condition, or IF part, to be called upon. Rule 1 being true caused the THEN part of the rule to be invoked, which is that the car will stall. The chaining continues: The IF part of rule 2 is triggered by the car actually stalling or because rule 1 is invoked. Your conclusion that a stall will cost money and make you late getting home can result from the stall itself or the observation of an overheating engine.

Why do we use the word "forward" in describing this problem? When a condition such as overheating takes place, something is affected by it (the THEN part, or conclusion). Since the condition *comes before* the conclusion, and we begin with conditions, we are going forward. Thereby we use the term forward chaining.

Now let's define what we mean by a forward chaining tool. The tool helps us find answers to questions by applying forward chaining principles to a knowledge base. In other words, the tool will ask you for conditions—engine overheating—and the name of the appropriate knowledge base—automobile mechanical problems—. Once you have supplied these answers to the tool's questions, the tool will refer to the information stored in the knowledge base and apply the forward chaining techniques we've just discussed. It will provide you with the conclusions or results you need, such as "the car will stall" or "a stall will cost you money, and you will be late getting home."

In order to explain the design of the tool in the simplest way, we will first lead you through the process you might use to solve a problem if no computer was available. This part of making the tool is known as developing an "algorithm," which is a logical step-by-step organization of the problem and all its aspects.

Since we know that computers do the same things people do, only faster, the second step is to transform this organized scheme of the problem into the tool itself—a computer program. This chapter will explain both steps clearly.

The C version of the expert tool is simple and is written in fundamental C so that it can be entered and run on almost any personal computer, including yours. You will be able to construct a knowledge base that covers a field of interest to you, and you can try it out by yourself. The design is also open-ended, so you can expand it in the future to make the tool more powerful for solving even more difficult and complex problems.

Sound simple? It is. In this chapter we'll diagram a problem carefully and then make an expert system tool out of it. If you follow our explanations carefully and then parallel them with a domain of interest to you, you will be on your way to being a knowledge engineer.

Example Using Forward Chaining

Here is a simple set of rules that might be part of a stock market expert system.

    10   IF INTEREST RATES = FALL
         THEN STOCK MARKET = RISE
    20   IF INTEREST RATES = RISE
         THEN STOCK MARKET = FALL
    30   IF DOLLAR EXCHANGE RATE = FALL
         THEN INTEREST RATES = RISE
    40   IF DOLLAR EXCHANGE RATE = RISE
         THEN INTEREST RATES = FALL

Using these rules, we ambitiously set up a stock market consulting company. Our first customer comes to us and tells us that the dollar exchange rate is declining (falling) against the money values of the major industrial nations. What should he do in the stock market? Obviously, the goal is to do well in the stock market, but whether or not our customer will make a profit will be decided by as yet undetermined conditions. Remember that forward chaining systems make predictions by considering conditions defined in clauses of the IF part of the rule and come to conclusions that are defined in the THEN part. In this case, the condition is

DOLLAR EXCHANGE RATE = FALL

Scanning our rules, we find that rule 30 contained DOLLAR EXCHANGE RATE in its IF clause. That is

    30   IF DOLLAR EXCHANGE RATE = FALL
         THEN INTEREST RATES = RISE

From it we can conclude that interest rates will rise. Scanning the rest of the IF-THEN rules for DOLLAR EXCHANGE RATE, we find it again in rule 40. But the IF clause

    40   IF DOLLAR EXCHANGE RATE = RISE

does not match the known condition of falling exchange rates. So rule 40 is not true. We are not yet finished since rule 30 introduced a new condition:

INTEREST RATES = RISE

We must now scan the rules to see if this condition leads to other conclusions, and we see that rule 10

    10   IF INTEREST RATES = FALL
         THEN STOCK MARKET = RISE

is not true but that rule 20 is:

    20   IF INTEREST RATES = RISE
         THEN STOCK MARKET = FALL

The chain continues by the introduction of a new condition:

    STOCK MARKET = FALL

Therefore, we are still not finished. We must check all the rules for this new condition. Scanning all the IF clauses, we see that none contains STOCK MARKET. We can go no further, and therefore the session is over. We hand our customer a report as follows:

> When the dollar exchange rate is falling, interest rates will rise and the stock market will fall.

The report, in reality, may need more complex rules, but the forward chaining system, like any system, acts only upon what is in the knowledge base.

From this example, we can describe the workings of a typical forward chaining system:

1. The system is presented with one or more conditions.
2. For each condition the system searches the rules in the knowledge base for those rules that correspond to the condition in the IF part.
3. Each rule can in turn *generate new conditions* from the conclusions of the invoked THEN part. These new conditions are added to the ones already existing.
4. Any conditions that have been added to the system are processed. If there are any such conditions, the system goes back to step 2 and searches the rules in the knowledge base again. If there are no more new conditions, this session ends.

The Knowledge Base

In this example you, as the expert, enter rules directly into the knowledge base and use these rules to direct your stock market decisions. But first you must create a variable name table, as shown in Figure

5-1, to make it easier to deal with long, clumsy variable names and to help you write the rules.

Using the variable name table you can write the following stock market rules:

10 IF INTEREST = FALL
    THEN STOCK = RISE

20 IF INTEREST = RISE
    THEN STOCK = FALL

30 IF DOLLAR = FALL
    THEN INTEREST = RISE

40 IF DOLLAR = RISE
    THEN INTEREST = FALL

50 IF FEDINT = FALL AND FEDMON = ADD
    THEN INTEREST = FALL

A word of caution: These rules are not a complete list of rules needed to do a proper stock market analysis but merely show the general principles involved. We must always remember that an expert system is only as good or as bad as the experts who formulate the rules. Keeping that in mind, let's continue to examine how the system uses the rules to arrive at answers.

Processing the Knowledge Base

Now that we have established the knowledge base using the variable name table, we are ready to begin processing that information using forward chaining principles. Our expert technique requires the construction of a number of useful tables that will aid in answering questions and making decisions about the problem we are trying to solve. These tables, or data structures, therefore serve an indispensable pur-

Variable name	Meaning
INTEREST	Interest rate direction
DOLLAR	Dollar exchange rate
FEDINT	Federal reserve interest rate goals
FEDMON	Federal reserve money circulation goals (i.e., add or remove reserves from the banking system)
STOCK	Stock market direction

Figure 5-1   Variable name table.

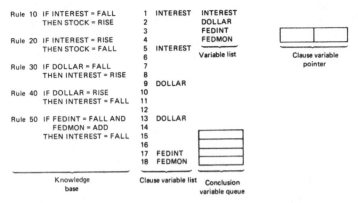

Figure 5-2   The knowledge base of the stock market expert system and its related data structure.

pose as they are derived directly from the knowledge base. A full description of each data structure will be provided in this chapter. The knowledge base with all its derived data structures is shown in Figure 5-2.

The first data structure we will use is the clause variable list. This simple list, as shown in Figure 5-3, lets us know which variables in our problem are associated with the IF parts of specific IF-THEN statements. The numbers 1 through 18 shown to the left of the variable names represent the array location in the data structure that the variable names are placed in. There are four array locations reserved for each rule. If a rule does not utilize all of these locations, they are left blank.

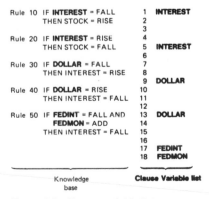

Figure 5-3   Clause variable list.

As an example of how the clause variable list is used, suppose we want to understand the effects of the dollar exchange rate falling, that is

DOLLAR = FALL

Rules 30 and 40 both contain clauses with DOLLAR as the variable. In order to always remember that DOLLAR is the variable in which we are interested, we will place this variable in a data structure we call the conclusion variable queue, shown in Figure 5-4.

Before continuing let us explain what a queue is and why we need one. People waiting on a supermarket checkout line are on a queue in which first come are first served. Shoppers enter a queue at the back of a line and are served when they reach the front. After being served, each person exits the queue. Why then must the conclusion variable queue be a queue? Let's use the variable DOLLAR as an example. We try to see if any statement containing DOLLAR meets the condition of DOLLAR = FALL. If it does, the THEN part of the statement is invoked and a new condition variable—INTEREST—is instantiated. In our case this would occur in rule 30:

30 IF DOLLAR = FALL
    THEN INTEREST = RISE

We would now have to see what the effect would be of interest rising after we finished processing all the rules containing DOLLAR. To remember that we are now dealing with a new variable, INTEREST, we place it on the conclusion variable queue after DOLLAR, as shown in Figure 5-5.

After we are through processing all the IF-THEN rules with IF parts

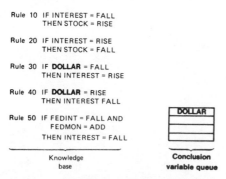

Rule 10 IF INTEREST = FALL
        THEN STOCK = RISE

Rule 20 IF INTEREST = RISE
        THEN STOCK = FALL

Rule 30 IF **DOLLAR** = FALL
        THEN INTEREST = RISE

Rule 40 IF **DOLLAR** = RISE
        THEN INTEREST FALL

Rule 50 IF FEDINT = FALL AND
        FEDMON = ADD
        THEN INTEREST = FALL

Knowledge base

DOLLAR

Conclusion variable queue

Figure 5-4 Conclusion variable queue.

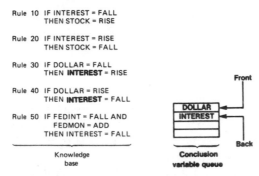

Figure 5-5 Conclusion variable queue.

containing DOLLAR, we remove it from our queue as shown in Figure 5-6. We are finished with checking the effects of a falling dollar, and now we want to see only the effects of rising interest rates. Since INTEREST has moved to the front of the queue, we will process it in the same way we processed DOLLAR. When there is nothing left on the queue, we have ended our forward chaining and are ready to provide the answers.

Let us examine the last two data structures needed for implementing forward chaining. These are the variable list and the clause variable pointer. The variable list tells us if a variable has been instantiated yet. Initially, before any questions are asked, the variable list will show that none of the variables have been instantiated, as shown in Figure 5-7. In our example so far, with DOLLAR and INTEREST instantiated, the variable list would look different, as shown in Figure 5-8.

The clause variable pointer keeps track of the clause within the rule we are examining and is made up of the rule number and the clause number. We need this pointer in our forward chaining tool to keep

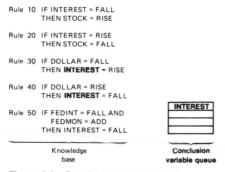

Figure 5-6 Conclusion variable queue.

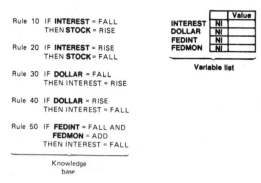

Rule 10 IF **INTEREST** = FALL
              THEN **STOCK** = RISE

Rule 20 IF **INTEREST** = RISE
              THEN **STOCK** = FALL

Rule 30 IF **DOLLAR** = FALL
              THEN INTEREST = RISE

Rule 40 IF **DOLLAR** = RISE
              THEN INTEREST = FALL

Rule 50 IF **FEDINT** = FALL AND
              FEDMON = ADD
              THEN INTEREST = FALL

Knowledge
base

	Value
INTEREST	NI
DOLLAR	NI
FEDINT	NI
FEDMON	NI

Variable list

Figure 5-7   Variable list.

track of where we are. That is, to know which rule and which clause within the rule we are now processing. Remember, the processing of each clause is a function of the variable in the front of the conclusion variable queue. For example, assume we have the variable DOLLAR in the front of the conclusion variable queue, that is, we want to see the consequence of the change in the dollar. The first rule in which DOLLAR appears as a condition (the IF part) is rule 30. We therefore want to process rule 30 to see if we can invoke a consequence of the dollar changing. The clause variable pointer will initially point to rule 30, as shown in Figure 5-9.

In short, the clause variable pointer actually points to an entry in the clause variable list. That entry contains the condition variable (DOLLAR, in this case) that we are interested in processing at the moment and that is at the front of the conclusion variable queue.

Let's take a moment to review these four data structures we have designed before we put them all together in a working example. All along we've said that artificial intelligence works because it imitates the way people actually think when they solve problems. Seen in this

Rule 10 IF **INTEREST** = FALL
              THEN **STOCK** = RISE

Rule 20 IF **INTEREST** = RISE
              THEN **STOCK** = FALL

Rule 30 IF **DOLLAR** = FALL
              THEN INTEREST = RISE

Rule 40 IF **DOLLAR** = RISE
              THEN INTEREST = FALL

Rule 50 IF **FEDINT** = FALL AND
              FEDMON = ADD
              THEN INTEREST = FALL

Knowledge
base

	Value
INTEREST	I	RISE
DOLLAR	I	FALL
FEDINT	NI	
FEDMON	NI	

Variable list

Figure 5-8   Variable list.

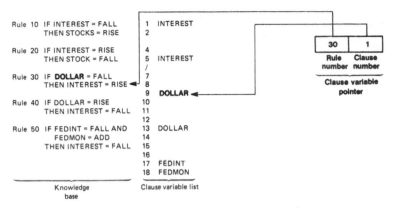

Figure 5-9   Clause variable pointer.

context, the structures we've just been working with do not simply comprise an abstract problem-solving method; they relate specifically to human thought processes. How?

When you set out to solve a problem in which you need to predict the consequences of various conditions, you first ponder all the variable conditions that could affect the end result (variable list). Then, you instantiate (establish conditions for) any of the variables for which you possess information (e.g., DOLLAR = FALL). Next, you consider all the rules you know that might help predict the outcome of the situation and see if any of the conditions you've come up with are consistent with any of the rules you know (clause variable list). The way you would "process" that information would be to put all the variable conditions in some kind of order (conclusion variable queue) and somehow focus on them, one at a time, to see how they might lead you to a possible conclusion (clause variable pointer).

In your mind, of course, all this happens automatically, very quickly, and in not so linear a manner. Most of the time, we aren't even aware that we are processing information and coming to conclusions about circumstances we encounter. As soon as you see the needle hovering at the high point of the temperature gauge of your car, you say "Oh, no!" because you've immediately come to the conclusion that the car might stall. The human brain works very fast because the neurons work together simultaneously. In parallel, when dealing with a highly complex problem containing many, many variables, a computer can work just as fast if the problem is organized into data structures like the ones we've discussed, and if algorithms are used in our expert tool to simulate the forward chaining inference process. If we are successful in designing the data structures and the expert tool, another person who sees the conclusions will judge that they make sense.

Forward Chaining Example

As an example, let's use the stock market knowledge base and pose the following question to the forward chaining tool:

> What is the effect of the Federal Reserve adding reserves to the banking system? That is: FEDMON = ADD

The forward chaining tool in the computer will read the stock market knowledge base from a peripheral storage device such as a disk and will conduct the lists, pointers, and queues, which we have already discussed, as shown in Figure 5-10. The conclusion variable queue will of course contain the initial condition variable, FEDMON, whose value is known. The tool searches the clause variable list for the first instance of FEDMON and finds that this occurs in rule 50. The clause variable pointer is therefore initially set to rule number 50, clause number 1. From the clause variable list we see that we have to instantiate two clause variables, FEDINT and FEDMON. We already know that FEDMON was instantiated to ADD as the original condition. Since FEDINT is not instantiated, the tool asks the user of the expert system the following question:

> Does the Federal Reserve want interest rates to rise or fall?

Let's say the user responds with "fall." This causes FEDINT to acquire the value FALL and be instantiated in the variable list. The clause number of the clause variable pointer is then incremented from 1 to 2. Since FEDMON, the second clause of rule 50, is already instantiated and there is no more rule 50 clauses, we can execute the entire IF part.

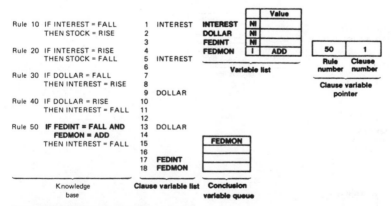

Figure 5-10 Forward chaining system.

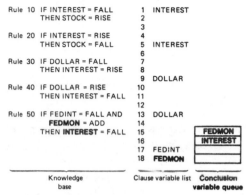

Figure 5-11   Conclusion variable queue.

Both conditions of the FEDINT = FALL and FEDMON = ADD are true. Therefore, the THEN part of the rule 50 is invoked, resulting in

INTEREST = FALL

Since INTEREST may represent a new condition, it is placed on the conclusion variable queue, which now looks like Figure 5-11, and the variable list is modified to look like Figure 5-12.

The remainder of the rules in the variable list are scanned for FED-MON. Since there are no more rules with FEDMON, it is removed from the conclusion variable queue. INTEREST now moves to the front. We search the clause variable list for INTEREST and find it in rule 10. The way our forward chaining system looks now is shown in Figure 5-13.

Rule 10 IF **INTEREST** = FALL
         THEN **STOCK** = RISE

Rule 20 IF **INTEREST** = RISE
         THEN **STOCK** = FALL

Rule 30 IF **DOLLAR** = FALL
         THEN INTEREST = RISE

Rule 40 IF **DOLLAR** = RISE
         THEN INTEREST = FALL

Rule 50 IF **FEDINT** = FALL AND
         FEDMON = ADD
         THEN INTEREST = FALL

Knowledge
base

		Value
INTEREST	I	FALL
DOLLAR	NI	
FEDINT	I	FALL
FEDMON	I	ADD

Variable list

Figure 5-12   Variable list.

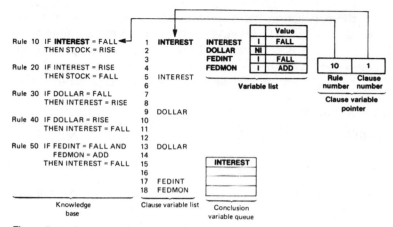

Figure 5-13 Forward chaining system.

You will note that both rules 10 and 20 contain INTEREST as conditions:

    10   IF INTEREST = FALL
         THEN STOCK = RISE

    20   IF INTEREST = RISE
         THEN STOCK = FALL

Since INTEREST is instantiated to FALL, the IF part of rule 10 is true. This causes the THEN part to be invoked, which instantiates STOCK to RISE. This will in turn result in STOCK being placed on the conclusion variable queue as shown in Figure 5-14. Rule 20 is not true because it contains the condition INTEREST = RISE while INTEREST has already been instantiated to FALL. INTEREST will then be

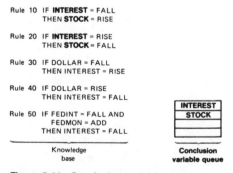

Figure 5-14 Conclusion variable queue.

removed from the conclusion variable queue since there are no more rules containing INTEREST, leaving STOCK in front as shown in Figure 5-15. Since STOCK is not in the IF part of any rule, the session ends. The answers to "What is the effect of the Federal Reserve adding reserves to the banking system and wanting interest rates to fall?" are

1. Interest rates will fall.
2. The stock market will rise.

Concepts for Design Implementation

Let us review the steps we have taken to implement the forward chaining structure:

1. The condition is identified.
2. The condition variable is placed on the conclusion variable queue and its value is marked on the variable list.
3. The clause variable list is searched for the variable whose name is the same as the one in the front of the queue. If found, the rule number and a 1 are placed into the clause variable pointer. If not found, go to step 6.
4. Each variable in the IF clause of the rule that is not already instantiated is now instantiated. The variables are in the clause variable list. If all the clauses are true, the THEN part is invoked.
5. The instantiated THEN part of the variable is placed in the *back* of the conclusion variable queue.
6. When there are no more IF statements containing the variable that is at the *front* of the conclusion variable queue, that variable is removed.

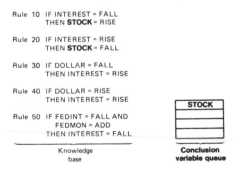

Rule 10 IF INTEREST = FALL
         THEN **STOCK** = RISE

Rule 20 IF INTEREST = RISE
         THEN **STOCK** = FALL

Rule 30 IF DOLLAR = FALL
         THEN INTEREST = RISE

Rule 40 IF DOLLAR = RISE
         THEN INTEREST = RISE

Rule 50 IF FEDINT = FALL AND
            FEDMON = ADD
         THEN INTEREST = FALL

| |
| STOCK |
| |
| |

Knowledge
base

Conclusion
variable queue

Figure 5-15 Conclusion variable queue.

7. If there are no more variables on the conclusion variable queue, end the session. If there are more variables, go to step 3.

We can use the above concepts to design, in C, a simple forward chaining expert tool.

Programming Applications

In this part of the chapter is a forward chaining tool for you to apply to your knowledge base (see Listing 5-1). This tool will allow you to insert a set of rules into comment locations 1500 through 1610 of the program, type forward, and obtain answers about your knowledge base.

Program Explanation

As an example to acquaint you with the way the program is used, we have inserted the rules governing the stock market and interest rates. This is the same example used to explain the forward chaining concepts. For example, the rule

IF interest rates fall
THEN stock market will rise

is covered by comments 1500 and 1510. The rule

IF dollar is falling
THEN interest rates will rise

is covered by comments 1540 and 1550.

Each variable in the variable list is specified in comment number 367. These are the condition variables that start a forward chaining operation. The clause variable list is constructed in comments 407 and 408.

The system responses have been abbreviated. For example:

ST = FALL means the stock market will fall.
IN = RISE means interest rates will rise.

Program Listing

Listing 5-1 is followed by a sequence of sample runs.

Listing 5-1   Forward chaining.

```
/******* FORWARD CHAINING *******/
/********************************/
/* INSTALL YOUR IF CLAUSES IN SEQUENCE IN THE MIDDLE OF
    THE PROGRAM WITHIN THE FIRST CASE STATEMENT
    EXAMPLE IF ((A1==2) && (A2==6) || (A3=='YES')) S=1;
            IF (J=='NO') S=1;
    THE THEN PART OF THE ABOVE CONSTRUCTION ALWAYS CONTAINS
    S=1. INSTALL YOUR THE CLAUSES IN SEQUENCE IN THE
    MIDDLE OF THE PROGRAM, WITHIN THE SECOND CASE STATEMENT */
#include <stdio.h>

int flag;
char cndvar [10][3];
char varlt[10][3] /* variable list */, clvarlt[40][3] /* clause variable list */;
char c[3], vp[3] /* condition variable */, v[3] /* variable */;
char fedint[10], interest[10], stock[10], dollar[10], fedmon[10];
char po[10] /* position */, qu[10] /* qualify */;

int instlt[10] /* instantiated list */, f, i, j, k, s, fp /* front pointer */;
int bp /* back pointer */, gr /* grade */, sn /* statement number */;
int cn /* clause number */;

void search(void);
void check_instantiation(void);
void instantiate(void);
main()
{
/************** INITIALIZATION SECTION ***************/
/* VARIABLE LIST (VARLIT), INSTANTIATED LIST (INSTLT),
    CLAUSE VARIABLE LIST (CLVARLT), CONDITIONAL VARIABLE QUEUE (CNDVAR) */
/* FRONT (FP) AND BACK (BP) CONDITION VARIABLE QUEUE POINTERS */
fp=1;
bp=1;
for (i=1; i < 41; i++)
 strcpy(clvarlt[i],"");
for (i=1; i < 11; i++)
 strcpy(cndvar[i],"");
for (i=1; i < 11; i++);
 strcpy(instlt[i],"");
for (i=1; i < 11; i++);
 strcpy(varlt[i],"");
for (i=1; i <11; i++);
 {
  strcpy(cndvar[i],"");
  strcpy(varlt[i],"");
  strcpy(instlt[i],"");
 }
/* enter variables which are in the if part, 1 at a time in
    the exact order that they occur. up to 3 variables per
    if statement. do not duplicate any variable names. any
    name is used only once. if no more variables left, just
    hit return key */
/********** comment 367 ********/
strcpy(varlt[1],"DO"); strcpy(varlt[2],"FT"); strcpy(varlt[3],"FM");
strcpy(varlt[4],"IN"); strcpy(varlt[5],"ST");
printf("*** VARIABLE LIST ***\n");
for (i=1; i<11; i++)
printf("ENTER VARIABLE   %d   %s\n" ,i ,varlt[i]);
printf("HIT RETURN KEY TO CONTINUE");
getchar();
/* enter variables as they appear in the if clauses. a
    maximum of 3 variables per if statement. if no more
    variables, hit return key. */
/********* comment 407, 408 ***********/
strcpy(clvarlt[1],"IN");
strcpy(clvarlt[5],"IN");
strcpy(clvarlt[9],"DO");
strcpy(clvarlt[13],"DO");
strcpy(clvarlt[17],"FT");
strcpy(clvarlt[18],"FM");
printf("*** CLAUSE-VARIABLE LIST ***\n");
for( i=1; i<9; i++)
 {
  printf("** CLAUSE %d\n",i);
  for( j=1; j<5; j++)
   {
```

```
      k=4*(i-1)+j;
      printf("VARIABLE %d  %s\n",j,clvarlt[k]);
      }
    if ( i==4)
      {
       printf("HIT RETURN KEY TO CONTINUE");
       getchar();
      }
}
/********************** INFERENCE SECTION ****************/
printf("ENTER CONDITION VARIABLE ? ");
gets(c);
/* place condition variable c on condition variable queue cndvar */
strcpy(cndvar[bp],c);
/* move backpointer (bp) back */
bp=bp+1;
/* set the condition variable pointer consisting of the
   statement number (sn) and the clause number (cn) */
sn=1; cn=1;
/* find the next statement number containing the condition variable
   which is in front of the queue (cndvar). this statement number
   is located in the clause variable list (clvarlt) */
/* start at the beginning */
f=1;
b496: search();
/* point to first clause in statement */
cn=1;
if (sn != 0)
/* more statements */
(
 /* locate the clause */
 i=4*(sn-1)+cn;
 /* clause variable */
 strcpy(v,clvarlt[i]);
 /* are there any more clauses for this statement */
 while (strcmp(v,""))
 /* more clauses */
  {
    /* check instantiation of this clause */
    check_instantiation();
    cn=cn+1;
    /* check next clause */
    i=4*(sn-1)+cn;
    strcpy(v,clvarlt[i]);
  }
 /* no more clauses check if part of statement */
 s=0;
 /* sample if-then statements from the position knowledge base */
 switch(sn)
 {
 /* statement 1 */
 /****** comment 1500 ******/
 case 1: if(strcmp(interest, "FALL") == 0) s=1;
         break;
 /* statement 2 */
 /****** comment 1510 *****/
 case 2: if(strcmp(interest,"RISE") == 0) s=1;
         break;
 /*statement 3 */
 /****** comment 1540 *******/
 case 3: if(strcmp(dollar,"FALL") == 0) s=1;
         break;
 /* statement 4 */
 /******* comment 1550 ******/
 case 4: if(strcmp(dollar,"RISE") == 0) s=1;
         break;
 /* statement 5 */
 case 5: if((strcmp(fedint,"FALL") == 0) && (strcmp(fedmon,"ADD")) == 0) s=1;
         break;
 /* statement 6 */
 case 6: if((strcmp(qu,"YES") == 0) && (gr >= 3.5) == 0) s=1;
         break;
 /******** comment 1610 *****/
 }
 /* see if the then part should be invoked i.e. s=1 */
 if(s!=1)
 (
```

Listing 5-1 (Continued)

```
         f=sn+1;
         goto b496;
       }
/* invoke then part */
switch (sn)
   {
   /******** comment 1500 ******/
   /* put variable on the conclusion variable queue */
   case 1:
    strcpy(stock,"RISE");
    printf("ST=RISE\n");
    strcpy(v,"ST");
    instantiate();
    break;
   /******** comment 1510 ******/
   /* put variable on the conclusion variable queue */
   case 2:
    strcpy(stock,"FALL");
    printf("ST=FALL\n");
    strcpy(v,"ST");
    instantiate();
    break;
   /* put variable on the conclusion variable queue */
   /******** comment 1540 *******/
   case 3:
    strcpy(interest,"RISE");
    printf("IN=RISE\n");
    strcpy(v,"IN");
    instantiate();
    break;
   /******* comment 1550 *****/
   /* put variable on the conclusion variable queue */
   case 4:
    strcpy(interest,"FALL");
    printf("IN=FALL\n");
    strcpy(v,"IN");
    instantiate();
    break;
   /* put variable on the conclusion variable list */
   case 5:
    strcpy(interest,"FALL");
    printf("IN=FALL\n");
    strcpy(v,"IN");
    instantiate();
    break;
   /* put variable on the conclusion variable queue */
   case 6:
    strcpy(po,"YES");
    printf("PO=YES\n");
    break;
    /********* comment 1610 ********/
   }
   f=sn+1;
   goto b496;
   }
/* no more clauses in the clause variable list (clvarlt)
   containing the variable in front of the queue (cndvar(fp))
   then remove front variable (cndvar(fp)) and replace it by
   the next variable (cndvar(fp+1)). if no more variables are
   at the front of the queue stop */
/* next queue variable */
fp=fp+1;
if(fp < bp)
   {
   /* check out this condition variable */
   f=1;
   goto b496;
   }
   /* no more conclusion variables on queue */
   }

void check_instantiation()
/* ROUTINE TO INSTANTIATE A VARIABLE (V) IF IT ISN'T ALREADY.
   THE INSTANTIATE INDICATION (INSTLT) IS A 0 IF NOT, A 1 IF IT
   IS. THE VARIABLE LIST (VARLT) CONTAINS THE VARIABLE (V) */

   {
   i=1;
   /* find variable in the variable list */
   while ((strcmp(v, varlt[i]) != 0) && (i <= 10)) i=i+1;
```

```
                        /* check if already instantiated */
                        if (instlt[i] != 1)
                          {
                          /* mark instantiated */
                           instlt[i] =1;
                          /* the designer of this knowledge base places the input
                              statements to instantiate the variables in this case
                              statement */
                          switch (i)
                            {
                          /* input statements for sample position knowledge base */
                            case 1:
                             printf("RISE OR FALL FOR DO ? ");
                             gets(dollar);
                             break;
                            case 2:
                             printf("RISE OR FALL FOR FT ? ");
                             gets(fedint);
                             break;
                            case 3:
                             printf("ADD OR SUBTRACT FOR FM ? ");
                             gets(fedmon);
                             break;
                            case 4:
                             printf("RISE OR FALL FOR IN ? ");
                             gets(interest);
                             break;
                            case 5:
                             printf("RISE OR FALL FOR ST ? ");
                             gets(stock);
                             break;
                            }
                          }
                        /* end of input statements for the position knowledge base */
                      }

void search()
/* SEARCH CLAUSE VARIABLE LIST FOR A VARIABLE (CLVARLT) EQUAL TO THE
   ONE IN FRONT OF THE CONCLUSION QUEUE (CNDVAR). RETURN THE STATEMENT
   NUMBER (SN). IF THERE IS NO MATCH I.E.. SN=0. THE FIRST STATEMENT
   NUMBER FOR THE SPACE IS F. */
{
 flag=0;
 sn=f;
 while ( (flag == 0) && (sn <= 10))
   {
   cn=1;
   k=(sn-1)*4+cn;
   while ( (strcmp(clvarlt[k], cndvar[fp]) !=0 ) && (cn<4) )
     {
     cn=cn+1;
     k=(sn-1)*4+cn;
     }
   if(strcmp(clvarlt[k], cndvar[fp]) == 0) flag=1;
   if (flag == 0) sn=sn+1;
   }
 if (flag == 0) sn=0;
}

void instantiate()
/* ROUTINE TO INSTANTIATE VARIABLE (V) AND THEN PLACE IT ON THE
   BACK OF THE QUEUE (CNDVAR[BP]) IF IT IS NOT ALREADY THERE. */
{
 i=1;
 /* find variable in the variable list (varlt) */
 while ((strcmp(v, varlt[i]) != 0) && (i <= 10)) i=i+1;
 /* instantiate it */
 instlt[i] = 1;
 i=1;
 /* determine if (v) is or already has been on the queue (cndvar) */
 while ((strcmp(v, cndvar[i]) != 0) && (i <= 10)) i=i+1;
 /* variable has not been on the queue. store it in back of the queue. */
 if (strcmp(v, cndvar[i]) != 0 )
   {
   strcpy(cndvar[bp],v);
   bp=bp+1;
   }
}
```

Sample Runs

When we enter forward, the following happens:

```
*** VARIABLE LIST ***
ENTER VARIABLE  1 DO
ENTER VARIABLE  2 FT
ENTER VARIABLE  3 FM
ENTER VARIABLE  4 IN
ENTER VARIABLE  5 ST
ENTER VARIABLE  6
ENTER VARIABLE  7
ENTER VARIABLE  8
ENTER VARIABLE  9
ENTER VARIABLE  10
HIT RETURN TO CONTINUE?
*** CLAUSE-VARIABLE LIST ***
** CLAUSE  1
VARIABLE  1 IN
VARIABLE  2
VARIABLE  3
VARIABLE  4
** CLAUSE  2
VARIABLE  1 IN
VARIABLE  2
VARIABLE  3
VARIABLE  4
** CLAUSE  3
VARIABLE  1 DO
VARIABLE  2
VARIABLE  3
VARIABLE  4
** CLAUSE  4
VARIABLE  1 DO
VARIABLE  2
VARIABLE  3
VARIABLE  4
HIT RETURN TO CONTINUE?
** CLAUSE  5
VARIABLE  1 FT
VARIABLE  2 FM
VARIABLE  3
VARIABLE  4
** CLAUSE  6
VARIABLE  1
VARIABLE  2
VARIABLE  3
VARIABLE  4
** CLAUSE  7
VARIABLE  1
VARIABLE  2
VARIABLE  3
VARIABLE  4
** CLAUSE  8
VARIABLE  1
VARIABLE  2
VARIABLE  3
VARIABLE  4
```

The preceding sample run appears with each of the following system-user interactions:

```
ENTER CONDITION VARIABLE ? DO
RISE OR FALL FOR DO-? RISE
IN = FALL
ST = RISE

ENTER CONDITION VARIABLE ? DO
RISE OR FALL FOR DO-? FALL
IN = RISE
ST = FALL

ENTER CONDITION VARIABLE ? IN
RISE OR FALL FOR IN-? FALL
ST = RISE

ENTER CONDITION VARIABLE ? FM
RISE OR FALL FOR FT-? RISE
ADD OR SUBTRACT FOR FM-? ADD
```

There are no conclusions for the above conditions since we can't satisfy any rule, i.e.,

IF   FT = FALL
           FM = ADD
THEN   IN = FALL

```
ENTER CONDITION VARIABLE ? FM
RISE OR FALL FOR FT-? FALL
ADD OR SUBTRACT FOR FM-? ADD
IN = FALL
ST = RISE
```

Forward Chaining Worksheet

The following worksheet is an aid to simplifying the process of placing a new knowledge base into the program to replace the one that is there now. It is included to allow you to validate the concepts of the relationship between the knowledge base and expert system data structures. As a future exercise, you can develop an input "compiler" which reads a knowledge base and makes transfers to the data structures automatically. You should do this only after understanding the concepts fully.

This worksheet will help you create and transfer the variables (variable 11, variable 12, etc.) and values (value 11, value 12, etc.) of your knowledge base into the program (it allows for *three* condition variables per rule). First create the rules for the IF-THEN statements below. Then transfer them onto the worksheets that follow.

IF (_____== _____   &&
Variable 11　　　　　　　Value 11

_____==_____   &&
Variable 12　　　　　　　Value 12

_____==_____   )
Variable 13　　　　　　　Value 13

_____ = _____ ;
Variable 14　　　　　　　Value 14

IF (_____==_____   &&
Variable 21　　　　　　　Value 21

_____==_____   &&
Variable 22　　　　　　　Value 22

_____==_____   )
Variable 23　　　　　　　Value 23

_____ = _____ ;
Variable 24　　　　　　　Value 24

IF (_____==_____   &&
Variable 31　　　　　　　Value 31

_____==_____   &&
Variable 32　　　　　　　Value 32

_____==_____   )
Variable 33　　　　　　　Value 33

_____ = _____ ;
Variable 34　　　　　　　Value 34

IF (_____==_____   &&
Variable 41　　　　　　　Value 41

_____==_____   &&
Variable 42　　　　　　　Value 42

_____==_____   )
Variable 43　　　　　　　Value 43

_____ = _____ ;
Variable 44　　　　　　　Value 44

IF (_____==_____   &&
Variable 51　　　　　　　Value 51

_____==_____   &&
Variable 52　　　　　　　Value 52

_____==_____   )
Variable 53　　　　　　　Value 53

_____ = _____ ;
Variable 54　　　　　　　Value 54

This worksheet inserts variables into the clause variable list (comments 407, 408).

CNDVAR[1]   = _____ ;
                  Variable 11

CNDVAR[2]   = _____ ;
                  Variable 12

CNDVAR[3]   = _____ ;
                  Variable 13

CNDVAR[5]   = _____ ;
                  Variable 21

CNDVAR[6]   = _____ ;
                  Variable 22

CNDVAR[7]   = _____ ;
                  Variable 23

CNDVAR[9]   = _____ ;
                  Variable 31

CNDVAR[10] = _____ ;
                  Variable 32

CNDVAR[11] = _____ ;
                  Variable 33

CNDVAR[13] = _____ ;
                  Variable 41

CNDVAR[14] = _____ ;
                  Variable 42

CNDVAR[15] = _____ ;
                  Variable 43

CNDVAR[17] = _____ ;
                  Variable 51

CNDVAR[18] = _____ ;
                  Variable 52

CNDVAR[19] = _____ ;
                  Variable 53

Use this worksheet to insert variables into the variable list (comment 367). Do not insert a variable name more than once.

VARLT[1] = _____ ;
                    Variable _____

VARLT[2] = _____ ;
                    Variable _____

VARLT[3] = _____ ;
                    Variable _____

VARLT[4] = _____ ;
                    Variable _____

VARLT[5] = _____ ;
                    Variable _____

This one is for insertion of the IF-THEN rules (see comments 1490–1611). The IF portions are listed first, followed by the THEN clause.

IF Rules

1500 IF (_____ == _____   &&
                Variable 11   Value 11

       _____ == _____   &&
            Variable 12   Value 12

       _____ == _____) S = 1;
            Variable 13   Value 13

    IF (_____ == _____   &&
            Variable 21   Value 21

       _____ == _____   &&
            Variable 22   Value 22

       _____ == _____) S = 1;
            Variable 23   Value 23

    IF (_____ == _____   &&
            Variable 31   Value 31

       _____ == _____   &&
            Variable 32   Value 32

       _____ == _____) S = 1;
            Variable 33   Value 33

IF (_____ == _____ &&
     Variable 41   Value 41

_____ == _____ &&
Variable 42   Value 42

_____ == _____) S = 1;
Variable 43   Value 43

IF (_____ == _____ &&
     Variable 51   Value 51

_____ == _____ &&
Variable 52   Value 52

_____ == _____) S = 1;
Variable 53   Value 53

THEN Rules

1500   _____ = _____ ;
       Variable 14   Value 14

printf("_____ = _____");
        Variable 14   Value 14

_____ = _____ ;
Variable 24   Value 24

printf("_____ = _____");
        Variable 24   Value 24

_____ = _____ ;
Variable 34   Value 34

printf("_____ = _____");
        Variable 34   Value 34

_____ = _____ ;
Variable 44   Value 44

printf("_____ = _____");
        Variable 44   Value 44

_____ = _____ ;
Variable 54   Value 54

printf("_____ = _____");
        Variable 54   Value 54

Backward Chaining

Suppose your car will not start. Is it because the battery is weak? Does the car need a tune-up? Or is the starter broken? We can state the problem in a more general way: We have a result or consequence (the car will not start) and want to determine the conditions causing the problem. In other words, we have a symptom (car doesn't start) and we want to discover what is wrong. Notice how this problem differs from the one we described in the previous chapter on forward chaining—in that car example, the car was overheating, and we didn't know what the outcome would be. The goal was to predict the possible result of the overheating. Here, the result has already happened, and the goal is to find out why.

We need rules to solve this problem as well. Some rules that might pertain to this situation are

Rule 1:
  IF the car is not tuned AND the battery is weak,
  THEN not enough current will reach the starter.
Rule 2:
  IF not enough current reaches the starter,
  THEN the car will not start.

How would you arrive at the conditions that have resulted in the car failing to start? There are two key words to keep in mind as we describe the situation: backward and chaining. The car did not start, triggering a chain of reasoning that led you backward in time from this car sequence to the set of conditions that caused it. Remember, a condition occurs earlier in time than its consequence; therefore, backward chaining works by searching for conclusions, instantiating causes, and seeing if these causes link to earlier conclusions. For example, rule 2 contains the conclusion clause "THEN the car will not start," so that rule, because we found out our car failed to start, is invoked first. Remember, backward chaining starts with the consequence (THEN part). The reason for the car not starting is a condition for rule 2, "IF not enough current reaches the starter." The chain of reasoning continues with the question, why is there not enough current? This question is addressed in rule 1 which identifies the conditions that prevent current from reaching the starter. These conditions are "IF the car is not tuned" and "the battery is weak." If these conditions are true, we have discovered the reason why the car did not start. If these conditions are false, we would need to find and invoke other pertinent rules and follow another chain in search of the cause.

If the conditions causing the problem are not contained in any other rules that pertain to the problem, you—the car owner—or a mechanic must provide additional information that will lead to the solution. To put it plainly, if the conditions suggested by the system are not true, the system needs to know if there are additional consequences (or symptoms) which, if they exist, will shed light on the problem.

You can now see that the word "chaining" signifies the linking of a set of rules. In our example, chaining began in rule 2 and ended in rule 1. What about the word backward? The car has to be untuned and the battery has to be weak before the car fails to start. Since we already know the car won't start—the consequence of these conditions—we try to find out why, that is, we try to pinpoint the conditions. Working from what occurred *last* to what occurred *first* is working backward.

Our backward chaining tool will help us solve diagnostic problems in which the conclusion is known and the causes are sought. We will construct a knowledge base and, using backward chaining principles, we will process the information in the knowledge base by answering questions put to us by the expert tool. And just as the forward chaining tool provided the conclusions or consequences to the condtiions presented, the backward chaining tool will find the conditions that led to the already known conclusions, consequences, or symptoms.

Backward chaining is just a bit trickier than forward chaining, but once again you will step through the design of an algorithm and the writing of the actual program for the tool.

A Procedure for Designing the Knowledge Base: The Decision Tree

The first thing to do is to state the problem that the expert system tool should solve. Let's consider an example suited to a backward chaining tool; it's one we will use as our central example throughout this chapter.

You are the personnel director for a large engineering firm, and an applicant, résumé in hand, comes to you for an interview. The applicant's qualifications are before you, as are the requirements of the job and the general standards of the company. Your problem is which position, if any, is this applicant qualified for?

This may not seem like a very complicated problem at first glance, but there are many factors that go into such a decision. Suppose the applicant has little experience in engineering but made an important discovery in his or her field. Or suppose the applicant did not do well in school but has several years of solid work experience. Each applicant is different, and although certain criteria must be met to land a job, there are several different combinations of factors in any applicant's history that may make that person qualified for a particular position.

The reason this problem is appropriate to backward chaining is that the goal is to select among a range of alternatives, in this case possible positions. The answer, in reality, already exists. The individual is sitting in the chair in front of you, perhaps with legs crossed, hands clasped nervously, trying to make a good impression on you. This individual, if qualified, is better suited for one position than another. Your job is to ask the right questions, drawn upon the knowledge you possess, and determine which position is best.

Once the problem has been stated, the next step is to somehow diagram the problem so that all its many aspects are illustrated as simply as possible. One of the most common diagrams used in working out problems of this sort is the decision tree. It is a very useful and effective type of diagram because it enables us to visualize all the factors that must be considered in reaching a decision and to see how one consideration leads to others, which then lead to still others, and so on.

The decision tree is so named because it branches off just like a tree, and at the very end of each branch or system of branches is a conclusion, in this case, should you or should you not offer this applicant a position and if so, which one? Because many problems are complex and difficult to conceptualize (or we wouldn't need expert systems to help solve them) we use the decision tree to illustrate the problem clearly.

Figure 6-1 is a decision tree for our job applicant dilemma. Study it for a few minutes. Notice that the flow diagram consists of circles and rectangles called "nodes"—the numbers in the nodes are for reference. The arrow lines that connect these nodes are known as "arcs" or "branches." The circles which contain questions are "decision nodes." The rectangular shapes contain the goals of the diagram, and they signify conclusions. The arrow lines designate the direction of the diagram. Many of the nodes have branches leaving them, providing pathways to other nodes. The path taken from each node is determined by

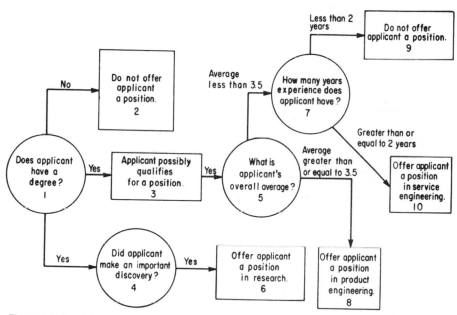

Figure 6-1   Decision tree for offering job position.

the response to the condition contained in the node's drawing. For example, node 5, shown in Figure 6-2, asks a question which has two possible answers and therefore two possible paths depending on what the applicant's school average is. If the average is 3.1, path 1 will be taken since 3.1 is less than 3.5. The applicant's average can be considered a variable and its value the instantiation of that variable. Therefore, each circular node contains a variable, and the paths are conditions placed upon the values of that variable. When we establish rules for this domain, these conditions will become clauses of the IF portion of an IF-THEN rule. The rectangles are conclusions or subconclusions. For example, the rectangular box in Figure 6-3 would be an answer to the problem statement "should we offer applicant a job position?" Our goal would be to provide the answer. Likewise, the rectangular box in Figure 6-4 would be a goal of the problem statement, "Does applicant possibly qualify for a position?" But it could also be a part of a path leading to another conclusion since it has a branch leaving its node. In that case, since the branch is not a condition, that is, it does not depend on anything and we can only emerge from that rectangle along that one branch, it is called a "subconclusion" of another goal. A subconclusion is also a clause in an IF statement. We will see an example of this shortly.

Now that we have carefully and thoroughly diagrammed the prob-

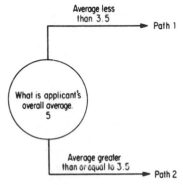

Average less
than 3.5

Path 1

What is applicant's
overall average.
5

Average greater
than or equal to 3.5

Path 2

Figure 6-2   Decision node path determination.

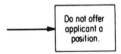

Do not offer
applicant a
position.

Figure 6-3   A conclusion.

lem, we're ready for the next step, creating a knowledge base that is comprised of IF-THEN rules.

Conversion to IF-THEN Rules

As we discussed in Chapter 2, IF-THEN rules are made up of two parts. The IF part is comprised of conditions called clauses connected to one another with words known as logical operators such as AND, OR, and NOT. The THEN part is evaluated only if the IF part is true. The combination of linked decision nodes (circles) and a conclusion node (rectangle) represents an IF-THEN rule. The IF part contains all the decision nodes in the path leading to a conclusion node; each decision node in the path leading to the conclusion contributes one clause to the IF portion. The conclusion itself forms the THEN portion. Figure 6-5 shows an example.

If we wish to determine if the applicant possibly qualifies for a position, node 3 is the conclusion. The only path leading to this conclusion

Application possibly
qualifies for a
position.

Figure 6-4   Another conclusion.

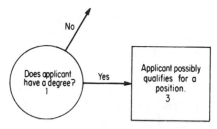

Figure 6-5   Path of IF-THEN conversion.

contains decision node 1, "Does applicant have a degree?" the rule that this path generates is

IF applicant has a degree = yes,
THEN applicant possibly qualifies for a position = yes

The clause "applicant has a degree" can have one of two values, namely, yes or no. Therefore, "applicant has a degree" is a variable. In fact, all the nodes contain variables.

Since it is too clumsy to refer to variables with such awkward, long names, we will give each node's variable a short, abbreviated name. Table 6-1 lists all the variable names in the nodes of the diagram in Figure 6-1, along with the variable's full meaning and the numbers of the nodes in which these variables can be found. These abbreviations will simply make creating our rules a little less cumbersome. We can use these simple variable names in the IF-THEN statements.

We are now ready to take a major step, generating all the rules for each of the possible conclusions. This is done according to the following technique.

1. Choose a conclusion (rectangular) node of the decision tree. Record it.

2. Choose a decision node with a connecting branch to the *left* of the node you chose in step 1. Record that node.

Table 6-1   Variable Name Table

Variable name	Meaning	Node(s)
DEGREE	Does applicant have a degree?	1
DISCOVERY	Did applicant make an important discovery?	4
EXPERIENCE	How many years experience does applicant have?	7
GRADE	What is applicant's overall school average?	5
POSITION	What position should be offered to applicant?	2, 6, 8, 9 ,10
QUALIFY	Applicant possibly qualifies for a position.	3

3. Continue doing step 2 until either there are no more nodes to the left or until a conclusion node is reached. If a conclusion (rectangular) node is reached, record it and stop. If there are no more nodes, stop.

4. Each decision node in the path is the variable part of an IF clause. The value associated with the branch is the condition. All connected clauses use the logical AND.

5. The conclusion becomes the THEN part.

Rule Generating Technique

As an example, consider the path shown in Figure 6-6. Following the steps just outlined, we would make the following listing:

Conclusion node 6

Path 6, 4, 1

Remember, this is a backward chaining technique. We start with the conclusion and move backward through the decision tree.

From this listing and the variable name table we arrive at the following rule:

    IF DEGREE = YES AND DISCOVERY = YES
    THEN POSITION = RESEARCH

That is, if the applicant has a degree *and* has made an important discovery, he or she should be offered a position as a researcher.

We are now ready to apply these principles to develop our knowledge base. You can do the same for your domain area, keeping in mind simply that there should be one IF-THEN rule for every unique path to each goal. The IF-THEN rules for Figure 6-1 are written out in Table 6-2. The rule numbers themselves are arbitrary; they simply serve as an easy means of identification.

The six rules cover all the paths leading to every goal of the decision tree of Figure 6-1. Now you can see why the decision tree comes in

Figure 6-6   A sample path.

Table 6-2 IF-THEN Rules

Rule	Path
10 IF DEGREE = NO THEN POSITION = NO	1, 2
20 IF DEGREE = YES THEN QUALIFY = YES	1,3
30 IF DEGREE = YES AND DISCOVERY = YES THEN POSITION = RESEARCH	1, 4, 6
40 IF QUALIFY = YES AND AVERAGE < 3.5 AND EXPERIENCE >= 2 THEN POSITION = SERVICE ENGINEER	3, 5, 7, 10
50 IF QUALIFY = YES AND AVERAGE < 3.5 AND EXPERIENCE < 2 THEN POSITION = NO	3, 5, 7, 9
60 IF QUALIFY = YES AND AVERAGE >= 3.5 THEN POSITION = PRODUCT ENGINEER	3, 5, 8

handy—it provides a simple and expedient method for establishing the rules that comprise the knowledge base. Without the knowledge base we cannot go forward.

Processing the Knowledge Base

Now we can implement our expert backward chaining techniques to answer questions based on our knowledge base. Technically, we can say that our knowledge base is used to lead us on a path toward reaching our conclusion. For example, if your path ended at conclusion node 9 of the decision tree, you will "not offer applicant a position." The conclusions contained in the decision (rectangular) nodes are equivalent to the variables contained in the THEN portion of the IF-THEN statements. The decision path we took to reach that conclusion provides an explanation of why we made it. In other words, the THEN portion represents a decision and the succession of IF clauses explains the reasoning.

Our expert technique requires construction of a number of useful tables, or data structures, that will aid in answering questions and making decisions about the problem we want to solve. These data structures are derived directly from the knowledge base, so they serve an indispensable purpose. The knowledge base with all its derived data structures is shown in Figure 6-7. When we have finally arrived at a way of solving this type of problem, we will be able to write a program to do the same thing in the same way.

Let's get on with the task of describing the algorithm and build some of the data structures that will help us along.

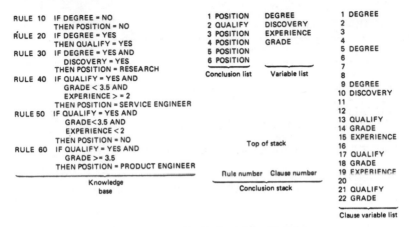

Figure 6-7   The knowledge base and its derived data structures.

Conclusion List

The first data structure is the conclusion list which merely lists all the possible conclusions in sequential order. The conclusion list contains three items: first is a rule number, second is the conclusion associated with that rule number, and third is the set of conditions which yield the conclusion. There will be one entry for every IF-THEN rule in our knowledge base. The completed conclusion list for the rules in our knowledge base is shown in Figure 6-8. Let's see how these entries are determined by examining rule 10. The THEN portion of rule 10 contains the variable POSITION; POSITION is therefore the variable associated with the conclusion of rule 10. When the conclusion in the THEN portion of each rule is placed in the same row as its rule number, the conclusion list is complete.

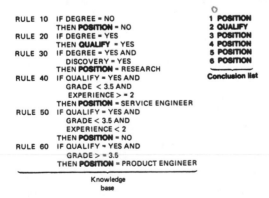

Figure 6-8   Conclusion list taken from THEN portion.

This structure is used solely to locate a conclusion by its corresponding rule number. If the IF part of the rule is true, we invoke the THEN part, thereby instantiating the conclusion. For example, if we want to know if an applicant should be offered a position, we would scan the conclusion list until we found POSITION. This is found right away in the first entry, that is, rule 10, which is:

IF DEGREE = NO
THEN POSITION = NO

If DEGREE is instantiated to NO, we cannot offer the applicant a position. If DEGREE equals YES, we cannot invoke the THEN part because YES differs from the condition for this statement. Therefore we have to scan the list for another rule containing the conclusion POSITION. For now, we are getting a little ahead of overselves; let's describe the other structures we need, and then we will pull them all together.

Variable List

The next structure we will discuss is the variable list. This structure also contains two items: one is a variable name for each variable contained in the IF part of the knowledge base rules, and the other item tells us whether or not the variable is instantiated. This list is shown in Figure 6-9. A variable only appears *once* in the list no matter how many condition clauses it appears in. It also cannot be a conclusion variable because the values of conclusion variables are determined by rules. The instantiated column is always initially set to not instantiated (NI). It will be changed to instantiated (I) as each variable is set

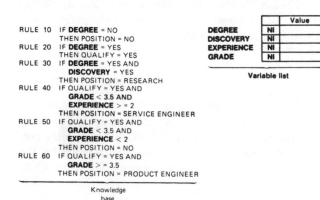

```
RULE 10   IF DEGREE = NO
             THEN POSITION = NO
RULE 20   IF DEGREE = YES
             THEN QUALIFY = YES
RULE 30   IF DEGREE = YES AND
              DISCOVERY = YES
             THEN POSITION = RESEARCH
RULE 40   IF QUALIFY = YES AND
              GRADE < 3.5 AND
              EXPERIENCE > = 2
             THEN POSITION = SERVICE ENGINEER
RULE 50   IF QUALIFY = YES AND
              GRADE < 3.5 AND
              EXPERIENCE < 2
             THEN POSITION = NO
RULE 60   IF QUALIFY = YES AND
              GRADE > = 3.5
             THEN POSITION = PRODUCT ENGINEER
```

Knowledge
base

		Value
DEGREE	NI	
DISCOVERY	NI	
EXPERIENCE	NI	
GRADE	NI	

Variable list

Figure 6-9   Variable list.

to a value, that is, as the applicant's qualifications are considered one by one. Before an IF-THEN statement can be executed, *all* the clause variables in the IF portion must be instantiated. If we are trying to execute an IF statement, we can see if any variable has already been instantiated by checking the variable list. If the variable is marked NI, the variable must first be instantiated. After the applicant has provided an answer and the variable is instantiated, we can set the instantiated value to I in the variable list. We are then in a position to compare the variable's value with the condition part of any clause containing the variable. Take rule 10 as an example:

IF DEGREE = NO
THEN POSITION = NO

Row 1 of the variable list contains DEGREE, which is not yet instantiated (NI). Therefore, the IF clause can't be executed. To instantiate DEGREE, we ask the applicant if he or she has a degree. The value of the answer, yes or no, which is stored in the variable, can then be compared with the condition part of the IF, that is,

IF DEGREE = NO

If DEGREE is instantiated to NO, the THEN part can be executed. In any case, after DEGREE is instantiated, NI is replaced with I in the DEGREE row of the variable list as follows:

Variable name	Instantiated	Value
DEGREE	I	NO

Now whenever the variable DEGREE is encountered in reference to any possible conclusion, it can be treated as having been instantiated in *any* clause of any IF-THEN statement. That is, once the applicant has answered the question, the answer will remain the same from that point on and will be available to other rules.

Clause Variable List

An IF statement can contain one or more variables. In our system, we allocate room for up to four variables. The variables are connected by logical operators AND, OR, or NOT. In this section we will only consider the AND operator since that is the one used most frequently. For example, rule 30 contains two clauses which are connected by an AND, namely

IF DEGREE = YES AND DISCOVERY = YES

In addition, note that rule 40 contains three clauses, as does rule 50, and so on. The following concept is important:

> If all the clauses in the IF part of a rule are connected by the logical operator AND, all the variables in these clauses must be instantiated before the IF part can be executed.

For example, using rule 30,

30   IF DEGREE = YES AND DISCOVERY = YES
     THEN POSITION = RESEARCH

you must have a value for both DEGREE and DISCOVERY before you can determine if the THEN part should be executed. You should therefore assemble a list of variables for the IF part of each IF-THEN rule. First, check each variable for instantiation in the variable list. Instantiate those that aren't and then execute the IF-THEN rule. The data structure containing the list of variables for each IF part of IF-THEN rules is called the clause variable list. The clause variable list for the six rules of our knowledge base is shown in Figure 6-10. To simplify the programming of the examples, each rule is allocated room for no more than four IF variables. The numbers, 1 through 22, shown to the left of the variable names represent the array location in the data structure that the variable names are placed in. If a rule does not utilize all of these four locations, they are left blank. Of course this number can always be increased beyond four with additional programming. There is a good reason for allocating the same number of loca-

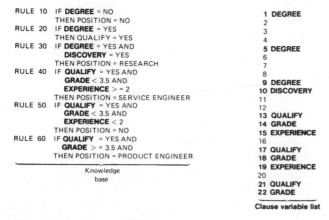

Figure 6-10   Clause variable list.

tions to each rule: The row number at the start of an IF-THEN rule can then be determined by a simple multiplication formula:

4 * (STATEMENT NUMBER / 10 − 1) + 1

For example, rule 50 starts at location 17:

4 * (50 / 10 − 1) + 1 = 17

Let's take a moment to review the three structures we've just designed. As we said in the chapter on forward chaining, these data structures relate specifically to thought processes you might go through when trying to solve a problem. The same is said for backward chaining. First you consider all the possible pathways that would lead to a conclusion (conclusion list). Then, you map out the conditions that constitute those various pathways (variable list and clause variable list). Because variable values often apply to more than one possible conclusion in a given situation, the data structures enable us to manage this information quickly and without repeating the same steps over and over. In other words, if you were considering hiring an applicant and you not only didn't have access to a computer but didn't even have a pencil and a piece of paper, you would probably have to review the same facts several times because they're simply too complicated to keep in one's head at one time. You could do it, of course, but it would just be harder and would take a lot longer.

Conclusion Stack

The fourth and last structure we will discuss is the conclusion stack. The conclusion stack is the central structure: It ties together all of the other structures we've discussed in the implementation of the backward chaining expert system tool. It is the conclusion stack that tells us which IF-THEN statement contains the conclusion we are trying to reach and which clause in the IF portion is being examined for instantiation.

In order to understand the conclusion stack, let's backtrack a second to the following rule again:

```
40   IF QUALIFY = YES AND      IF clause 1
        GRADE < 3.5     AND     IF clause 2
        EXPERIENCE >= 2         IF clause 3
     THEN POSITION = SERVICE ENGINEERING
```

This rule has three IF clauses, which are numbered 1 to 3, and one THEN clause. In order to evaluate the rule to see if we should invoke the THEN clause, we must examine each IF clause one at a time. If all the IF clauses are true, we can invoke the THEN clause which directs us to offer the applicant a position in service engineering. If any of the IF clauses are false, we must discard this rule. Let's see how we can keep track of the rule by its number and keep track of each clause as it is examined. The conclusion stack data structure will help us do this, as shown in Figure 6-11. We see from this figure that we are examining rule 40 and its clause 1. This tells us that we are examining

QUALIFY = YES

But the value of QUALIFY is determined by rule 20 which is

IF DEGREE = YES   (IF clause 1)
THEN QUALIFY = YES

Therefore we must now examine rule 20 to determine the value of QUALIFY. We place rule 20 on top of the conclusion stack as shown in Figure 6-12. The clause number tells us to look at clause 1 of rule 20 which is

DEGREE = YES

DEGREE will be instantiated to a value of YES or NO by the applicant. Since there are no more IF clauses in rule 20, we can instantiate QUALIFY to YES only if DEGREE = YES. Assume the applicant has a degree (DEGREE = YES); then QUALIFY = YES. Now that we are finished with rule 20, we can remove it from the stack. Since QUALIFY = YES, we are now finished with clause 1 of rule 40 and next must examine clause 2, as shown in Figure 6-13. This interaction of the

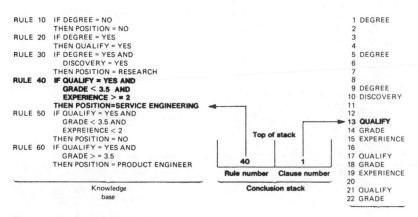

Figure 6-11 Conclusion stack.

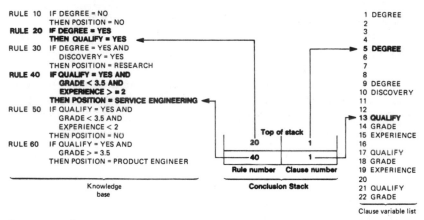

Figure 6-12   Conclusion stack compares additional rule.

conclusion stack with the knowledge base continues throughout the backward chaining process.

In review, the conclusion stack is the place for keeping track of which rule and which clause within that rule we are trying to verify.

An Example Using the Knowledge Base

In order to pull all these concepts together, let's examine a typical request to our expert system tool from start to finish. A user will first enter a conclusion that the system can verify. For this example, it is

Should applicant be offered a position?

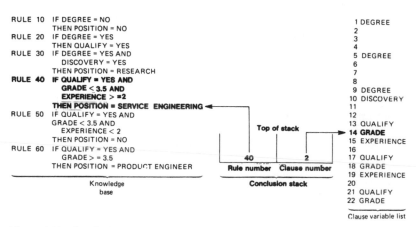

Figure 6-13   Conclusion stack advances.

The conclusion variable, taken from the variable name table, is

POSITION

The tool will place on the top of the conclusion stack the number of the next rule that contains POSITION as a conclusion variable. Since this is the first time POSITION has been encountered, we search the conclusion list starting with rule 10. We immediately find POSITION is the conclusion variable of rule 10. Therefore, the conclusion stack will initially contain one item and look like Figure 6-14.

By looking at the clause variable list, we see that the number 1 variable in rule 10 is DEGREE. By scanning the variable list, we see DEGREE is not yet instantiated, that is, it is designated NI. Since DEGREE is also *not* a conclusion variable, it is not on the conclusion list, and the applicant must instantiate it with the following question:

Does applicant have a degree?

The answer—let's say it is yes—causes a change in the variable list as shown in Figure 6-15.

This answer makes rule 10,

10   IF DEGREE = NO
      THEN POSITION = NO

false since DEGREE = YES. We must now remove the false conclusion from the conclusion stack and scan the condition list for the next use of POSITION as a conclusion variable. This is found in rule 30 which is

30   IF DEGREE = YES AND DISCOVERY = YES
      THEN POSITION = RESEARCH

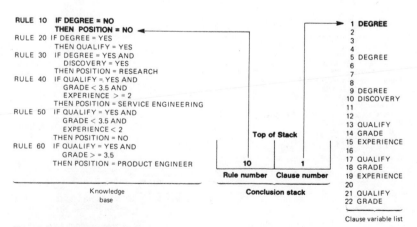

Figure 6-14   Initial conclusion stack.

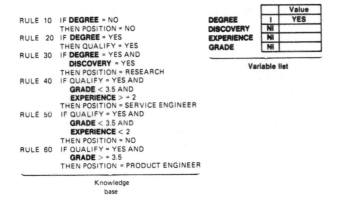

Figure 6-15 Updated variable list.

We would place rule 30 on top of the conclusion stack as shown in Figure 6-16.

We will now try to instantiate all the condition variables in rule 30, as shown in the clause variable list in Figure 6-17. The clause number of the conclusion stack points to DEGREE in the clause variable list, which we see has already been instantiated (I) in the variable list. Therefore the clause number is incremented to 2, pointing to DISCOVERY in the clause variable list. The updated stack is shown in Figure 6-18.

From the variable list we see DISCOVERY is not instantiated (NI) and is not a conclusion since it is not on the conclusion list. We therefore ask the applicant

Did applicant make an important discovery?

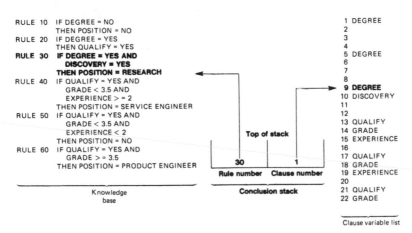

Figure 6-16 Stack operation.

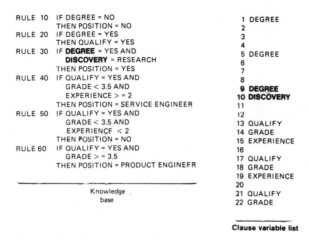

Figure 6-17   Clause variable list snapshot.

to which, let's say, the answer is no. Since DISCOVERY is now instantiated to NO, we can update the variable list as shown in Figure 6-19.

Now that the first two variables have been instantiated, the clause number of the conclusion stack is updated to 3. Since there is no variable in location 3 of rule 30 in the clause variable list, all of the variables for rule 30 have evidently been instantiated. We are ready to execute the IF-THEN rule,

30   IF DEGREE = YES AND DISCOVERY = YES
       THEN POSITION = YES

The second clause of rule 30 is false because DISCOVERY has been instantiated to NO. We therefore remove rule 30 from the top of the

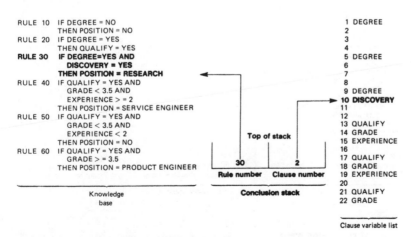

Figure 6-18   Further updated conclusion stack.

```
RULE 10   IF DEGREE = NO
          THEN POSITION = NO
RULE 20   IF DEGREE = YES
          THEN QUALIFY = YES
RULE 30   IF DEGREE = YES AND
             DISCOVERY = RESEARCH
          THEN POSITION = YES
RULE 40   IF QUALIFY = YES AND
             GRADE < 3.5 AND
             EXPERIENCE >.= 2
          THEN POSITION = SERVICE ENGINEER
RULE 50   IF QUALIFY = YES AND
             GRADE < 3.5 AND
             EXPERIENCE < 2
          THEN POSITION = NO
RULE 60   IF QUALIFY = YES AND
             GRADE > = 3.5
          THEN POSITION = PRODUCT ENGINEER
```

		Value
DEGREE	I	YES
DISCOVERY	I	NO
EXPERIENCE	NI	
GRADE	NI	

Variable list

Knowledge
base

Figure 6-19   Variable list.

conclusion stack. Searching the remainder of the conclusion list, we
see that POSITION is also a conclusion variable of rule 40 which is

> 40   IF QUALIFY = YES AND GRADE < 3.5 AND
> EXPERIENCE >= 2
> THEN POSITION = SERVICE ENGINEER

We place rule 40 on the conclusion stack as shown in Figure 6-20.

The first clause of rule 40 is QUALIFY. Since QUALIFY has not
been instantiated in the variable list and is also in the conclusion list,
we find QUALIFY to be a conclusion variable of rule 20. We place a
new unit on top of the conclusion stack as shown in Figure 6-21. Rule
20's first and only clause variable is DEGREE. Since DEGREE has

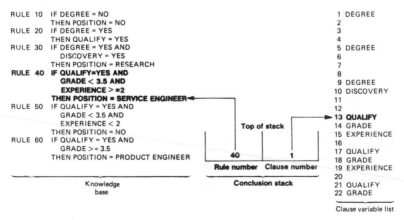

Figure 6-20   Latest conclusion stack.

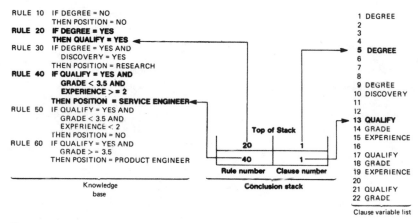

Figure 6-21   Multiunit conclusion stack.

already been instantiated to YES, as shown in the variable list, we can go ahead and execute rule 20

20   IF DEGREE = YES
     THEN QUALIFY = YES

which causes the THEN part to be invoked and QUALIFY to be instantiated to YES. Since QUALIFY is now instantiated, we can remove its unit from the top of the stack and get back to rule 40. The clause number for the unit on top of the stack is incremented to 2 as shown in Figure 6-22.

Since the variable GRADE of rule 40 is not on the conclusion list, it has not yet been instantiated and the applicant is asked

What is your average grade?

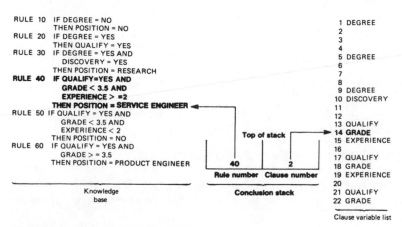

Figure 6-22   Updated conclusion stack.

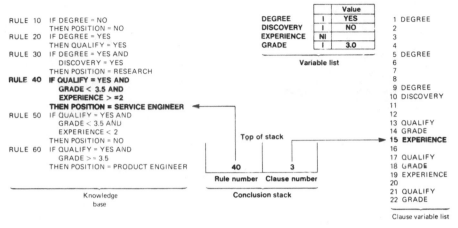

Figure 6-23   Example status.

The applicant answers 3.0, which instantiates GRADE. The clause number is incremented to 3 and the conclusion stack and variable list as they look now are shown in Figure 6-23.

EXPERIENCE, the third clause, has still not been instantiated and is not a conclusion variable. Therefore, the applicant is asked the question

How many years experience do you have?

The reply, 4.5, instantiates EXPERIENCE, causing the variable list to change to an I and the clause number to be incremented to 4. Since there are no more variables in the clause variable list for rule 40, the IF part can now be executed. Since

QUALIFY = YES
GRADE = 3.0
EXPERIENCE >= 2

when rule 40's IF clause

IF QUALIFY = YES AND GRADE < 3.5 AND EXP >= 2

is executed, we find it true, POSITION is instantiated to SERVICE ENGINEERING, because of the THEN part:

THEN POSITION = SERVICE ENGINEERING

This is the moment we have been waiting for. The goal has been reached. We can offer the applicant a position in the service engineering department.

Concepts for Design Implementation

Let us review the steps we have taken to implement the backward chaining structure:

1. Identify the conclusion.

2. Search the conclusion list for the first instance of the conclusion's name. If found, place the rule on the conclusion stack using the rule number and a (1) to represent the clause number. If not found, notify the user that an answer cannot be found.

3. Instantiate the IF clause (i.e., each condition variable) of the statement.

4. If one of the IF clause variables is not instantiated, as indicated by the variable list, and is not a conclusion variable, that is, not on the conclusion list, ask the user to enter a value.

5. If one of the clauses is a conclusion variable, place the conclusion variable's rule number on the top of the stack and go back to step 3.

6. If the statement on top of the stack cannot be instantiated using the present IF-THEN statement, remove the unit from the top of the stack and search the conclusion list for another instance of that conclusion variable's name.

7. If such a statement is found, go back to step 3.

8. If there are no more conclusions left on the conclusion stack with that name, the rule for the previous conclusion is false. If there is no previous conclusion, then notify the user that an answer cannot be found. If there is a previous conclusion, go back to step 6.

9. If the rule on top of the stack can be instantiated, remove it from the stack. If another conclusion variable is underneath, increment the clause number, and for the remaining clauses go back to step 3. If no other conclusion variable is underneath, we have answered our question. The user can come to a conclusion.

The Tool Itself

We can use the above concepts to design, in C, our expert system tool. We can insert a set of IF-THEN rules into its knowledge base and use it to answer our questions. So put away your pencil and paper and run the program in Listing 6-1. It will solidify your understanding of all the concepts we have covered.

Programming Applications

In this part of the chapter we will supply you with a backward chaining tool for you to apply to your knowledge base. This tool will allow you to insert a set of rules into comments 1500 through 1680 of the program, type backward, and obtain answers from your knowledge base.

Program Explanation

As an example to acquaint you with the way the program is used, we have inserted the rules for determining if we should give an applicant a position in our company. This is the same example we used to explain the backward chaining concepts. For example, the rule

    IF DEGREE = NO
    THEN POSITION = NO

is covered by comments 1500 and 1510. The rule

    IF (QUALIFY = YES) AND (GRADE < 3.5) AND
    (EXPERIENCE >= 2)
    THEN POSITION = SERVICE ENGINEERING

is covered by comments 1560 and 1570.

Each variable in the variable list is found in one of the condition clauses (the IF part) but is not a conclusion variable (the THEN part). The variable list is constructed in comment 367. Each of these variables must be instantiated by the backward chaining system. This is done in comments 1700 and 1715. The order in which the variables are placed is determined by the order in comment 367. The conclusion list is constructed in comment 305. The clause variable list is constructed in comments 407 and 409.

Program Listing

Listing 6-1 is followed by a sequence of sample runs. Note that the system responses have been abbreviated. For example, PO = RE-SEARCH (or SERVICE ENGINEERING or PRODUCT ENGINEER-ING) means "offer the applicant a position in that department"; PO = NO means "do not offer applicant a position"; QU = YES means "the applicant is qualified but we're not sure as yet for what."

Listing 6-1   Backward chaining.

```
/********************* backward chaining *************/
/* install your IF clauses in sequence in the first case
   statement of the main program
   example: if((a1==2) && (a2==6)) s=1;
            if(strcmp(j,"NO") != 0) s=1;
   the then part of the above construction always
   contains s=1;
   install your the clauses in sequence in the second
   case statement of the main program
   example strcpy(po,"YES");

/* conclusion list */
char conclt[10][3];
/* variable list */
char varlt[10][3];
/* clause variable list */
char clvarlt[40][3];
char varble[3];
char /* qualify */ qu[4], /* degree */ de[4];
char /* discovery */ di[4], /* position */ po[4];

/* instantiated list */
int instlt[11];
/* statement stack */
int statsk[11];
int /* clause stack */ clausk[11], sn,f,i,j,s,k, /* stack pointer */ sp;

float /* grade */ gr, /* experience */ ex;

void determine_member_concl_list(void);
void push_on_stack(void);
void instantiate(void);

main()
{
/********* initialization section *******/
/* stack space is 10 we initially place stack space at 10+1 */
sp=11;
for(i=1;i<11;i++)
{
  strcpy(conclt[i],"");
  strcpy(varlt[i],"");
  instlt[i]=0;
  statsk[i]=0;
  clausk[i]=0;
}
for(i=1;i<41;i++) strcpy(clvarlt[i],"");
/* enter conclusions which are the variables in the then part, 1 at a
   time. enter the conclusions in exact order starting at the 1st if-then.
   after last conclusion hit return key for rest of conclusions */
/******* comment 305 **********/
  strcpy(conclt[1],"PO");
  strcpy(conclt[2],"QU");
  strcpy(conclt[3],"PO");
  strcpy(conclt[4],"PO");
  strcpy(conclt[5],"PO");
  strcpy(conclt[6],"PO");
  printf("*** CONCLUSION LIST ***\n");
  for(i=1;i<11;i++) printf("CONCLUSION %d  %s\n",i,conclt[i]);
  printf("HIT RETURN TO CONTINUE");
  gets();
  /* enter variables which are in the if part, 1 at a time in the exact
     order that they occur. up to 3 variables per if statement. do not
     duplicate any variable names. any name is used only once. if no
     more variables left just hit return key. */
  printf("*** VARIABLE LIST ***\n");
/********** comment 367 **********/
  strcpy(varlt[1],"DE");
  strcpy(varlt[2],"DI");
  strcpy(varlt[3],"EX");
  strcpy(varlt[4],"GR");
  for(i=1;i<11;i++) printf("VARIABLE %d  %s\n",i,varlt[i]);
  printf("HIT RETURN KEY TO CONTINUE");
  gets();
  /* enter variables as they appear in the if clauses. a maximum of 3
     variables per if statement. if no more variables hit return key.*/
  printf("*** CLAUSE VARIABLE LIST ***\n");
```

Listing 6-1 *(Continued)*

```
/************ comment 407 though 409 *********/
   strcpy(clvarlt[1],"DE");
   strcpy(clvarlt[5],"DE");
   strcpy(clvarlt[9],"DE");
   strcpy(clvarlt[10],"DI");
   strcpy(clvarlt[13],"QU");
   strcpy(clvarlt[14],"GR");
   strcpy(clvarlt[15],"EX");
   strcpy(clvarlt[17],"QU");
   strcpy(clvarlt[18],"GR");
   strcpy(clvarlt[19],"EX");
   strcpy(clvarlt[21],"QU");
   strcpy(clvarlt[22],"GR");
   for(i=1;i<9;i++)
   {
    printf("** CLAUSE %d\n",i);
    for(j=1;j<5;j++)
    { k=4*(i-1)+j; printf("VARIABLE %d  %s\n",j,clvarlt[k]); }
    if(i==4)
    { printf("HIT RETURN KEY TO CONTINUE"); gets(); }
   }
/*************** inference section ***************/
  printf("** ENTER CONCLUSION ? "); gets(varble);
  /* get conclusion statement number (sn) from the conclusion list (conclt) */
  /* first statement starts search */
  b520: f=1;
  determine_member_concl_list();
  if(sn != 0) {
   /* if sn=0 then no conclusion of that name */
   do
   /* push statement number (sn) and clause number=1 on goal stack which is
      composed of the statement stack (statsk) and clause stack (clausk) */
   {
    push_on_stack();
    do
    {
    /* calculate clause location in clause-variable list */
  b545: i=(statsk[sp]-1)*4 + clausk[sp];
       /* clause variable */
       strcpy(varble,clvarlt[i]);
       if(strcmp(varble,"") != 0) {
        /* is this clause variable a conclusion? */
        f=1;
        determine_member_concl_list();
        if(sn != 0)
        /* it is a conclusion push it */
          goto b520;
          /* check instantiation of this clause */
          instantiate();
          clausk[sp]=clausk[sp]+1;
        }
    } while(strcmp(varble,"") != 0); /* do-while statement */
    /* no more clauses check if part of statement */
    sn=statsk[sp];
    s=0;
    /*********** if then statements ************/
    /* sample if parts of if then statements from the position
       knowldge base */
    switch (sn) {
    /* if part of statement 1 */
 /********* comment 1500 *********/
     case 1: if (strcmp(de,"NO") == 0) s=1;
             break;
     /* if part of statement 2 */
 /********* comment 1510 *********/
     case 2: if(strcmp(de,"YES") == 0) s=1;
             break;
     /* if part of statement 3 */
     case 3: if((strcmp(de,"YES") == 0) && (strcmp(di,"YES") ==0)) s=1;
             break;
     /* if part of statement 4 */
 /********* comment 1560 *********/
     case 4: if((strcmp(qu,"YES") == 0) && (gr<3.5) && (ex >= 2)) s=1;
             break;
```

```
/********** comment 1570 **********/
    /* if part of statement 5 */
    case 5: if((strcmp(qu,"YES") == 0) && (gr<3) && (ex<2)) s=1;
            break;
    /* if part of statement 6 */
    case 6: if((strcmp(qu,"YES") == 0) && (gr >=3.5)) s=1;
              break;
/********** comment 1680 **********/
    }
  /* see if the then part should be invoked */
  if( s!= 1) {
  /* failed..search rest of statements for same conclusion */
  /* get conclusion */
  i=statsk[sp];
  strcpy(varble,conclt[i]);
  /* search for conclusion starting at the next statement number */
  f=statsk[sp]+1;
  determine_member_concl_list();
  sp=sp+1;
  }
  /* pop old conclusion and put on new one */
  } while((s != 1) && (sn != 0));  /* outer do-while loop */
if(sn != 0) {
/* if part true invoke then part */
/* then part of if-then statements from the position knowledge base */
switch (sn) {
/* then part of statement 1 */
/************* comment 1500 ***********/
 case 1: strcpy(po,"NO");
           printf("PO=NO\n");
           break;
 /* then part of statement 2 */
/************* comment 1510 **********/
 case 2: strcpy(qu,"YES");
           printf("QU=YES\n");
           break;
 /* then part of statement 3 */
 case 3: strcpy(po,"YES");
           printf("PO=RESEARCH\n");
           break;
 /* then part of statement 4 */
/************* comment 1560 ***********/
 case 4: strcpy(po,"YES");
           printf("PO=SERVICE ENGINEER\n");
           break;
 /* then part of statement 5 */
/************* comment 1570 ***********/
 case 5: strcpy(po,"NO");
           printf("PO=NO\n");
           break;
 /* then part of statement 6 */
 case 6: strcpy(po,"YES");
           printf("PO=PRODUCT ENGINEER\n");
           break;
/************* comment 1680 ***********/
 }
/* pop the stack */
sp=sp+1;
if(sp >= 11)
/* finished */
 printf("*** SUCCESS\n");
else {
 /* stack is not empty */
 /* get next clause then continue */
  clausk[sp]=clausk[sp]+1;
  goto b545;
  }
 }
}
```

Listing 6-1 *(Continued)*

```
void determine_member_concl_list() {
/* routine to determine if a variable (varble) is a member of the conclusion
   list (conclt). if yes return sn !=0. if not a member sn=0; */
/* initially set to not a member */
sn=0;
/* member of conclusion list to be searched is f */
i=f;
while(( strcmp(varble, conclt[i]) != 0) && (i<8))
/* test for membership */
 i=i+1;
if ( strcmp(varble, conclt[i]) == 0) sn=i; /* a member */
}

void push_on_stack()
/* routine to push statement number (sn) and a clause number of 1 onto the
   conclusion stack which consists of the statement stack (statsk) and the
   clause stack (clausk)..to push decrement stack pointer (sp) */
{
sp=sp-1;
statsk[sp]=sn;
clausk[sp]=1;
}

void instantiate()
/* routine to instantiate a variable (varble) if it isn't already. the
   instantiate indication (instlt) ia a 0 if not, a 1 if it is. the
   variable list (varlt) contains the variable (varble). */
{
i=1;
/* find variable in the list */
while((strcmp(varble, varlt[i]) !=0) && (i<10)) i=i+1;
if((strcmp(varble,varlt[i]) == 0) && (instlt[i] != 1))
 /* found variable and not already instantiated */
 {
 instlt[i]=1; /* mark instantiated */
 /* the designer of the knowledge base places the input statements to
    instantiate the variables below in the case statement */
 switch (i)
  {
/****** input statements *******/
/* input statements for sample position knowledge base */
/***** comment 1700 ********/
  case 1: printf("INPUT YES OR NO FOR DE-? ");
          gets(de);
          break;
  case 2: printf("INPUT YES OR NO FOR DI-? ");
          gets(di);
          break;
  case 3: printf("INPUT A REAL NUMBER FOR EX-? ");
          scanf("%f",&ex);
          break;
  case 4: printf("INPUT A REAL NUMBER FOR GR-? ");
          scanf("%f",&gr);
          break;
 /******** comment 1715 *********/
 }
 /* end of inputs statements for sample position knowledge base */
 }
}
```

Sample Runs

Let's see how the program works in giving us answers. When we enter backward, the following happens:

```
***  CONCLUSION LIST  ***
CONCLUSION  1 PO
CONCLUSION  2 QU
CONCLUSION  3 PO
CONCLUSION  4 PO
CONCLUSION  5 PO
CONCLUSION  6 PO
CONCLUSION  7
CONCLUSION  8
CONCLUSION  9
CONCLUSION  10
HIT RETURN TO CONTINUE?

***  VARIABLE LIST  ***
VARIABLE  1 DE
VARIABLE  2 DI
VARIABLE  3 EX
VARIABLE  4 GR
VARIABLE  5
VARIABLE  6
VARIABLE  7
VARIABLE  8
VARIABLE  9
VARIABLE  10
HIT RETURN TO CONTINUE?

***  CLAUSE-VARIABLE LIST  ***
**  CLAUSE  1
VARIABLE  1 DE
VARIABLE  2
VARIABLE  3
VARIABLE  4
**  CLAUSE  2
VARIABLE  1 DE
VARIABLE  2
VARIABLE  3
VARIABLE  4
**  CLAUSE  3
VARIABLE  1 DE
VARIABLE  2 DI
VARIABLE  3
VARIABLE  4
**  CLAUSE  4
VARIABLE  1 QU
VARIABLE  2 GR
VARIABLE  3 EX
VARIABLE  4
HIT RETURN TO CONTINUE?

**  CLAUSE  5
VARIABLE  1 QU
VARIABLE  2 GR
VARIABLE  3 EX
VARIABLE  4
```

```
**  CLAUSE  6
VARIABLE  1 QU
VARIABLE  2 GR
VARIABLE  3
VARIABLE  4
**  CLAUSE  7
VARIABLE  1
VARIABLE  2
VARIABLE  3
VARIABLE  4
**  CLAUSE  8
VARIABLE  1
VARIABLE  2
VARIABLE  3
VARIABLE  4
```

The preceding printout appears with each of the following runs:

Run 1
```
**  ENTER THE CONCLUSION ? PO
INPUT YES OR NO FOR DE-? NO
PO = NO
***  SUCCESS
```

Run 2
```
**  ENTER THE CONCLUSION ? PO
INPUT YES OR NO FOR DE-? YES
INPUT YES OR NO FOR DI-? NO
QU = YES
INPUT A REAL NUMBER FOR GR-? 3.0
INPUT A REAL NUMBER FOR EX-? 2.8
PO = SERVICE ENGINEER
***  SUCCESS
```

Run 3
```
**  ENTER THE CONCLUSION ? PO
INPUT YES OR NO FOR DE-? YES
INPUT YES OR NO FOR DI-? NO
QU = YES
INPUT A REAL NUMBER FOR GR-? 2.0
INPUT A REAL NUMBER FOR EX-? 4.0
PO = SERVICE ENGINEER
***  SUCCESS
```

Run 4
```
**  ENTER THE CONCLUSION ? QU
INPUT YES OR NO FOR DE-? NO
```

In this run, there is no rule with QU as a conclusion for the condition DE = NO.

Run 5
```
**  ENTER THE CONCLUSION ? QU
INPUT YES OR NO FOR DE-? YES
QU = YES
***  SUCCESS
```

Backward Chaining Worksheet

The following worksheet is an aid to simplifying the process of placing a new knowledge base into the program to replace the one that is there now. This is included to allow the reader to validate the concepts of the relationship between the knowledge base and expert system data structures. As a future exercise, the reader can develop an input compiler which reads a knowledge base and makes transfers to the data structures automatically. The reader should do this only after understanding the concepts fully.

This worksheet will help you create and transfer the variables and values of your knowledge base into the program (it allows for *three* condition variables per rule). First create the rules for the IF-THEN statements below. Then transfer them to the worksheets that follow.

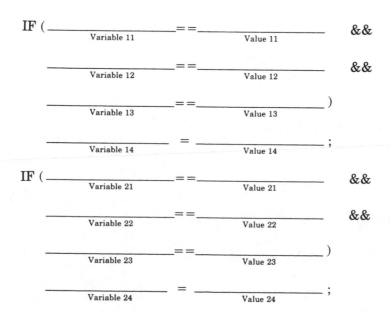

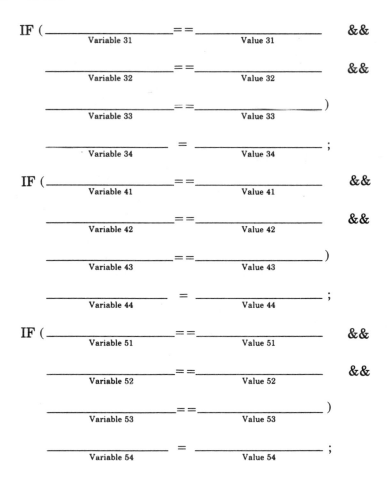

IF (_____== _____   &&
　　　　Variable 31　　　　　　　Value 31

_____== _____   &&
　　　Variable 32　　　　　　　Value 32

_____== _____)
　　　Variable 33　　　　　　　Value 33

_____ = _____ ;
　　　Variable 34　　　　　　　Value 34

IF (_____== _____   &&
　　　Variable 41　　　　　　　Value 41

_____== _____   &&
　　　Variable 42　　　　　　　Value 42

_____==_____)
　　　Variable 43　　　　　　　Value 43

_____ = _____ ;
　　　Variable 44　　　　　　　Value 44

IF (_____==_____   &&
　　　Variable 51　　　　　　　Value 51

_____==_____   &&
　　　Variable 52　　　　　　　Value 52

_____==_____)
　　　Variable 53　　　　　　　Value 53

_____ = _____ ;
　　　Variable 54　　　　　　　Value 54

This worksheet inserts variables into the clause variable list (comments 407 through 409).

CLVARLT[1]   = _____ ;
　　　　　　　　Variable 11

CLVARLT[2]   = _____ ;
　　　　　　　　Variable 12

CLVARLT[3]   = _____ ;
　　　　　　　　Variable 13

CLVARLT[5]   = _____ ;
　　　　　　　　Variable 21

CLVARLT[6]   = _____ ;

Variable 22

CLVARLT[7]   = _____ ;

Variable 23

CLVARLT[9]   = _____ ;

Variable 31

CLVARLT[10] = _____ ;

Variable 32

CLVARLT[11] = _____ ;

Variable 33

CLVARLT[13] = _____ ;

Variable 41

CLVARLT[14] = _____ ;

Variable 42

CLVARLT[15] = _____ ;

Variable 43

CLVARLT[17] = _____ ;

Variable 51

CLVARLT[18] = _____ ;

Variable 52

CLVARLT[19] = _____ ;

Variable 53

Use this worksheet to insert variables into the variable list (comment 367). Do not insert a variable name more than once.

VARLT[1] = _____ ;

Variable _____

VARLT[2] = _____ ;

Variable _____

VARLT[3] = _____ ;

Variable _____

VARLT[4] = _____ ;

Variable _____

VARLT[5] = _____ ;

Variable _____

Use this worksheet to insert variables into the conclusion list (comments 305 and 306).

CONCLT[1] = $\underline{\hspace{3cm}}$;
Variable 14

CONCLT[2] = $\underline{\hspace{3cm}}$;
Variable 24

CONCLT[3] = $\underline{\hspace{3cm}}$;
Variable 34

CONCLT[4] = $\underline{\hspace{3cm}}$;
Variable 44

CONCLT[5] = $\underline{\hspace{3cm}}$;
Variable 54

This worksheet is used to insert the IF-THEN rules (see comments 1490 through 1611) into the program.

IF Rules

1500   IF ($\underline{\hspace{2cm}}$ == $\underline{\hspace{2cm}}$ &&
Variable 11   Value 11

$\underline{\hspace{2cm}}$ == $\underline{\hspace{2cm}}$ &&
Variable 12   Value 12

$\underline{\hspace{2cm}}$ == $\underline{\hspace{2cm}}$)   S = 1;
Variable 13   Value 13

IF ($\underline{\hspace{2cm}}$ == $\underline{\hspace{2cm}}$ &&
Variable 21   Value 21

$\underline{\hspace{2cm}}$ == $\underline{\hspace{2cm}}$ &&
Variable 22   Value 22

$\underline{\hspace{2cm}}$ == $\underline{\hspace{2cm}}$)   S = 1;
Variable 23   Value 23

IF ($\underline{\hspace{2cm}}$ == $\underline{\hspace{2cm}}$ &&
Variable 31   Value 31

$\underline{\hspace{2cm}}$ == $\underline{\hspace{2cm}}$ &&
Variable 32   Value 32

$\underline{\hspace{2cm}}$ == $\underline{\hspace{2cm}}$)   S = 1;
Variable 33   Value 33

IF (_____ == _____ &&
Variable 41 Value 41

_____ == _____ &&
Variable 42 Value 42

_____ == _____) S = 1;
Variable 43 Value 43

IF (_____ == _____ &&
Variable 51 Value 51

_____ == _____ &&
Variable 52 Value 52

_____ == _____) S = 1;
Variable 53 Value 53

THEN Portion

1500 _____ = _____ ;
Variable 14 Value 14

printf("_____ = _____");
Variable 14 Value 14

_____ = _____ ;
Variable 24 Value 24

printf("_____ = _____");
Variable 24 Value 24

_____ = _____ ;
Variable 34 Value 34

printf("_____ = _____");
Variable 34 Value 34

_____ = _____ ;
Variable 44 Value 44

printf("_____ = _____");
Variable 44 Value 44

_____ = _____ ;
Variable 54 Value 54

printf("_____ = _____");
Variable 54 Value 54

Use of Probability and Fuzzy Logic in Expert Systems

When we discussed heuristic rules in Chapter 3, we said they were a special kind of rule that experts use. Many heuristic rules are based upon the likelihood of certain events occurring, a likelihood that only an expert has the knowledge and experience to calculate. In everyday language, we might say that experts make educated guesses about things in their domain.

What this really means is that "something" is known to work in a certain way according to statistical evidence of some kind. The something could be the diagnosis a doctor makes because of the presence of some supporting data. The doctor's educated guess in this case really means that a large percentage of the time, based upon doctors' observations, there is a high probability that the patient has a particular illness. Of course, there is also a probability that the patient does *not* have that illness, and that is why we often seek a second opinion.

Similarly, an oil company may decide to drill for oil based upon certain evidence provided by extensive research that points to an oil deposit. But, the drilling might produce a dry hole.

Probability techniques that are based on predicting that something will happen because of the evidence of something else happening in the past were developed by a man named Bayes. The area of probability that contains these theories is called "conditional probability." Statistical decisions based on Bayes' theories are used extensively in expert systems. We will describe how they are used in a very simple way.

Let's first consider another aspect of probability theory. It is not always possible to describe an event with rules that are absolutely defined. For example, we might say someone has a mild illness when his temperature is more than 99 degrees Fahrenheit but is less than 101 degrees Fahrenheit. A fever that is greater than 101 degrees Fahrenheit gets to be more serious. People cannot always express themselves with exact answers. Can you give me an exact temperature when someone says its mild outside? Probably not. Terms such as tall, hot, and mild are linguistic variables that cannot be defined with single values. The use of these terms in formulating systems is called "fuzzy logic."

This chapter will describe a methodology for incorporating fuzzy concepts into an expert system using bayesian techniques.

Fundamentals of Probability

Probability is the study of degrees of randomness. We frequently make an educated guess and express a conclusion in terms of probabilities without even realizing we are doing it. How often do you hear someone say something like, "I think it is okay, but I am only 80 percent sure."

Probability may be defined as

$$P = \frac{\text{Total number of ways a specific event can occur}}{\text{Total number of ways any event can occur}}$$

For example, suppose we toss a coin two times. The following is a listing of the total number of ways the two-coin tosses can occur:

First toss	Second toss
1. Head	Head
2. Head	Tail
3. Tail	Head
4. Tail	Tail

The probability that a tail would appear in one of the two tosses is

$$P = \frac{\text{Total number of ways a tail can occur in two tosses}}{\text{Total number of different tosses that can occur}} = \frac{3}{4}$$

that is, a tail appears in second, third, and fourth possibilities. As another example, the probability that a tail appears in the first toss of two tosses is ¾. The tail appears in the first toss of possibilities 3 and 4. The probability that no tail appears in two tosses in ¼. This occurs in the first possibility. As you may have noticed, the denominator of the probability equation always has a number *not* less than the numerator. This is always true because the total number of ways any event can occur is always greater than or equal to, but never less than, the total ways a specific event can occur. Therefore, the probability of something occurring must always be greater than or equal to 0 but less than or equal to 1.

Bayesian Probability

Bayes developed some of the basic theories of conditional probability. Conditional probability is a type of probability based on the existence of evidence. For example, consider again the two-coin tosses. The probability of having a head followed by a tail occurs only in possibility 2 and is ¼. But the probability of getting a tail in the second toss, already knowing that we received a head in the first toss, is ½. This is so because knowing that a head has already come up creates a new set of possibilities:

First toss	Second toss
1. Head	Head
2. Head	Tail

We have eliminated all cases with tail occurring in the first toss because we have evidence that a head already occurred. Therefore, there is only one case out of two with a tail in the second toss. This occurs in possibility 2. Hence, the conditional probability of getting a tail in the second toss, knowing we have a head in the first toss, is ½.

We will define conditional probability as the probability of something occurring, which we will designate as s, with the evidence that something else has already occurred, which we will designate as e. This probability is represented as $P(s|e)$. The probability equation of two things occurring is:

$$P(e \text{ and } s) = P(s|e) * P(e)$$

This is read as follows: the probability of e and s happening, where e happens first, is equal to the probability of s happening if we *know* e has already happened, times the probability of e happening. Let's see how this equation is used with an example. Suppose we have two Is and two Os, as shown, which we can choose at random whenever we need an I or an O.

    I I O O

Using our equation, we will calculate the probability of picking an O first and then an I in two picks. Substituting O and I into our equation, we get

$$P(O \text{ and } I) = P(I|O) * P(O)$$

Since there are two Is and two Os, which make four objects, the probability of picking an O, P(O), is ¾. The probability of picking an I on the assumption that an O was already picked, P(I|O), is ⅔. To see how this works, we would have the following situation on the assumption that one O was already picked and no longer available to us:

I I O

Since there are two Is out of the three remaining items, the probability of choosing an I is ⅔. The probability P(O and I) is

$$P(I|O) * P(O) = ⅔ * ¾ = ⅓.$$

Another conditional probability equation that we will make use of in our expert system is

$$P(s) = P(s|e) * P(e) + P(s|\text{NOT } e) * P(\text{NOT } e) \tag{1}$$

This equation reads as follows: The probability of s, P(s), is equal to the conditional probability of s on the assumption e occurred, P(s|e), times the probability of e occurring, P(e), plus the probability of s occurring on the assumption e *does not* occur, P(s|NOT e), times the probability of e *not* occurring, P(NOT e). We will refer to this equation as Equation 1 in all of our following examples.

Example

As an example, in the use of these probability theories let us consider these stock market rules (and assume these are the only rules affecting the stock market).

    10 IF INTEREST RATES = FALL
        THEN STOCK = RISE
    20 IF INTEREST RATES = RISE
        THEN STOCK = FALL
    30 IF DOLLAR = FALL
        THEN INTEREST RATES = RISE
    40 IF DOLLAR = RISE
        THEN INTEREST RATES = FALL

For this example we would like to know the probability of the stock market rising. Of course, we know the situation is more complex, but we want to illustrate a solution approach in a simple way. Our backward chaining system would scan the rules for STOCK = RISE in the THEN part of our rules. This occurs in rule 10. Rule 10 tells us that STOCK = RISE on the condition that INTEREST RATES = FALL.

We can evaluate these conditions using the probability equation, Equation 1, with s being replaced by STOCK = RISE and e, by INTEREST = FALL. This gives us Equation 2:

$$P(STOCK = RISE) = P(STOCK = RISE|INTEREST = \quad (2)$$
$$FALL) * P(INTEREST = FALL) + P(STOCK =$$
$$RISE|INTEREST = NOT\ FALL) * P(INTEREST = NOT\ FALL)$$

In order to determine if INTEREST = FALL, we must backward chain to rule 40, which is

    40   IF DOLLAR = RISE
           THEN INT = FALL   (We have abbreviated INTEREST RATES
                            to INT.)

This statement translates into the following probability, shown in Equation 3:

$$P(INT = FALL) = P(INT = FALL|DOLLAR = RISE) \quad (3)$$
$$* P(DOLLAR = RISE) + P(INT = FALL|DOLLAR =$$
$$NOT\ RISE) * P(DOLLAR = NOT\ RISE)$$

Since DOLLAR is not in any THEN part, that is, its value can't be determined by a rule, its probability must come directly from the user. Similarly, the conditional probabilities are also not included in the THEN part of the rules and therefore the conditional probabilities also come from the user. Let's assign some numbers to the probabilities to see how things work. We assume the following probabilities based upon our understanding of the problem, which is our educated guess.

$$P(DOLLAR = RISE) = 0.6$$

In fundamental probability theory the sum of the probability of something happening and the probability of it not happening equals 1. We will refer to this as the fundamental probability rule. Therefore a variation of this is

$$P(DOLLAR = NOT\ RISE) = 1 - P(DOLLAR = RISE) = 1 - 0.6$$
$$= 0.4$$

The user estimates each of the conditional probabilities, which are

$$P(INT = FALL|DOLLAR = RISE) = 0.8$$
$$P(INT = FALL|DOLLAR = NOT\ RISE) = 0.1$$

You should note that conditional probabilities based on different evidence conditions do *not* have to add up to 1. The two different evidence conditions above are DOLLAR = RISE and DOLLAR = NOT RISE.

Substituting these values in the conditional probability equation, Equation 3, we get

$$P(INT = FALL) = 0.8 * 0.6 + 0.1 * 0.4 = 0.52 \qquad (3)$$

From the fundamental probability rule, we get

$$P(INT = NOT\ FALL) = 1 - 0.52 = 0.48$$

In order to solve the problem of the P(STOCK = RISE) the user must supply the conditional probabilities, which are

$$P(STOCK = RISE|INT = FALL) = 0.85$$
$$P(STOCK = RISE|INT = NOT\ FALL) = 0.1$$

We can now calculate the probability using Equation 2 for P(STOCK = RISE) which is

$$P(STOCK = RISE) = 0.85 * 0.52 + 0.1 * .48 = 0.49\ or\ 49\%$$

The user can now decide how to invest based on this probability. It is interesting to note that there is less than a 50 percent chance of the stock market rising in this example. This is due directly to the selection of probabilities. If the user increased the conditional probability of the stock market rising when interest rates do not fall, that is, P(STOCK = RISE|INT = NOT FALL), there would be a higher probability of P(STOCK = RISE).

Fuzzy Concepts

So far we have been talking about terms such as "rise" and "fall." In addition, we have used some of these terms with more than one variable. For example, we used the term "rise" with both the variables STOCK and DOLLAR. When used with STOCK, the word "rise" might mean 10 to 30 points on the Dow Jones average. But the word "rise" when used with DOLLAR might mean that the dollar rises between 20 and 30 Japanese yen. Such a use of the word "rise" is referred to as a "linguistic variable." It is a variable that can not only take on any value in a range of values, but the range might change depending on circumstance. For example, if we use the word "cold," it may have a different range when used in the winter than when used in spring.

Another linguistic variable we used in our rules is the word "fall." Since it is usually too much to ask of a user of an expert system to supply probability values, we will show you how to use linguistic variables to accomplish the same thing. In order to do that we must be a little more specific with our linguistic variables. We must allow the user of our expert system to hedge these variables with prefixes such as low or medium. That is, the user can specify a low rise for the dollar, and we will know exactly what he means. Let's see, with the stock market as an example, how we can determine the probabilities.

Probability Membership Table

In order to determine if the stock market will rise we encountered two rules and their associated probabilities. These rules are

    10   IF INT = FALL
         THEN STOCK = RISE
    40   IF DOLLAR = RISE
         THEN INT = FALL

with probabilities

P(STOCK = RISE) = P(STOCK = RISE|INT = FALL) * P(INT = FALL) + P(STOCK = RISE|INT = NOT FALL) * P(INT = NOT FALL)

P(INT = FALL) = P(INT = FALL|DOLLAR = RISE) * P(DOLLAR = RISE) + P(INT = FALL|DOLLAR = NOT RISE) * P(DOLLAR = NOT RISE)

In order to solve these equations we will use an expert to construct a table for the user. This table will contain hedge words, that is, words that will be used to define what the user means by, for example, "a medium rise." On the same row as each hedge word we will specify the percentage change represented by the linguistic variable and the probability and conditional probability of that change taking place. Here is the table; an example of how to use it follows.

	Column 1	Column 2	Column 3
Linguistic variable	Dollar equal rise value in table	P(INT = FALL| DOLLAR = RISE)	P(DOLLAR = RISE)
Low	1–2%	0.2	0.5
Medium	3–4%	0.5	0.3
High	Greater than 4%	0.8	0.1

For simplicity let's assume that the expert who provides all these values decides that the dollar either rises by the amount shown in column 1 of the table or does not rise at all. There is no in between. The expert, therefore, has to only calculate two types of values. One is related to the dollar rising and has already been recorded in the table. The other occurs when the dollar does not rise. That is, the expert calculates the conditional probability of interest rates falling when the dollar is not rising and records this value as:

P(INT = FALL|DOLLAR = NOT RISE) = 0.07

The probability of stocks rising if interest rates fall is recorded by the expert as

P(STOCK = RISE|INT = FALL) = 0.2

The probability of stocks rising if interest rates do not fall is recorded by the expert as

P(STOCK = RISE|INT = NOT FALL) = 0.1

These tables and values have to be constructed by an expert. They become part of the knowledge base and may change from time to time. That is, the expert needs to change these tables when the interest rates or dollar probabilities change. The expert making these changes may be another expert system.

When the user of the system asks for the probability of the stock market rising, the expert system will ask the user to respond to the following question:

```
DO YOU WANT TO CALCULATE THE EFFECTS IF THE RISE OF THE
DOLLAR IS

1-LOW

2-MEDIUM

3-HIGH

ENTER ONE NUMBER - ? 2
```

In this case assume that the user responds with 2, which is MEDIUM. From the table, we see this means that the user expects the dollar to rise 3 to 4 percent. The probabilities needed to solve P(INT = FALL) are taken from the table and the values provided by the expert. These are

Probability	Source
P(DOLLAR = RISE) = 0.3	Row 2, column 3 of table
P(DOLLAR = NOT RISE) = 1 − 0.3 = 0.7	Fundamental rule
P(INT = FALL|DOLLAR = RISE) = 0.5	Row 2, column 2 of table
P(INT = FALL|DOLLAR = NOT RISE) = 0.07	Expert
P(INT = FALL) = 0.5 * 0.3 + 0.07 * 0.7 = 0.199	Equation 3

Let's now calculate P(STOCK = RISE). We repeat the previous calculation result:

Probability	Source
P(INT = FALL) = 0.199	Previous calculation
P(INT = NOT FALL) = 1 − 0.199 = 0.811	Fundamental rule
P(STOCK = RISE|INT = FALL) = 0.2	Expert
P(STOCK = RISE|INT = NOT FALL) = 0.1	Expert

We can now calculate the probability of the stock market rising from equation 3.

$$P(STOCK = RISE) = 0.2 * 0.1999 + 0.1 * 0.811 = .121$$

or a probability of 12.1 percent.

By using an expert to construct the table and provide all the values we relieved the user from this chore.

Summary

Let us review the concepts discussed in this chapter.

1. In order to assess the probability of an event taking place, we calculate that probability according to a specific formula that takes into account the total number of ways a specific event can occur divided by the total number of ways any event can occur. Bayesian probability, which analyzes conditional probability, goes one step further to analyze what will happen based on what has already happened. This can be applied to a backward chaining system in which probability formulas are applied to the rules of a knowledge base.

2. The same terms that are analyzed for their probability of occurrence can be analyzed via fuzzy concepts by analyzing linguistic variables, that is, by analyzing the value of specific words, such as "rise" and "fall" of the stock market, used in a knowledge base to make decisions. Again, the use of formulas is implemented, this time analyzing the variable measures of the terms low, medium, high.

The user must remember that each time a situation is calculated, it is based on the probability values assigned to that situation.

Programming Applications

Let's examine a program written in C which allows us to apply the bayesian probability concepts we have just discussed.

Program Explanation

The rules we use in the program are the same two used in the concept description. These are shown in comments 10 through 60. The corresponding probability equations are shown in comments 70 and 105. The program simply asks the users to supply the values for the probabilities within the equations and then arrives at the probability of the stock market rising.

Program Listing

Listing 7-1 is followed by a set of runs.

Listing 7-1   Bayesian probabilities.

```
/* bayesian probabilities. in this example the following two rules are used
********** comment 10 *************
 10 if int=fall
    then stock=rise
 40 if dollar=rise
    then int=fall
  the bayesian equations are:
   for rule 10
 p(stock=rise)=p(stock=rise;int=fall)*p(int=fall)
             +p(stock=rise;int=not fall)*p(int=not fall)
    for rule 40
 p(int=fall)=p(int=fall;dollar=rise)*p(dollar=rise)
            +p(int=fall;dollar=not rise)*p(dollar=not rise)
********** comment 60 *************
the following abbreviations will be used
********** comment 70 *************
i1=p(int=fall)              i2=p(int=not fall)
i3=p(int=fall;dollar=rise)  i4=p(int=fall;dollar=not rise)
s1=p(stock=rise)            s2=p(stock=rise;int=fall)
s3=p(stock=rise;int=not fall)
d1=p(dollar=rise)           d2=p(dollar=not rise)
re-writing the probabilities for the rules we get
s1=s2*i1+s3*i2   (3)
i1=i3*d1+i4*d2   (4)
*********** comment 105 *************
*********************** inference mechanism ****************
for this example we want to determine the probability of the
"stock=rise". by backward chaining we come to rule 10. the
condition part of 10 has the variable "int". by continuing
backward chaining we come to rule 40. the condition part of
rule 40 has the variable "dollar" which is not part of any
other rule. therefore the user instantiates each probability
variable in equation (3). */

#include <stdio.h>

 float s1, d1,d2,i3,i4,s2,i1,i2,s3;

main() {
 printf("WHAT IS THE PROBABILITY OF THE DOLLAR RISING? ");
 scanf("%f",&d1);
 d2=1-d1;
 printf("WHAT IS THE PROBABILITY OF INTEREST RATES FALLING IF THE DOLLAR RISES? ");
 scanf("%f",&i3);
 printf("WHAT IS THE PROBABILITY OF INTEREST RATES FALLING IF THE\n");
 printf("DOLLAR DOES NOT RISE? ");
 scanf("%f",&i4);
 i1=i3*d1+i4*d2;
 printf("*** THE PROBABILITY OF INTEREST RATES FALLING IS %f\n",i1);
 printf("WHAT IS THE PROBABILITY OF STOCKS RISING IF INTEREST RATES FALL? ");
 scanf("%f",&s2);
 i2=1-i1;
 printf("WHAT IS THE PROBABILITY OF STOCKS RISING IF INTEREST RATES DO NOT FALL? ");
 scanf("%f",&s3);
 s1=s2*i1+s3*i2;
 printf("*** THE PROBABILITY OF THE STOCK MARKET RISING IS %f\n",s1);
}
```

Sample Runs

```
WHAT IS THE PROBABILITY OF THE DOLLAR RISING? .6
WHAT IS THE PROBABILITY OF INTEREST RATES FALLING IF THE
DOLLAR RISES? .5
WHAT IS THE PROBABILITY OF INTEREST RATES FALLING IF THE
DOLLAR DOES NOT RISE? .5
** THE PROBABILITY OF INTEREST RATES FALLING IS .5
WHAT IS THE PROBABILITY OF STOCKS RISING IF INTEREST RATES FALL? .7
WHAT IS THE PROBABILITY OF STOCKS RISING IF INTEREST RATES
DO NOT FALL? .5
** THE PROBABILITY OF THE STOCK MARKET RISING IS .6

WHAT IS THE PROBABILITY OF THE DOLLAR RISING? .7
WHAT IS THE PROBABILITY OF INTEREST RATES FALLING IF THE
DOLLAR RISES? .4
WHAT IS THE PROBABILITY OF INTEREST RATES FALLING IF THE
DOLLAR DOES NOT RISE? .5
** THE PROBABILITY OF INTEREST RATES FALLING IS .43
WHAT IS THE PROBABILITY OF STOCKS RISING IF INTEREST RATES FALL? .5
WHAT IS THE PROBABILITY OF STOCKS RISING IF INTEREST RATES
DO NOT FALL? .7
** THE PROBABILITY OF THE STOCK MARKET RISING IS .614
```

We have included in Listing 7-2 the bayesian probability equations. The program is followed by a sample run.

Listing 7-2   Bayesian backward chaining.

```
/********************* backward chaining ************/
/* install your IF clauses in sequence in the first case
   statement of the main program
   example: if((a1==2) && (a2==6)) s=1;
            if(strcmp(j,"NO") != 0) s=1;
   the then part of the above construction always
   contains s=1;
   install your the clauses in sequence in the second
   case statement of the main program
   example strcpy(po,"YES"); */

/* conclusion list */
char conclt[10][3];
/* variable list */
char varlt[10][3];
/* clause variable list */
char clvarlt[40][3];
char varble[3];
char interest[5], dollar[5],stock[5];

/* instantiated list */
int instlt[11];
/* statement stack */
int statsk[11];
int /* clause stack */ clausk[11], sn,f,i,j,s,k, /* stack pointer */ sp;

float s1,s4,s5,i1,i2;

void determine_member_concl_list(void);
void push_on_stack(void);
void instantiate(void);

main()
{
/********* initialization section *******/
/* stack space is 10 we initially place stack space at 10+1 */
sp=11;
for(i=1;i<11;i++)
{
 strcpy(conclt[i],"");
 strcpy(varlt[i],"");
 instlt[i]=0;
 statsk[i]=0;
 clausk[i]=0;
}
for(i=1;i<41;i++) strcpy(clvarlt[i],"");
/* enter conclusions which are the variables in the then part. 1 at a
   time. enter the conclusions in exact order starting at the 1st if-then.
   after last conclusion hit return key for rest of conclusions */
strcpy(conclt[1],"ST");
strcpy(conclt[2],"ST");
strcpy(conclt[3],"IN");
strcpy(conclt[4],"IN");
printf("*** CONCLUSION LIST ***\n");
for(i=1;i<11;i++) printf("CONCLUSION %d   %s\n",i,conclt[i]);
printf("HIT RETURN TO CONTINUE");
gets();
/* enter variables which are in the if part. 1 at a time in the exact
   order that they occur. up to 3 variables per if statement. do not
   duplicate any variable names. any name is used only once. if no
   more variables left just hit return key. */
printf("*** VARIABLE LIST ***\n");
strcpy(varlt[1],"DO");
for(i=1;i<11;i++) printf("VARIABLE %d   %s\n",i,varlt[i]);
printf("HIT RETURN KEY TO CONTINUE");
gets();
/* enter variables as they appear in the if clauses. a maximum of 3
   variables per if statement. if no more variables hit return key.*/
printf("*** CLAUSE VARIABLE LIST ***\n");
strcpy(clvarlt[1],"IN");
strcpy(clvarlt[5],"IN");
strcpy(clvarlt[9],"DO");
strcpy(clvarlt[13],"DO");
for(i=1;i<9;i++)
{
```

Listing 7-2 (Continued)

```
            printf("** CLAUSE %d\n",i);
            for(j=1;j<5;j++)
            { k=4*(i-1)+j; printf("VARIABLE %d  %s\n",j,clvarlt[k]); }
            if(i==4)
            { printf("HIT RETURN KEY TO CONTINUE"); gets(); }
        }
/*************** inference section ***************/
    printf("** ENTER CONCLUSION ? "); gets(varble);
    /* get conclusion statement number (sn) from the conclusion list (conclt) */
    /* first statement starts search */
    b520: f=1;
    determine_member_concl_list();
    if(sn != 0) {
     /* if sn=0 then no conclusion of that name */
     do
     /* push statement number (sn) and clause number=1 on goal stack which is
        composed of the statement stack (statsk) and clause stack (clausk) */
     {
      push_on_stack();
      do
      {
      /* calculate clause location in clause-variable list */
    b545: i=(statsk[sp]-1)*4 + clausk[sp];
          /* clause variable */
          strcpy(varble,clvarlt[i]);
          if(strcmp(varble,"") != 0) {
           /* is this clause variable a conclusion? */
           f=1;
           determine_member_concl_list();
           if(sn != 0)
           /* it is a conclusion push it */
              goto b520;
              /* check instantiation of this clause */
              instantiate();
              clausk[sp]=clausk[sp]+1;
          }
      } while(strcmp(varble,"") != 0); /* do-while statement */
      /* no more clauses check if part of statement */
      sn=statsk[sp];
      s=0;
      /*********** if then statements ************/
      /* sample if parts of if then statements from the position
         knowldge base */
      switch (sn) {
       /* if part of statement 1 */
       case 1: if (strcmp(interest,"FALL") == 0) s=1;
               break;
       /* if part of statement 2 */
       case 2: if (strcmp(interest,"RISE") == 0) s=1;
               break;
       /* if part of statement 3 */
       case 3: if (strcmp(dollar,"FALL") == 0) s=1;
               break;
       /* if part of statement 4 */
       case 4: if (strcmp(dollar,"RISE") == 0) s=1;
               break;
      }
     /* see if the then part should be invoked */
     if( s!= 1) {
      /* failed..search rest of statements for same conclusion */
      /* get conclusion */
      i=statsk[sp];
      strcpy(varble,conclt[i]);
      /* search for conclusion starting at the next statement number */
      f=statsk[sp]+1;
      determine_member_concl_list();
      sp=sp+1;
     }
     /* pop old conclusion and put on new one */
    } while((s != 1) && (sn != 0)); /* outer do-while loop */
    if(sn != 0) {
    /* if part true invoke then part */
    /* then part of if-then statements from the position knowledge base */
    switch (sn) {
```

```c
/* then part of statement 1 */
 case 1: i2=1-i1;
         printf("P(INTEREST=NOT FALL)= %f\n",i2);
         printf("WHAT IS THE PROBABILITY OF STOCKS RISING ");
         printf("IF INTEREST RATES FALL? ");
         scanf("%f",&s4);
         printf("WHAT IS THE PROBABILITY OF STOCKS RISING ");
         printf("IF INTEREST RATES DO NOT FALL? ");
         scanf("%f",&s5);
         s1=s4*i1+s5*i2;
         printf("P(STOCK=RISE)=%f\n",s1);
         strcpy(stock,"RISE");
         printf("ST=RISE\n");
         break;
/* then part of statement 2 */
case 2: i2=1-i1;
         printf("P(INTEREST=NOT RISE)=%f\n",i2);
         printf("WHAT IS THE PROBABILITY OF STOCKS FALLING ");
         printf("IF INTEREST RATES RISE? ");
         scanf("%f",&s4);
         printf("WHAT IS THE PROBABILITY OF STOCKS FALLING ");
         printf("IF INTEREST RATES DO NOT RISE? ");
         scanf("%f",&s5);
         s1=s4*i1+s5*i2;
         printf("P(STOCK=FALL)=%f\n",s1);
         strcpy(stock,"FALL");
         printf("ST=FALL\n");
         break;
/* then part of statement 3 */
case 3: printf("WHAT IS THE PROBABILITY OF THE VALUE ");
         printf("OF THE DOLLAR FALLING? ");
         scanf("%f",&i1);
         printf("P(DOLLAR=NOT FALL)=%f\n",i2);
         printf("WHAT IS THE PROBABILITY OF INTEREST RATES ");
         printf("RISING IF THE DOLLAR FALLS? ");
         scanf("%f",&s4);
         printf("WHAT IS THE PROBABILITY OF INTEREST RATES ");
         printf("RISING IF THE DOLLAR DOES NOT FALL? ");
         scanf("%f",&s5);
         s1=s4*i1+s5*i2;
         printf("P(INTEREST=RISE)=%f\n",s1);
         i1=s1;
         strcpy(interest,"RISE");
         printf("IN=RISE\n");
         break;
/* then part of statement 4 */
case 4: printf("WHAT IS THE PROBABILITY OF THE VALUE ");
         printf("OF THE DOLLAR RISING? ");
         scanf("%f",&i1);
         i2=1-i1;
         printf("P(DOLLAR=NOT RISE)=%f\n",i2);
         printf("WHAT IS THE PROBABILITY OF INTEREST RATES ");
         printf("FALLING IF THE DOLLAR RISES? ");
         scanf("%f",&s4);
         printf("WHAT IS THE PROBABILITY OF INTEREST RATES ");
         printf("FALLING IF THE DOLLAR DOES NOT RISE? ");
         scanf("%f",&s5);
         s1=s4*i1+s5*i2;
         printf("P(INTEREST=FALL)+%f\n",s1);
         i1=s1;
         strcpy(interest,"FALL");
         printf("IN=FALL\n");
         break;
 }
/* pop the stack .. if it reached the initial point we had
   our success. if not just keep going to verify the old
   conclusion */
/* pop the stack */
sp=sp+1;
if(sp >= 11)
/* finished */
 printf("*** SUCCESS\n");
else {
```

Listing 7-2 *(Continued)*

```
         /* stack is not empty */
         /* get next clause then continue */
          clausk[sp]=clausk[sp]+1;
          goto b545;
          }
         }
     }
 }

 void determine_member_concl_list() {
 /* routine to determine if a variable (varble) is a member of the conclusion
    list (conclt). if yes return sn !=0. if not a member sn=0; */
 /* initially set to not a member */
 sn=0;
 /* member of conclusion list to be searched is f */
 i=f;
 while(( strcmp(varble, conclt[i]) != 0) && (i<8))
 /* test for membership */
  i=i+1;
 if ( strcmp(varble, conclt[i]) == 0) sn=i; /* a member */
 }

 void push_on_stack()
 /* routine to push statement number (sn) and a clause number of 1 onto the
    conclusion stack which consists of the statement stack (statsk) and the
    clause stack (clausk)..to push decrement stack pointer (sp) */
 {
 sp=sp-1;
 statsk[sp]=sn;
 clausk[sp]=1;
 }

 void instantiate()
 /* routine to instantiate a variable (varble) if it isn't already. the
    instantiate indication (instlt) ia a 0 if not. a 1 if it is. the
    variable list (varlt) contains the variable (varble). */
 {
 i=1;
 /* find variable in the list */
 while((strcmp(varble, varlt[i]) !=0) && (i<10)) i=i+1;
 if((strcmp(varble,varlt[i]) == 0) && (instlt[i] != 1))
  /* found variable and not already instantiated */
  {
  instlt[i]=1; /* mark instantiated */
  /* the designer of the knowledge base places the input statements to
     instantiate the variables below in the case statement */
  switch (i)
   {
  /****** input statements *******/
  /* input statements for sample position knowledge base */
  /***** comment 1700 ********/
   case 1: printf("IS THE DOLLAR EXPECTED TO RISE OR FALL? ");
            gets(dollar);
            break;
   }
  }
 }
```

Sample Run

```
*** CONCLUSION LIST ***
CONCLUSION  1 ST
CONCLUSION  2 ST
CONCLUSION  3 IN
CONCLUSION  4 IN
CONCLUSION  5
CONCLUSION  6
CONCLUSION  7
CONCLUSION  8
CONCLUSION  9
CONCLUSION  10
HIT RETURN TO CONTINUE?
*** VARIABLE LIST ***
VARIABLE  1 DO
VARIABLE  2
VARIABLE  3
VARIABLE  4
VARIABLE  5
VARIABLE  6
VARIABLE  7
VARIABLE  8
VARIABLE  9
VARIABLE  10
HIT RETURN TO CONTINUE?

*** CLAUSE-VARIABLE LIST ***
** CLAUSE  1
VARIABLE  1 IN
VARIABLE  2
VARIABLE  3
VARIABLE  4
** CLAUSE  2
VARIABLE  1 IN
VARIABLE  2
VARIABLE  3
VARIABLE  4
** CLAUSE  3
VARIABLE  1 DO
VARIABLE  2
VARIABLE  3
VARIABLE  4
** CLAUSE  4
VARIABLE  1 DO
VARIABLE  2
VARIABLE  3
VARIABLE  4
HIT RETURN TO CONTINUE?

** CLAUSE  5
VARIABLE  1
VARIABLE  2
VARIABLE  3
VARIABLE  4
** CLAUSE  6
VARIABLE  1
VARIABLE  2
VARIABLE  3
VARIABLE  4
```

```
** CLAUSE  7
VARIABLE  1
VARIABLE  2
VARIABLE  3
VARIABLE  4
** CLAUSE  8
VARIABLE  1
VARIABLE  2
VARIABLE  3
VARIABLE  4
** ENTER THE CONCLUSION ? ST
IS THE DOLLAR EXPECTED TO RISE OR FALL? RISE
WHAT IS THE PROBABILITY OF THE VALUE OF THE DOLLAR RISING? .6
P(DOLLAR=NOT RISE)= .4
WHAT IS THE PROBABILITY OF INTEREST RATES FALLING IF THE DOLLAR RISES? .5
WHAT IS THE PROBABILITY OF INTEREST RATES FALLING IF THE DOLLAR DOES
NOT RISE? .5
P(INTEREST=FALL)= .5
IN=FALL
P(INTEREST=NOT FALL)= .5
WHAT IS THE PROBABILITY OF STOCKS RISING IF INTEREST RATES FALL? .7
WHAT IS THE PROBABILITY OF STOCKS RISING IF INTEREST RATES DO NOT FALL? .5
P(STOCK=RISE)= .6
ST=RISE
*** SUCCESS
```

Expert Systems:
Knowledge Plus Inference

Section 3 discusses three actual expert systems. We examine the different ways each system represents its solution. To further develop your understanding we have provided programming examples. This sets the stage for you to construct your own expert systems.

8

Financial Planning Expert System

Now that you understand some of the concepts of artificial intelligence and expert systems, you are ready to learn how to construct a knowledge base for an actual expert system.

We will now describe a simple financial planning system that anyone can use for making financial decisions. This system is not comprehensive and we certainly don't recommend that you plan your financial future using the limited database supplied here. What we have attempted to give you is a framework for creating a thorough financial planning expert system or another decision-making system based upon the same principles. To put it simply, we can't make you a financial planning expert, but we can make you a knowledge engineer.

We must first address three questions:

1. How do you choose a domain?
2. How do you research your domain?
3. How do you represent (organize) the relevant facts for the chosen domain?

The simplest way to answer these questions is to lead you through the development of an actual system and then write an expert system with you. We will take you step by step, just as we have done up until now.

First, let us review the basic definition of an expert system. Remember the description in Chapter 3 of how to create a domain of knowledge for an expert system? As described, the goals can be reached via facts, rules, pruning, and an inference mechanism. You select, as your domain, a special area of interest within the subject matter. You then collect all the goals, facts, and rules related to that small domain and put all this knowledge together with an inference mechanism and a pruning structure to create an expert system.

How Do You Choose a Domain?

Two things go into choosing a domain. One, of course, is that it be of interest to you. Two is that the knowledge base be small enough so that a manageable amount of information can be gathered. This chapter is devoted to a specific domain within the broad field of financial planning. We chose this topic because it affects just about everyone. Managing your money wisely may be the single most important thing you can do today. In the complex age in which we live, with the unpredictable rise and fall of the dollar, it is essential to learn to make the most out of what you have. Besides, everyone is interested in making money.

So let's get started. Your first step is to visit the local library and bookstore and think of any professionals you know who are knowledgeable in this area. Before reviewing the research and/or interviewing knowledgeable people, keep in mind what aspect of the topic is of personal interest to you. In other words, always think about your own goals.

How Do You Research Your Topic?

At this point you are probably thinking that financial planning is a vast topic, much too difficult for a simple computer program. Not so. Let's move along the following path. We went to our local library and took out several books on the topic—about five or six comprehensive ones were enough. We then thought of professionals that we knew, chose two that we felt were competent, and spent some time with each of them. At first, we came away with a lot of information but without a solid form. We had learned about stocks, real estate, and money market funds. We had learned about various financial services, such as discount brokerage services offered by the banks. We had learned about the many types of professionals that offer services. Some books analyzed the world financial situation from various angles. For example, some books advocated different creative means for investing money. Others stressed investment in real estate as the most profitable means of making money. One book stressed "crisis investment," that is, how to handle your money strategically in the event of an economic crisis. With all this deluge of information, we again asked ourselves the more specific question, "What would be of personal interest to us, what would be most beneficial for us to learn about?" When we thought about it at some length, we realized that professionals and the literature were both saying the same thing: Explore your own financial needs because that is what is most important.

So we decided the best approach would be to take much of the information we had learned and combine it into a meaningful whole. More specifically, we studied our financial needs and tailored a financial program to suit these needs based upon age and life-style. One of the best books we found that addressed the topic was *The Lifetime Book of Money Management* by Grace Weinstein (New American Library, 1983). The book describes a typical person's life cycle in terms of finances in four to five stages and outlines the most salient aspects of each stage. The goal that we chose for our expert system was to learn the best financial strategies available for a given age group.

Organizing the Relevant Facts for the Domain

Once the goal had been established, the next step was to organize or partition that data into several primary but independent categories. For example, age groups would be one category. This partitioning would allow us to prune irrelevant categories from consideration by our inference mechanism. For example, by partitioning our knowledge base into age groups, we could eliminate (prune) age groups not included in our expert analysis of a specific person's financial needs. If the person's age is 50, for example, we would not consider the age 18 to 24 knowledge base. Based on literature suggestions, we have established the following age categories:

Ages 18 to 24 (young adult)

Ages 25 to 45 (adult)

Ages 46 to 64 (mature adult)

Ages 65 and over (senior adult)

This partition divides a life span into four different age groups. The goal for each age group is to determine where investments should be made. What are the facts associated with each age group? Knowing what our goal is, we can sort out the facts related to our goal. Compiling all of our research, we now listed from our notes various pieces of gathered information from a wide variety of sources.

Let us now begin to list these facts. Under the first age group, 18 to 24, we reviewed our research and listed the following facts in the form of a taxonomy, which is a classification of similar items into a system. This will be elaborated on after we list the facts for this age group.

A. Ages 18 to 24
    A-1   Train for a career
    A-2   Enter a vocational program
    A-3   Enter a college or graduate school
    A 4   Establish plan for a personal life
        A-4.1   Remain single
            A-4.1.1   Start savings plan with money devoted to own needs
            A-4.1.2   Establish credit identity
            A-4.1.3   Establish financial record-keeping system
        A-4.2   Marry with no children
            A-4.2.1   Start savings plan with joint goals
            A-4.2.2   Establish credit identity
            A-4.2.3   Establish financial record-keeping system
            A-4.2.4   Establish residential plans for life-style
        A-4.3   Marry with children
            A-4.3.1   Start savings plans with long-range plan to include children
            A-4.3.2   Establish credit identity for large future investments
            A-4.3.3   Establish financial record-keeping system
            A-4.3.4   Establish residential plans for life-style

Let us take a moment to explain the other structure used. Notice that the numbers to the left of the facts highlight the categories and subdivisions. For example, "Establish plans for a personal life" is numbered A-4 and all the supporting points related to "Establish plans for a personal life" are numbered A-4.1, A-4.2, etc. "Establish credit identity" is numbered A-4.1.2, a further subdivision of "Remain single" which is numbered A-4.1, which is a subdivision of "Establish plans for a personal life," which is numbered A-4. This numerical system (also called taxonomy) will be utilized later on in the chapter in order to guide us in the creation of a decision tree structure.

We now move on to the next age group, 25 to 45. What are the facts associated with this group? It is within this age group that a lot of planning is put into motion since these are the years when adult life-styles are established. These are the child-rearing years, years for putting aside money for educational needs of children, and years for expanded residential planning. These are also the years that people begin to earn larger incomes and must allocate their money in different directions. For this reason we have devoted more attention to this age group than to the others. First, we divided this age group into four categories of life-style in order to make it more manageable. Then we

expanded on each category, listing all the pertinent facts. A taxonomy of the facts follows.

B. Ages 25 to 45
    B-1   Single adult
        B-1.1   Expand career goals
        B-1.2   Invest for capital growth
            B-1.2.1   Money market
            B-1.2.2   Time securities
            B-1.2.3   Savings bonds
        B-1.3   Plan for housing investment—buy apartment, condominium, or small house
    B-2   Single adults living together
        B-2.1   Expand career goals
        B-2.2   Invest for capital growth
            B-2.2.1   Joint accounts
            B-2.2.2   Separate accounts
        B-2.3   Plan for housing investment—buy apartment, condominium, or small house
            B-2.3.1   Joint ownership
                B-2.3.1.1   Draw up legal contracts
                B-2.3.1.2   Spell out obligations and responsibilities
    B-3   Single parent families
        B-3.1   Establish new career goals for former nonearning spouse
        B-3.2   Invest for capital growth
            B-3.2.1   Obtain credit for new purchases
            B-3.2.2   Meet insurance needs—insure supplementary income in the event of death of spouse, etc.
        B-3.3   Plan for housing
            B-3.3.1   Establish who will remain in house of origin (which divorced spouse)
            B-3.3.2   Establish what happens if house is sold
    B-4   Husband and wife families with children
        B-4.1   Provide for child-bearing and child-care expenses
            B-4.1.1   Provide for health insurance (1982 statistics show birth costs from $3,000 to $4,000.)
            B-4.1.2   Assess child-care expenses (They depend on whether mother works outside house or not.)
        B-4.2   Provide for expanded housing needs
            B-4.2.1   Apartments—rent stabilized (more control over living expenses)
            B-4.2.2   Private homes—more space, tax deductions, equity
                B-4.2.2.1   Assess schools in neighborhood to determine if school taxes will rise
                B-4.2.2.2   Estimate taxes and interest costs
        B-4.3   Increase insurance to meet expanding costs
            B-4.3.1   Working couples need to provide for income replacement to protect one another

               B-4.3.2   Buy life insurance that can later meet college needs
               B-4.3.3   Insurance to plan for retirement needs
     B-4.4   Build an education fund
               B-4.4.1   Determine specific costs
               B-4.4.2   Determine what your options are, based on income
                        B-4.4.2.1   Low income—financial aid
                        B-4.4.2.2   Middle income
                                  B-4.4.2.2.1   Savings plan—put away monthly
                                  B-4.4.2.2.2   Tax shelter
                                  B-4.4.2.2.3   Tax scholarship-custodial account to save in child's name
                                  B-4.4.2.2.4   Income splitting—sharing income with a family member in lower income bracket

The last two age groups have been divided into ages 46 to 64 and ages 65 and over. We have limited the facts for these age groups to a few basic ones as our intention is to focus more on the 25 to 45 age group. In addition, financial planning in later years tends to be a natural outgrowth of that which was done in earlier years and therefore involves fewer new financial planning considerations.

C. Ages 46 to 64
    C-1   Continue career development
    C-2   Diversify investments
    C-3   Develop estate plans
    C-4   Explore retirement goals
D. Ages 65 and over
    D-1   Re-evaluate budget to meet retirement needs
    D-2   Investigate part-time or volunteer work for retirement
    D-3   Review will

Let's review for a moment and see how the steps we have taken so far apply to *your* needs:

1. Choose your topic to create a knowledge base—one that is of personal interest to you and in so doing specify your goals.

2. Research your topic; read books on the topic, talk with respected professionals, and use your own expertise if you are also knowledgeable.

3. Categorize your information and properly organize your facts into a taxonomy.

As you will soon see, we will create a decision tree from the taxonomy of facts from which we will create the actual knowledge base.

Decision Tree

So far we have a list of facts organized into a taxonomy. The next step we must take is to design a decision tree. A decision tree, as we saw in the chapter on backward chaining, is a grouping of questions that are related to the facts and that follow a path. The path may take us in several directions and explore several possibilities for those facts, but once we have reached the end of the path, we have come to a decision about those facts and thereby reached our goal. A path may move in several directions, and therefore several decisions will be made. As you will see on the decision tree in Figure 8-1, the end of the path is signified by a square, surrounding the statement, at the end of the path. Since we do not have enough space in this book to develop a decision tree for all the possible combinations of age groups and subdivisions within those age groups, we will take a part of the taxonomy and develop a small portion of the whole tree. You will be able to fill in the rest very easily.

Let's now take two hypothetical cases. The first is a single adult, the second is single adult living together (living with another single adult). How should the single adult, age 25 to 45, handle investments for capital growth? Under this category we've suggested that a person in that age group and life-style consider money market funds (B-1.2.1), time deposit securities (B-1.2.2), and savings bonds (B-1.2.3).

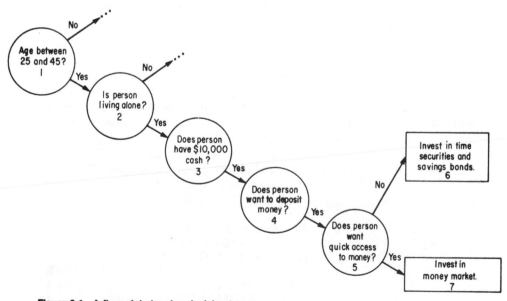

Figure 8-1 A financial planning decision tree.

The following questions will help us make decisions about the facts:

1. How much money does this single adult have?
2. Does this single adult want to deposit money for savings?
3. Does this single adult want quick access to money or is single adult willing to put money away for a longer period of time to accumulate interest?
4. Does single adult want security in investments?

The decision tree in Figure 8-1 illustrates these facts and the questions that will help reach our goal.

Notice that a few paths (the ones ending in three dots) are started but then trail off into space. These are included to give you an idea of how several paths are often interwoven into a decision tree and to show you how you might expand on this small tree if you wished to.

Now let us take the second hypothetical person, who is a single adult living together between the ages of 25 and 45. How would this person decide upon housing? Under the category "plan for housing investment" (B-2.3) we listed buy apartment, condominium, private house (B-2.3); joint ownership (B-2.3.1); draw up legal contracts (B-2.3.1.1); and spell out obligations and responsibilities (B-2.3.1.2). The following important questions are related to the facts:

1. How much money does the single adult living together have?
2. Does the single adult living together want to buy assets?
3. Does the single adult living together believe in joint ownership?

A larger portion of our small decision tree is shown in Figure 8-2.

From the decision tree we can directly write the rules for our knowledge base. This is done by tracing *all* paths leading to each terminated node of the tree. A terminated node is one that has a square drawn around it and one that does not have any branches leaving. For example, we have labeled some of our nodes with numbers. The node marked no. 6, invest in money market, is a terminated node. The path leading to this node is via the nodes labeled 1, 2, 3, 4, and 5. We can write a rule for arriving at this node as follows:

```
IF AGE >= (is more than or equal to) 25 AND          (Node 1)
   AGE <= (is less than or equal to) 45 AND          (Node 1)
   PERSON'S LIFE-STYLE = LIVING ALONE AND            (Node 2)
   PERSON'S CASH > $10,000 AND                       (Node 3)
   PERSON DEPOSIT CASH = YES                          (Node 4)
THEN PERSON INVEST = MONEY MARKET        (Terminal Node 6)
```

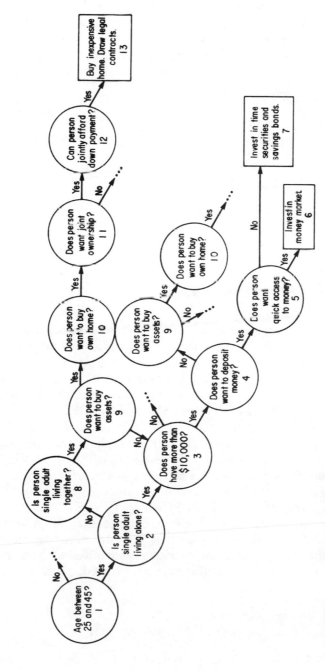

Figure 8-2 A bigger portion of the decision tree.

119

Notice that we invented simple variable names such as PERSON INVEST. Remember to always be consistent with variable names and use them in other rules in which they apply. For example, terminal node 13 has the following rule that is generated by the path 1, 2, 8, 9, 10, 11, and 12:

```
IF AGE > = 25 AND                                    (Node 1)
   AGE < = 45 AND                                    (Node 1)
   PERSON LIFE-STYLE = SINGLE ADULT
   LIVING TOGETHER                             (Node 2 and 8)
   PERSON BUY ASSETS = YES AND                       (Node 9)
   PERSON WANT OWN HOME = YES AND                   (Node 10)
   PERSON WANT JOINT OWNERSHIP
   = YES AND                                        (Node 11)
   PERSON HAS DOWN PAYMENT = YES                    (Node 12)
THEN PERSON INVEST = INEXPENSIVE HOME AND DRAW
LEGAL CONTACT
```

Backward and Forward Chaining Considerations

We can now place these rules in a knowledge base of either a backward or forward chaining system and then arrive at certain decisions. We would use a backward chaining system to see if a particular financial plan—or goal—is appropriate to a particular individual. We select a goal, such as finding the type of investments a person should make for capital growth. This is the one called PERSON INVEST. Once the goal has been identified, we search the THEN part of all the rules for the first instance of the goal's name. In our example of the single adult (living alone) we would study the rule related to PERSON INVEST: IF a person is more than age 25 *and* less than age 45 *and* is a single adult *and* has more than $10,000 cash *and* wants to deposit cash *and* wants to have quick access to cash, THEN PERSON INVEST in money market. All of the clauses after the IF statement and after the AND statements are clause variables that cannot be determined by invoking other rules (that is, they are not conclusion variables of other rules). We therefore must instantiate the variables by asking specific questions:

Is person more than age 25?

Is person less than age 45?

Is person single adult (living alone)?

Does person have more than $10,000 cash?

Does person want to deposit cash?

Does person want quick access to money?

A value (yes or no) must be provided for each question. Once this is done, each clause variable has been instantiated. If any of the questions are answered no, the statement for this goal is false. We then scan the rules for another statement that contains the conclusion variable PERSON INVEST. Since there are no other instances of that goal in our example, we are finished with this goal. In other words, such an investment is not a good idea for this individual. Of course, in a larger system there might be many other rules with instances of this goal.

If, however, all of the answers to our questions are yes, we have met this goal and the user can make a decision based upon the answer invest in money market.

In a forward chaining system rather than trying to satisfy a conclusion, we would try to recommend a financial path for an individual to take based upon that person's age, life-style, etc. We would do this by asking questions to satisfy the IF part of the rules in order to arrive at the conclusions generated by the THEN part. If we take the example of the single adult living together who is age 42 and is considering buying a home, we would ask the following questions:

Is person more than age 25?

Is person less than age 45?

Is this a single adult living together?

Does person want to buy assets?

Does person want to buy own home?

Does person want joint ownership?

Can person jointly afford down payment?

If all of the above conditions are met for this rule, that is, yes is answered to each question, the decision would be made to "buy an inexpensive home and draw up a legal agreement." If all the conditions are not met, that is, no is provided as an answer to at least one of the questions, we would have to look for another IF-THEN rule in which the conditions could be satisfied and an appropriate decision made.

From what you have read in this chapter, along with the chapters on the implementation theories of backward and forward chaining structures, you are now ready to undertake the development of a full-blown financial planning system.

Programming Applications

The rules for financial planning as derived from the decision tree can be inserted into either the forward or backward chaining tools outlined in the previous chapters. The user, of course, should remove the sample knowledge base used for backward chaining and replace it with the knowledge base for financial planning. A discussion of the statements to be replaced follows.

Let us consider one of the rules to show how this is done.

```
IF AGE > = 25 AND
   AGE < = 45 AND
   LIFE-STYLE = LIVING ALONE AND
   CASH > $10,000 AND
   DEPOSIT = YES
THEN INVEST = MONEY MARKET
```

The first thing we must do is abbreviate each variable, as for example

AG for AGE

LF for LIFE-STYLE

CA for CASH

DE for DEPOSIT

IN for INVEST

If we now refer to either the backward or forward chaining listing (Listings 5-1 and 6-1), we can replace comment 367 with

```
/* COMMENT 367 */

strcpy(VARLT[1],"AG");strcpy(VARLT[2],"LF");strcpy(VARLT[3],"CA");
strcpy(VARLT[4],"DE");
```

This places the condition variables of the rule into the variable list. We can now insert the rule into the IF-THEN statement section starting at comment 1500 for either the backward or forward chaining program as follows:

```
/* COMMENT 1500 */

IF (AG>=25) && (AG<=45) && (strcmp(LF,"LIVING ALONE")==0)T=1;

/* COMMENT 1501 */

IF (T=1) && (CA>10,000) && (strcmp(DE,"YES")==0)S=1;
```

The reason the rule was separated into two parts at comments 1500 and 1501 has to do with the limitation of the length of a C comment on some popular computers. Some computers limit a statement length. Briefly, the way the two statements tie together is

1. All three clauses of comment 1500 must be true for T: = 1.
2. All three clauses of comment 1501, including T: = 1 and the last two clauses, must be true for S: = 1.
3. Therefore all five clauses of the rule must be true for S: = 1, which is what we require.

For the backward chaining program the THEN part at comment 1510 would look like

```
strcpy(IN, "MONEY MARKET"); printf("IN=MONEY MARKET");
strcpy(VARBLE; "IN");
```

For the forward chaining program the THEN part at comment 1510 would look like

```
strcpy(IN, "MONEY MARKET"); printf("IN=MONEY MARKET");
strcpy(VARBLE, "IN");

INSTANTIATE
```

In addition, the following lists must be filled in. For backward chaining the conclusion variable list must contain the conclusion variable IN. This is done at comment number 305 as CLVART[1]: = 'IN'. In addition, the input statements must be modified to contain the condition variables. For example

```
printf("INPUT AGE NUMBER FOR AG?"); gets(&AG);

printf("INPUT LIFESTYLE e.g., "LIVING ALONE" FOR LF?"); gets(&LF);

printf("INPUT A DOLLAR NUMBER FOR CA?"); gets(&CA);

printf("INPUT YES OR NO FOR DE?"); gets(&DE);
```

For both backward and forward chaining the clause variable list must be filled in at comment 407. Unfortunately both tools have a limitation of four variables per clause. As an exercise, it will be very instructive for you to do the following:

Expand both the forward and backward chaining tools so that the clause variable list can hold nine variables per statement. Then enter the rule into the knowledge base for both tools and run the program.

Sales Expert System

The success of any business depends on how well it sells its product to its customers, be it automobiles, consulting services, feed grain, or insurance policies. The one-to-one relationship between a salesperson and a customer is still the basic unit of our sales-oriented economic system. Selling is anything but an exact science; the salesperson and the customer are individuals with different needs, different aspirations, and different considerations on their minds. Personalities play a major role in sales success. A poor mix of personalities has been known to ruin a sale to someone who was genuinely in need of the offered product, while just the right blend of characters often clinches a sale to a customer who probably didn't even need the product.

In business, computers are too often seen as no more than a tool for the most objective tasks: keeping records, compiling data, organizing statistical information. But in reality, computers can help make business more efficient even in an intangible and subjective area such as the effect of personality on sales performance.

The expert system we are about to describe is designed to assess the likelihood of a sale being closed based upon the personalities of both the salesperson and the customer. This assessment can help the salesperson determine what sort of approach should be taken with a particular customer and how much time and energy should reasonably be applied given the likelihood of a successful sale being made.

Needless to say, the variability of the human character is too complex a subject to be rendered neatly into an expert domain. But it is possible to include enough personality traits that are related to this specific area of human interrelationship to create a simple expert system that will give well-founded guidance to the salesperson.

Establishing the Facts

The first thing that must be done in designing an expert system for the salesperson-customer personality domain is to collect all the relevant facts. The personality facts domain will be divided into its two component parts: the salesperson's personality and the customer's personality. For each personality, a set of facts will be recorded that will allow the expert system to classify a salesperson or a customer into one of a number of personality categories. The facts were gathered for this expert system through extensive research in the most current marketing and psychological studies available on the subject of sales performance and sales and customer personality traits.

Salesperson Personality Types

What personality categories are there? In order to categorize sales personalities, we took from the literature various attributes that appeared to surface continually and formed them into general groupings. They were grouped into three main personality types which are

1. Dominant-aggressive
2. Submissive-pleasant
3. Assertive

We then made note of the most salient attributes (or characteristics) associated with these three personality types. In collecting attributes for a personality type we used both attributes that contributed greatly and those that contributed somewhat less. Naturally, there were also some attributes that belonged to more than one personality type. From this research we drew the following list of facts for each personality type. Each fact is assigned an identification number, such as 1-1, so we can refer to it for our later discussions. In addition, to the right of each fact in parenthesis is a weighting factor. The meaning of the weighting factor will be explained later.

Personality type 1—dominant-aggressive
    1-1 Likes to compete for a sale (5)
    1-2 Presentation is energetic and dynamic (5)
    1-3 Absorbed with own advancement (5)
    1-4 Hates to fail or lose a sale (10)
    1-5 Ambitious about moving up in company or meeting sales productivity demands (2.5)
    1-6 Decisive (2.5)

Personality type 2—submissive-pleasant
   2-1   Lacks assertiveness with customers (10)
   2-2   Feels the best offense is a good defense (5)
   2-3   Looks for security within job structure (5)
   2-4   Displays warm and affectionate behavior (5)
   2-5   Tries to be agreeable (2.5)
   2-6   Frequently wants to be available (2.5)

Personality type 3—assertive
   3-1   Likes to compete for a sale (2.5)
   3-2   Makes decisions easily (5)
   3-3   Open and honest with coworkers and customers (10)
   3-4   Ambitious to meet productivity demands (2.5)
   3-5   Presentation is energetic and dynamic (5)
   3-6   Welcomes another's opinion (5)

For purposes of simplicity, and to explain in clear, precise terms how to construct this sort of system, we have limited ourselves to only six attributes per personality type. In reality, of course, there are many more.

Instantiating the Facts

The next step is to develop a set of questions that will instantiate the facts relating to the personality type attributes. These questions are shown below.

Do you like to compete for a sale?

Is your presentation energetic and dynamic?

Are you absorbed with your own advancement?

Do you hate to fail or lose a sale?

Are you ambitious about moving up in the company or meeting sales productivity demands?

Are you decisive?

Do you lack assertiveness with customers?

Do you feel that the best offense is a good defense?

Do you look for security within your job structure at all cost?

Do you display warm and affectionate behavior?

Do you always try to be agreeable?

Do you frequently want to be available?

Do you make decisions easily?

Are you open and honest with coworkers and customers?

Do you welcome another's opinion?

Weighting Factors

Within a personality type, certain attributes are more important than others in determining whether an individual has that personality type. For example, when considering the dominant-aggressive personality, the attribute "hates to fail or lose a sale" (1-4) is more important than "decisive" (1-6). What is meant by the term "important?" A person with the attribute "hates to fail or lose a sale" would be more likely to be identified as a dominant-aggressive personality than one with the attribute "decisive." We can therefore rate each attribute on an importance scale of 1 to 10. The higher the number, the greater the importance. We call this number a weighting factor. Therefore "hates to fail or lose a sale" with a weighting factor of 10 has a higher value than "decisive" with a weighting factor of 2.5.

How Are the Weighting Factors Used?

When an answer to a question is yes, the fact associated with the question also becomes yes. In order to get a weighting factor score for each personality, we sum those weighting factors instantiated to yes. The score is called the "sum weighting factor." If all the facts are instantiated to yes, the sum weighting factor we get is called the "maximum sum weighting factor." In our example, the maximum sum weighting factor is 30 and occurs when all facts for a given salesperson's personality are yes. For example, the sum weighting factors of all the facts in the dominant-aggressive personality are

$$5 + 5 + 5 + 10 + 2.5 + 2.5 = 30$$

An Example of the System at Work

Since pictures are worth a thousand words, we will use an example to show you how those concepts we have already explained, plus additional concepts that will be explained in the following example, are used by the expert system.

The user, who in this case is the salesperson, sits at the computer terminal to answer all the personal questions. Our hypothetical salesperson's responses are indicated after the question mark.

1-1 Do you like to compete for a sale?   YES
1-2 Is your presentation energetic and dynamic?   YES

1-3 Are you absorbed with your own advancement? NO
1-4 Do you hate to fail or lose a sale? YES
1-5 Are you ambitious about moving up in the company or meeting sales productivity demands? NO
1-6 Are you decisive? NO
2-1 Do you lack assertiveness with customers? NO
2-2 Do you feel that the best offense is a good defense? NO
2-3 Do you look for security within your job structure at all cost? NO
2-4 Do you display warm and affectionate behavior? NO
2-5 Do you always try to be agreeable? YES
2-6 Do you frequently want to make yourself available? NO
3-2 Do you make decisions easily? YES
3-3 Are you open and honest with coworkers and customers? NO
3-6 Do you welcome another's opinions? NO

You should note that question 3-1 is identical to question 1-1 and therefore does not have to be repeated. But it is also important to note that question 1-1 has a weighting of 5 and question 3-1 has a weighting factor of 2.5. The difference is their relative importance within the personality type they are included in. This is an important point. Similarly, questions 3-4 and 3-5 are already answered in questions 1-5 and 1-2, respectively. Table 9-1 summarizes the responses and provides the weighting factor calculations.

It is now quite apparent that people do not fit neatly into one type of personality structure but may contain characteristics of several types. There is obviously a great deal of overlap and variability within individuals, and this simple system highlights only a small degree of it.

We have now drawn a picture of the following salesperson's personality:

Likes to compete (personality 1 and 3)

Presentation is energetic and dynamic (personality 1 and 3)

Hates to fail or lose a sale (personality 1)

Always tries to be agreeable (personality 2)

Makes decisions easily (personality 3)

Assessing the Salesperson Personality Scores

As seen in Table 9-1, the sum weighting factors for the three personality types are

Sales personality 1	Dominant-aggressive	20.0
Sales personality 2	Submissive-pleasant	2.5
Sales personality 3	Assertive	12.5
Total		35.0

Table 9.1   Results of Example Expert System for Sales

Personality attributes	Answers to questions	Weighting factor
Dominant-aggressive		
1-1	Yes	5.0
1-2	Yes	5.0
1-3	No	0
1-4	Yes	10.0
1-5	No	0
1-6	No	0
Sum weighting factor		20.0
Submissive-pleasant		
2-1	No	0
2-2	No	0
2-3	No	0
2-4	No	0
2-5	Yes	2.5
2-6	No	0
Sum weighting factor		2.5
Assertive		
3-1	Yes	2.5
3-2	Yes	5.0
3-3	No	0
3-4	No	0
3-5	Yes	5.0
3-6	No	0
Sum weighting factor		12.5

We see that a salesperson may have a tendency to exhibit any one of the personalities. The higher the sum weighting factors for a given personality, the greater the tendency to exhibit that personality. For example, there is a much greater tendency to exhibit a dominant-aggressive personality with a sum weighting factor of 20 than to exhibit a submissive-pleasant one with a sum weighting factor of 2.5. If these two personalities were the only personalities we had to deal with, we could say that the possibility of this salesperson exhibiting a dominant-aggressive versus submissive-pleasant personality would be 20.0 divided by 22.5. The value 22.5 is the total of both sum weighting factors. The possibility of being submissive-pleasant would be 2.5/22.5. We have in effect compared one personality with another. This has been accomplished by comparing the score of the individual personality with the combined scores of both personalities. In our example we have three personalities. The same procedure would hold true for any number of personalities considered. We will define the possibility that the salesperson will exhibit a particular personality with the following equation:

$$POS = \frac{\text{Sum weighting factor for a personality}}{\text{Total of all sum weighting factors}}$$
$$\text{for all three personalities}$$

Therefore for each salesperson personality we get the following possibility

POS 1 = 20/35 = .571 = 57.1%
POS 2 = 2.5/35 = .071 = 7.1%
POS 3 = 12.5/35 = .357 = 35.7%

These possibility values will be combined with the customer's personality possibility value to determine the likelihood of a successful sale.

The Customer

We now move on to assess the various types of customer personalities. Again, we sort out all our research of the various customer personalities from the literature. Once again, for purposes of simplicity, we have organized our research into four customer personalities and listed those facts—four facts per personality—that we judged to belong to each of the personalities. They are listed with their associated weighting factors in parenthesis to the right of the fact:

Personality type 1—motivated by needs for independence and self-esteem
    1-1 Conversation is filled with reference to oneself (5)
    1-2 Is self-congratulatory or boastful (3)
    1-3 Does not seek advice of salesperson (2)
    1-4 Thinks he knows better than anyone else (5)
Personality type 2—motivated by needs for security
    2-1 Cautious (5)
    2-2 Slow to make decisions (5)
    2-3 Unwilling to share or provide information (3)
    2-4 Unwilling to reveal opinions or feelings (2)
Personality type 3—motivated by needs for social acceptance
    3-1 Goes out of way to please (5)
    3-2 Is very submissive (5)
    3-3 Dodges any hint of disagreement or argument (2)
    3-4 Comes across as pleasant, cooperative, sympathetic (3)
Personality type 4—motivated by needs for independence and self-realization
    4-1 Gets involved with presentation (5)
    4-2 Offers ideas and opinions freely (2)

4-3   Wants involvement as codecision-maker with salesperson (3)
4-4   Flexible approach (5)

A maximum sum weighting factor of 15 has been assigned to each customer personality type. For each customer, the salesperson will answer the following questions according to how the customer is observed:

1-1   Is customer's conversation filled with references to oneself?
1-2   Is customer self-congratulatory or boastful?
1-3   Does customer seek advice of salesperson?
1-4   Does customer think he knows better than anyone else?
2-1   Is customer cautious?
2-2   Is customer slow to make decisions?
2-3   Is customer unwilling to share or provide information?
2-4   Is customer unwilling to reveal opinions or feelings?
3-1   Does customer go out of way to please?
3-2   Is customer very submissive?
3-3   Does customer dodge any hint of disagreement or argument?
3-4   Does customer come across as pleasant, cooperative, or sympathetic?
4-1   Does customer get involved with presentation?
4-2   Does customer offer ideas and opinions freely?
4-3   Does customer want involvement as codecision-maker with salesperson?
4-4   Does customer have a flexible approach?

Each customer personality question is used to instantiate a fact in the same way the salesperson personality questions were used. A yes answer causes the weighting associated with that question to be evaluated. A no causes the weighting factor to be ignored. As an example, Table 9-2 was constructed for a particular customer based on the customer personality questions listed above.

It is apparent that customers, as well as salespersons, have personalities that can overlap into more than one personality type. For the customer example, these are sum weighting factors for customer personalities 2 and 3.

We have now drawn a picture of the following customer personality.

Cautious (personality 2)

Slow to make decisions (personality 2)

Goes out of way to please (personality 3)

Very submissive (personality 3)

Dodges any hint of disagreement or argument (personality 3)

Comes across as pleasant, cooperative, and sympathetic (personality 3)

Table 9-2   Results of Example Expert System for Customer

Personality attributes	Answers to questions	Weighting factor
Customer type 1		
1-1	No	0
1-2	No	0
1-3	No	0
1-4	No	0
Sum weighting factor		0
Customer type 2		
2-1	Yes	5
2-2	Yes	5
2-3	No	0
2-4	No	0
Sum weighting factor		10
Customer type 3		
3-1	Yes	5
3-2	Yes	5
3-3	Yes	2
3-4	Yes	3
Sum weighting factor		15
Customer type 4		
4-1	No	0
4-2	No	0
4-3	No	0
4-4	No	0
Sum weighting factor		0

Assessing Customer Personality Scores

In summary the sum weighting factor for each customer personality is

Customer personality 1	Conversation is filled with references to oneself	0
Customer personality 2	Motivated by need for security	10
Customer personality 3	Motivated by need for social acceptance	15
Customer personality 4	Motivated by need for independence and self-realization	0
Total		25

Therefore using

$$POS = \frac{Sum\ weighting\ factor}{Total\ of\ all\ sum\ weighting\ factors}$$

we can calculate the possibilities of the customer being

POS 1 =   0/25 = 0.00 =   0%
POS 2 = 10/25 = 0.40 = 40%
POS 3 = 15/25 = 0.60 = 60%
POS 4 =   0/25 = 0.00 =   0%

Assessing the Possible Sales and Customer Combinations

Now that we have values for the possibilities of a person being a particular sales type and a customer being a particular customer type, we must determine the possibilities of having a specific combination when the two interact with one another. It is quite clear that salesperson personality 1 and customer personality 3 are the most likely for our two examples. But what if the values were closer or there was a tie? What if there was disagreement with the values? We must therefore consider all possibilities and allow the expert system user to make the final decision. To do this, we arrive at the combination possibilities by multiplying the possibility of the salesperson being a particular sales type by the possibility of the customer being a particular customer type for all the personality types. In normal probability-possibility theory when we have two events that are mutually exclusive of the other and we want to find out the possibility of event 1 and event 2 occurring together, we multiply the probability-possibility of each individual event.

This product is shown in Table 9-3.

Table 9.3   Table of Combination Possibilities

Sales type	Customer type	Sales possibility	Customer possibility	Combination possibility
1	1	0.571	0	0
1	2	0.571	0.4	0.2284
1	3	0.571	0.6	0.3426
1	4	0.571	0	0
2	1	0.071	0	0
2	2	0.071	0.4	0.0284
2	3	0.071	0.6	0.0426
2	4	0.071	0	0
3	1	0.355	0	0
3	2	0.357	0.4	0.1428
3	3	0.357	0.6	0.2142
3	4	0.357	0	0

The system user can now study the combination possibilities to determine which sales and customer personalities are present and make corresponding decisions.

Expert System Assessments

The user of the expert system may now want to assess, in simple narrative, what happens when a specific type of sales personality encounters a specific customer type. For example, since the possibility is highest that salesperson personality 1 and customer personality 3 are present, we might want to know the computer's "sales outcome" prediction for this combination. For this combination the expert system would print the following:

```
Sales result: Above average; salesperson dominates, customer admires
salesperson and complies.
```

This assessment by the expert system would come from the following list, which gives sales assessments by a human expert of each personality combination. SP (number) and CP (number) is a shorthand notation for salesperson personality (number) and customer personality (number).

SP 1 and CP 1	Sales result: Average; high mutual regard, interaction seen as a contest.
SP 1 and CP 2	Sales result: Below average; salesperson disdains, customer withdraws.
SP 1 and CP 3	Sales result: Above average; salesperson dominates, customer admires salesperson and complies.
SP 1 and CP 4	Sales result: Average; salesperson respects customer, but customer suspicious of salesperson's forcefulness.
SP 2 and CP 1	Sales result: Below average; salesperson withdraws, customer in control, low mutual regard.
SP 2 and CP 2	Sales result: Below average; both withdraw, low-key interaction.
SP 2 and CP 3	Sales result: Average; salesperson neutral toward customer, customer is eager to be nice guy.
SP 2 and CP 4	Sales result: Below average; salesperson is aloof and passive; customer tries to gain information; salesperson has high regard for customer, but customer has mixed regard for salesperson.
SP 3 and CP 1	Sales result: Above average; high mutual regard.
SP 3 and CP 2	Sales result: Average; rapport easily established, salesperson patient, and customer trusts salesperson.

SP 3 and CP 3   Sales result: Above average; salesperson responds to customer's social needs, customer responds.

SP 3 and CP 4   Sales result: Above average; excellent rapport, both function as partners, high mutual regard.

Let us now summarize the procedure for designing the expert system that is described in this chapter:

1. Research and organize gathered information.
2. List categories and the facts associated with each category.
3. List questions in order to attain the information for each fact.
4. Assign weighting factors.
5. Compute the sum weighting factor.
6. Assess possibilities based on the sum weighting factors.
7. Provide combination possibilities based on each category.
8. Provide strategic predictions based on the decision made.

You have just finished reading about one approach to creating an expert system for the salesperson-customer domain. You are now ready to expand upon this system or create another one within this domain but with a different thrust.

Programming Applications

Let us examine a methodology for implementing this expert system in C. Listing 9-1 is used to determine the sum weighting factors and possibilities for all of the personalities discussed.

Program Explanation

The program is organized into four parts which are

1. Initialization
2. Salesperson, data acquisition, analysis
3. Customer, data acquisition, analysis
4. A combined salesperson-customer analysis

Program Listing

Listing 9-1 is followed by a sample run.

Listing 9-1 Sales expert system.

```
/*************** sales expert system **************/
#include <stdio.h>

char s[4][21], c[5][61], a[21][2] /* answer array */;

float sw[4] ; /* sum weighting factor array for salesperson */
float cw[5] ; /* sum weighting factor array for customer */
float sf[19] ; /* salesperson weighting factor */
float cf[17] ; /* customer weighting factor */
float ps[4], pc[5], sum ;

int i, j, k ;

main() {
/* initialization section */
/* salesman personality name */
strcpy(s[1],"DOMINANT/AGRESSIVE");
strcpy(s[2],"SUBMISSIVE/PLEASANT");
strcpy(s[3],"ASSERTIVE");
/* customer personality name */
strcpy(c[1],"MOTIVATED BY NEEDS FOR INDEPENDENCE AND SELF ESTEEM");
strcpy(c[2],"MOTIVATED BY NEEDS FOR SECURITY");
strcpy(c[3],"MOTIVATED BY NEEDS FOR SOCIAL ACCEPTANCE");
strcpy(c[4],"MOTIVATED BY NEEDS FOR INDEPENDENCE AND SELF-REALIZATION");
sf[1]=5; sf[2]=5; sf[3]=5; sf[4]=10; sf[5]=2.5; sf[6]=2.5;
sf[7]=10; sf[8]=5; sf[9]=5; sf[10]=5; sf[11]= 2.5; sf[12]=2.5;
sf[13]=2.5; sf[14]=5; sf[15]=10; sf[16]=2.5; sf[17]=5; sf[18]=5;
cf[1]=5; cf[2]=3; cf[3]=2; cf[4]=5; cf[5]=5; cf[6]=5; cf[7]=3;
cf[8]=2; cf[9]=5; cf[10]=5; cf[11]=2; cf[12]=3; cf[13]=5; cf[14]=2;
cf[15]=3; cf[16]=5;
/****************************************************/
/***** data acquisition section ******/
/******** salespersons data **********/
printf("**** SALESPERSONS DATA ****\n");
printf("DO YOU LIKE TO COMPETE FOR A SALE? ");
gets(a[1]);
printf("IS YOUR PRESENTATION ENERGETIC AND DYNAMIC? ");
gets(a[2]);
printf("ARE YOU ABSORBED WITH YOUR OWN ADVANCEMENT? ");
gets(a[3]);
printf("DO YOU HATE TO FAIL OR TO LOSE A SALE? ");
gets(a[4]);
printf("ARE YOU AMBITIOUS ABOUT MOVING UP IN THE COMPANY OR\n");
printf(" MEETING SALES PRODUCTIVITY DEMANDS? ");
gets(a[5]);
printf("ARE YOU DECISIVE? ");
gets(a[6]);
printf("DO YOU LACK ASSERTIVENESS WITH CUSTOMERS? ");
gets(a[7]);
printf("DO YOU FEEL THE BEST OFFENSE IS A GOOD DEFENSE? ");
gets(a[8]);
printf("DO YOU LOOK FOR SECURITY WITHIN YOUR JOB STRUCTURE AT ALL COSTS? ");
gets(a[9]);
printf("DO YOU DISPLAY WARM AND AFFECTIONATE BEHAVIOR? ");
gets(a[10]);
printf("DO YOU ALWAYS TRY TO BE AGREEABLE? ");
gets(a[11]);
printf("DO YOU FREQUENTLY WANT TO BE AVAILABLE? ");
gets(a[12]);
strcpy(a[13],a[1]);
printf("DO YOU MAKE DECISIONS EASILY? ");
gets(a[14]);
printf("ARE YOU OPEN AND HONEST WITH CO-WORKERS AND CUSTOMERS? ");
gets(a[15]);
strcpy(a[16],a[5]);
strcpy(a[17],a[2]);
printf("DO YOU WELCOME ANOTHER'S OPINION? ");
gets(a[18]);
printf("\n");
/* calculate sum-weighting factor and possibility factor */
for(i=1;i<4;i++) {
```

```
                      /* calculate sum weighting factor */
                      sum=0;
                      for(j=1;j<7;j++) {
                      k=(i-1)*6+j;
                      if(strcmp(a[k],"Y") == 0) sum=sum+sf[k];
                      }
                      sw[i]=sum;
                      }
                      /* calculate the possibilities of being a personality type */
                      /* total sum weighting factors */
                      sum=sw[1]+sw[2]+sw[3];
                      for(i=1;i<4;i++) {
                       printf("%s\n",s[i]);
                       printf("SUM WEIGHTING FACTOR=%f\n",sw[i]);
                       ps[i]=sw[i]/sum;
                       printf("POSSIBILITY=%f\n\n",ps[i]);
                      }
                      /*******************************************/
                      /******** customer data ********/
                      printf("**** CUSTOMER DATA ****\n");
                      printf("IS CUSTOMERS CONVERSATION FILLED WITH REFERENCE TO ONESELF? ");
                      gets(a[1]);
                      printf("IS CUSTOMER SELF CONGRATULATORY/BOASTFUL? ");
                      gets(a[2]);
                      printf("DOES CUSTOMER SEEK ADVICE OF SALESPERSON? ");
                      gets(a[3]);
                      printf("DOES CUSTOMER THINK HE KNOWS BETTER THAN ANYONE ELSE? ");
                      gets(a[4]);
                      printf("IS CUSTOMER CAUTIOUS? ");
                      gets(a[5]);
                      printf("IS CUSTOMER SLOW TO MAKE DECISIONS? ");
                      gets(a[6]);
                      printf("IS CUSTOMER WILLING TO SHARE OR PROVIDE INFORMATION? ");
                      gets(a[7]);
                      printf("IS CUSTOMER UNWILLING TO REVEAL OPINIONS OR FEELINGS? ");
                      gets(a[8]);
                      printf("DOES CUSTOMER GO OUT OF WAY TO PLEASE? ");
                      gets(a[9]);
                      printf("IS CUSTOMER VERY SUBMISSIVE? ");
                      gets(a[10]);
                      printf("DOES CUSTOMER DODGE ANY DISAGREEMENT OR ARGUMENT? ");
                      gets(a[11]);
                      printf("DOES CUSTOMER COME ACROSS AS PLEASANT-COOPERATIVE ");
                      printf(" OR SYMPATHETIC? ");
                      gets(a[12]);
                      printf("DOES CUSTOMER GET INVOLVED WITH PRESENTATION? ");
                      gets(a[13]);
                      printf("DOES CUSTOMER OFFER IDEAS AND OPINIONS FREELY? ");
                      gets(a[14]);
                      printf("DOES CUSTOMER WANT INVOLVEMENT AS CO-DECISION MAKER ");
                      printf(" WITH SALESMAN? ");
                      gets(a[15]);
                      printf("DOES CUSTOMER HAVE FLEXIBLE APPROACH? ");
                      gets(a[16]);
                      printf("\n");
                      /* calculate sum weighting factor and possibility factor */
                      for(i=1;i<5;i++) {
                      /* calculate sum weighting factor */
                      sum=0;
                       for(j=1;j<5;j++) {
                        k=(i-1)*4+j;
                        if(strcmp(a[k],"Y") == 0) sum=sum+cf[k];
                       }
                       cw[i]=sum;
                      }
                      printf("ENTER RETURN TO CONTINUE?");
                      gets();
                      /* calculate the possibilities of being a personality type */
                      /* total sum weighting factors */
                      sum=cw[1]+cw[2]+cw[3];
                      for(i=1;i<5;i++) {
```

Listing 9-1   *(Continued)*

```
/* print results */
printf("%s\n",c[i]);
printf("SUM WEIGHTING FACTOR=%f\n",cw[i]);
pc[i]=cw[i]/sum;
printf("POSSIBILITY=%f\n",pc[i]);
printf("\n");
}
for(i=1;i<4;i++) {
 for(j=1;j<5;j++)
  printf("SALES %d   CUSTOMER %d   POSSIBILITY=%f\n",i,j,ps[i]*pc[j]);
 printf("ENTER RETURN TO CONTINUE?");
 gets();
}
}
```

Sample Run

```
**** SALESPERSONS DATA ****
DO YOU LIKE TO COMPETE FOR A SALE? Y
IS YOUR PRESENTATION ENERGETIC AND DYNAMIC? Y
ARE YOU ABSORBED WITH YOUR OWN ADVANCEMENT? N
DO YOU HATE TO FAIL OR LOSE A SALE? Y
ARE YOU AMBITIOUS ABOUT MOVING UP IN THE COMPANY OR
 MEETING SALES PRODUCTIVITY DEMANDS? N
ARE YOU DECISIVE? N
DO YOU LACK ASSERTIVENESS WITH CUSTOMERS? N
DO YOU FEEL THAT THE BEST OFFENSE IS A GOOD DEFENSE? N
DO YOU LOOK FOR SECURITY WITHIN YOUR JOB STRUCTURE
 AT ALL COSTS? N
DO YOU DISPLAY WARM AND AFFECTIONATE BEHAVIOR? N
DO YOU ALWAYS TRY TO BE AGREEABLE? Y
DO YOU FREQUENTLY WANT TO BE AVAILABLE? N
DO YOU MAKE DECISIONS EASILY? Y
ARE YOU OPEN AND HONEST WITH CO-WORKERS AND CUSTOMERS? N
DO YOU WELCOME ANOTHER'S OPINION? N

DOMINANT/AGGRESSIVE
SUM WEIGHTING FACTOR= 20
POSSIBILITY= .5714286

SUBMISSIVE/PLEASANT
SUM WEIGHTING FACTOR= 2.5
POSSIBILITY= .0714285

ASSERTIVE
SUM WEIGHTING FACTOR= 12.5
POSSIBILITY= .3571429


**** CUSTOMERS DATA ****
IS CUSTOMERS CONVERSATION FILLED WITH REFERENCE TO ONESELF? N
IS CUSTOMER SELF CONGRATULATORY/BOASTFUL? N
DOES CUSTOMER SEEK ADVICE OF SALESPERSON? N
DOES CUSTOMER THINK HE KNOWS BETTER THAN ANYONE ELSE? N
IS CUSTOMER CAUTIOUS? Y
IS CUSTOMER SLOW TO MAKE DECISIONS? Y
IS CUSTOMER UNWILLING TO SHARE OR PROVIDE INFORMATION? N
IS CUSTOMER UNWILLING TO REVEAL OPINIONS OR FEELINGS? N
```

```
DOES CUSTOMER GO OUT OF WAY TO PLEASE? Y
IS CUSTOMER VERY SUBMISSIVE? Y
DOES CUSTOMER DODGE ANY DISAGREEMENT OR ARGUMENT? Y
DOES CUSTOMER COME ACROSS AS PLEASANT-COOPERATIVE OR
 SYMPATHETIC? Y
DOES CUSTOMER GET INVOLVED WITH PRESENTATION? N
DOES CUSTOMER OFFER IDEAS AND OPINIONS FREELY? N
DOES CUSTOMER WANT INVOLVEMENT AS CO-DECISION MAKER WITH
 SALESPERSON? N
DOES CUSTOMER HAVE FLEXIBLE APPROACH? N

ENTER RETURN TO CONTINUE?
MOTIVATED BY NEEDS FOR INDEPENDENCE AND SELF ESTEEM
SUM WEIGHTING FACTOR= 0
POSSIBILITY = 0

MOTIVATED BY NEEDS FOR SECURITY
SUM WEIGHTING FACTOR= 10
POSSIBILITY = .4

MOTIVATED BY NEEDS FOR SOCIAL ACCEPTANCE
SUM WEIGHTING FACTOR= 15
POSSIBILITY = .6

MOTIVATED BY NEEDS FOR INDEPENDENCE AND SELF-REALIZATION
SUM WEIGHTING FACTOR= 0
POSSIBILITY - 0

SALES  1    CUSTOMER  1    POSSIBILITY= 0
SALES  1    CUSTOMER  2    POSSIBILITY- .2285714
SALES  1    CUSTOMER  3    POSSIBILITY= .3428572
SALES  1    CUSTOMER  4    POSSIBILITY= 0
ENTER RETURN TO CONTINUE?
SALES  2    CUSTOMER  1    POSSIBILITY= 0
SALES  2    CUSTOMER  2    POSSIBILITY= .0285714
SALES  2    CUSTOMER  3    POSSIBILITY= .0428571
SALES  2    CUSTOMER  4    POSSIBILITY= 0
ENTER RETURN TO CONTINUE?
SALES  3    CUSTOMER  1    POSSIBILITY= 0
SALES  3    CUSTOMER  2    POSSIBILITY= .1428572
SALES  3    CUSTOMER  3    POSSIBILITY= .2142857
SALES  3    CUSTOMER  4    POSSIBILITY= 0
ENTER RETURN TO CONTINUE?
```

Chapter

10

Learning Evaluation
Expert System

This chapter will describe how an expert system can be used to pinpoint the existence of an educational problem. Statistics show that a large number of English-speaking native born American adults read or write so poorly that they have trouble holding jobs. Some of them may suffer from specific learning disorders. Statistics also show that many children in this country also suffer from some organically based learning disability.

A learning problem or disability can most profitably be seen as spanning a continuum from mild to severe. We will use the term "learning disability" to define the more severe and the term "learning problem" to define the milder educational problem. The severity of the learning problem depends on the number and severity of processes affected.

Reading and other academic skills are not the only issues to address when studying the field of educational problems. Katrina De Hirsch, in her article, "Learning Disabilities, an Overview," states

> Psychological and physiological factors, the child's genetic endowment, including his vulnerability to stress, his prenatal, neonatal, and postnatal history, the emotional climate in which he is reared, and the social milieu of which he is a part, all interact in complex ways.

The literature therefore makes it clear that disabilities or learning problems are the result of complex interacting forces. Assessment and evaluation, which is the accepted method of diagnosis in the field today, must therefore take into account many factors in order to make a correct evaluation.

Today, the accepted method of educational assessment is implemented by administering standardized tests and gathering pertinent data. In general these tests evaluate specific academic skills such as reading, spelling, and arithmetic. They also assess vocabulary and expressive writing skills. In addition the evaluator gathers background information related to preschool history and present functioning. The testee's school and home environment is assessed as are those psychological and social attributes that relate to the learning process. The evaluator computes the educational test scores, studies the responses on the test in order to pinpoint educational deficits, summarizes all the data gathered regarding background information and present social and psychological functioning, and forms an overall assessment of the person's total learning capacity.

An expert system that assesses the incidence of a learning problem must take all these procedures into consideration. We have created such a system called the Learning Evaluating System (LES). It organizes the process of evaluation systematically so that a thorough and exact analysis is made. As you can well understand, evaluations that are administered by human beings, i.e., professional evaluators, can often be very subjective. People too often consider one or two facts and draw final conclusions swiftly and erroneously. This is not to say that human beings do not evaluate professionally or that computers do a better job. But a system like LES can guide the evaluator in a carefully constructed process by highlighting all of the important facts to be assessed and providing guidelines on how to make decisions about those collected facts. The human mind simply cannot process all of that information simultaneously or as systematically as a computer can.

LES does not make any black and white decisions. It pinpoints specific areas of educational dysfunction and appraises the extent of the deficit, but it allows the evaluator to make the final decisions and recommendations.

This was accomplished via the following format:

1. Organizing the data into topics and subtopics

2. Listing facts associated with each subtopic

3. Assigning weighting factors to the facts and establishing decision levels

4. Verifying the data

Organizing the Data into Topics and Subtopics

Via a literature search, extensive experience, and the collaboration of several professionals, the system has been divided into the following topics:

Educational

Biological and physical

Psychological

Social

These topics represent some of the determinants or causative contributors to learning problems and disabilities. Since they encompass a great deal of material, several subtopics were devised for each general topic. The topics and subtopics are as follows:

A. Educational
   A-1   Reading
   A-2   Arithmetic
B. Biological and physical
   B-1   Hereditary factors
C. Psychological
   C-1   Self-confidence

Listing the Facts

We took the topics and subtopics and listed the facts associated with each. Please remember that there are many more topics and facts associated with an educational evaluation than the ones listed below. These facts are but a very small sample of those used in the Learning Evaluation System.

The number in parentheses after each fact is the weighting factor, which will be discussed later in this chapter.

A. Educational
   A-1   Reading
      A-1.1   Pronunciation
         A-1.1.1   Recognizes letters of the alphabet (1)
         A-1.1.2   Pronounces words without reversing or omitting letters (1)
         A-1.1.3   Knows where to place the accent (1)
         A-1.1.4   Breaks different words into proper syllable division (1)
         A-1.1.5   Retains and evokes sound equivalent of letters in words (1)
      A-1.2   Comprehension
         A-1.2.1   Retains facts (1)
         A-1.2.2   Draws inferences (1)
         A-1.2.3   Familiar with vocabulary (1)
         A-1.2.4   Familiar with concepts presented (1)
   A-2   Arithmetic
      A-2.1   Adds numbers in a single column (1)
      A-2.2   Adds numbers in multiple columns (1)

A-2.3 Subtracts with single-column borrowing (1)
A-2.4 Subtracts with multiple-column borrowing (1)
A-2.5 Multiplies single digits (1)
A-2.6 Multiplies multiple digits (1)
A-2.7 Divides and finds a quotient without remainders (1)
A-2.8 Divides and finds a quotient with remainders (1)
B. Biological and physical
   B-1 Hereditary factors
      B-1.1 Parents with learning disabilities (1)
      B-1.2 Sibling (not a twin) with learning disabilities (1)
      B-1.3 Twin with learning disabilities (1)
      B-1.4 Incidence of chromosome anomalies or hereditary disorders in family (1)
C. Psychological
   C-1 Self-confidence
      C-1.1 Withdraws from activities (1)
      C-1.2 Lacks motivation (1)
      C-1.3 Exhibits defeatism (1)

Assigning Weighting Factors and Establishing Decision Levels

The numbers in parentheses following each of the facts are the weighting factors. Weighting factors help us make decisions because they assign specific values to the facts. Notice that in this system all the factors have been given the weight 1. Since weighting factors are equivalent to importance in their contribution to a problem or lack of one, this means that all the listed facts have equal importance. How do we then make decisions as to whether there is an educational problem? In this system we have established decision levels. Each fact can contribute to a learning problem or disability. If there are many contributing facts, we say the student has a learning problem. If a small number of facts contribute, we might say the student is just missing the point. The way we determine this is by adding the weighting factors of each fact that contributes to that topic, i.e., arithmetic, attention span, etc., being a problem. We call the sum of these facts the sum weighting factor. The lowest sum weighting factor within a subtopic that we determine causes a learning problem is the decision level. If a person scores a sum weighting factor within a subtopic that equals or exceeds the decision level, we assert that there is a problem in that area. For example, the decision level for hereditary factors is 1. If a person received a score of 2 or more in that subtopic, there is probably a problem. Since each fact has a weighting factor of 1, any one or more facts in this topic will cause the decision level to be reached.

The values that we assign to decision levels are determined by testing and research. By testing a sample population, the researcher learns what degree of difficulty indicates a problem area. Of course ongoing, more comprehensive research might modify our selection of weighting factors and decision levels. We have designed an expert system which uses the best guesses of present-day experts and experimentation, but its simple organization will allow us to make easy modifications, should they be needed in the future.

Now that we have the facts and our inference mechanism in hand— the weighting factors and decision levels—let's start out with the implementation.

The procedure for implementing this system is as follows. We formulate questions for each fact of each topic. The questions are formulated so that a yes answer indicates that the fact contributes to a learning problem or deficiency. A no answer indicates that there is no problem or deficiency. The evaluator will sit at the computer and answer specific questions about a subject's performance. The evaluator's response of yes will indicate that the weighting factor, which in this case is always 1, is to be added to the score. A response of no does not add anything to the score. Within a subtopic the final sum weighting factor is tabulated. If the sum weighting factor equals or exceeds the decision level for that subtopic, we state that this subtopic constitutes a problem and inform the evaluator. We may find, of course, that several subtopics are problem areas. We therefore note the number of subtopics that equaled or exceeded the decision levels. If too many exceeded, we definitely have a learning problem. For our simplistic purposes, we can hypothetically establish that if three subtopics exceed the weighting factors, there is a severe problem; if two, there is a mild learning problem; and if one or zero, either there is no learning problem or there is a need for future exploration. To summarize

1. We compute the sum weighting factor by adding the weighting factor of all of the questions that received a yes within a subtopic.

2. We establish whether the sum weighting factor for a subtopic equals or exceeds the decision level for that same subtopic.

3. We print the number and the names of those subtopics that equal or exceed the decision levels.

4. Depending on the number of topics that indicate a problem, we determine whether an individual has a learning problem, a learning disability, or neither.

An Example of the System at Work

We will now show you how the system works with the following example of a sample case. The evaluator's responses are contained after the question marks below.

Name of person to be evaluated?   Sara Green
Age of person to be evaluated?   12 years, 8 months
Grade level (if applicable)?   7th grade, 10th month
Date of evaluation?   June 7, 1985
Name of evaluator?   Diane Drang

A. Educational
  A-1   Reading
    A-1.1   Pronunciation
    Is person unable to
    A-1.1.1   Recognize letters of the alphabet?   No
    A-1.1.2   Pronounce words without reversing and omitting letters?   Yes
    A-1.1.3   Know where to place the accent?   Yes
    A-1.1.4   Break difficult words into proper syllable division? Yes
    A-1.1.5   Retain and evoke sound equivalent of letters in words?   Yes
      Sum weighting factor = 4
      Decision level = 2
      Test score = Grade 5 years, 8 months
    A-1.2   Comprehension
    Is person unable to
    A-1.2.1   Retain facts?   No
    A-1.2.2   Draw inferences?   Yes
    A-1.2.3   Handle difficult vocabulary?   No
    A-1.2.4   Handle concepts presented?   Yes
      Sum weighting factor = 2
      Decision level = 1
      Test score = Grade 4 years, 8 months
  A-2   Arithmetic
  Is person unable to
  A-2.1   Add numbers in a single column?   No
  A-2.2   Add numbers in multiple columns?   No
  A-2.3   Subtract with single column borrowing?   No
  A-2.4   Subtract with multiple column borrowing?   No
  A-2.5   Multiply single digits?   No
  A-2.6   Multiply multiple digits?   No
  A-2.7   Divide to find quotient without remainders?   No
  A-2.8   Divide to find quotient with remainders?   No
    Sum weighting factor = 0
    Decision level = 2
    Test score = Grade 8 years, 2 months
B. Biological and physical
  B-1   Hereditary factors
    B-1.1   Does either parent have a learning disability?   Yes
    B-1.2   Is there a sibling (not a twin) with a learning disability?   No
    B-1.3   Is there a twin with a learning disability?   No

B-1.4 Is there any familial history of chromosome anomalies or hereditary disorders in family? No
     Sum weighting factor = 1
     Decision level = 1

C. Psychological
   C-1 Self-confidence
   Does person
     C-1.1 Withdraw from activities? No
     C-1.2 Lack motivation? Yes
     C-1.3 Exhibit defeatism? No
          Sum weighting factors = 1
          Decision level = 3

Summary of evaluation:
   Names of subtopics that equal or exceed decision level:
   1. Reading pronunciation   2. Reading comprehension
   3. Hereditary factors
Total of subtopics that equal or exceed decision level: 3
   A score of 3 indicates possible incidence of severe learning disability.
   A score of 2 indicates possible incidence of mild learning problem.
   A score of 1 or 0 indicates no learning disability or learning problem.
Sara Green displays a problem in 3 subtopics and therefore shows evidence of
having a severe learning disability.

Verification Using the Inference Mechanism

Once we have totaled the sum weighting factors and assessed which
subtopics are problem areas, we can say that we have reached our goal.
But to further determine if it was reached accurately, we must check
one more thing. We must create some method for verifying the yes and
no responses that we provided. In other words, how do we know that
the answers we have provided are correct? We need some measure of
verification. Verification is achieved by taking new data and matching
it with original data. The mechanism that matches the two sets of data
is part of the inference mechanism.

As noted earlier in the chapter, one of the important aspects of an
educational evaluation is the administering of educational tests. The
test scores are in the form of age levels and grades. Naturally a person
is expected to score at appropriate grade or age levels chronologically.
An 8-year-old, for example, should achieve an equivalent score of
grade 3 or age 8. If a person scores below age or grade level, we can
state that the person has some problem in that area. The lower the
score, the greater the problem. Consequently the higher the score, the
fewer the problems. It is then safe to say that if a test score falls below
age and grade expectation, there must be deficiencies in that area. For
example, our 12-year-old testee scored grade 4.8 in reading com-

prehension. That score is much lower than her chronological grade level. This means that there must be deficiencies in reading comprehension and *at least* one fact associated with reading comprehension must be answered with a yes. Remember, yes signifies a deficiency.

Verification has a dual purpose. We are trying to verify whether or not a deficiency exists. The verification that a deficiency exists will occur for a specific subtopic when a test score for that specific subtopic shows a deficiency *and* the sum weighting factor for that specific subtopic equals or exceeds the decision level. A deficiency does not exist if the test score does not show a deficiency *and* the decision level has not been achieved. If we are inconsistent in our judgment, i.e., we note a deficient test score and the decision level is not achieved, or we note a high test score and the decision level *is* achieved, the system will tell us that we have made an error. We can use IF-THEN rules to make our verification determination. The rules are the new data which will be matched with the sum weighting factors.

The following are examples of these rules:

1. IF a person scores below age and/or grade level on tests of reading pronunciation, THEN there must be at least one deficiency noted in reading pronunciation.

2. IF a person scores below age and/or grade level on tests of reading comprehension, THEN there must be at least one deficiency noted in reading comprehension.

3. IF a person scores more than 2 years below age and/or grade level on tests for reading pronunciation, THEN that person will equal or exceed the decision level for reading pronunciation.

4. IF a person scores more than 2 years below age and/or grade level on tests for reading comprehension, THEN that person will equal or exceed the decision level for reading comprehension.

The same kinds of rules can be written for all of the educational subtopics. If the evaluator makes an error (for example, suppose all the questions in reading pronunciation are answered no, which indicates no problem, but the score fell below age or grade level on the test for reading pronunciation), the system will print the following error message:

```
Error: Go back and check response to the questions
       related to reading pronunciation.
```

The user would then return to that section and re-evaluate the responses to the questions. Once the errors were corrected, the system would then proceed to evaluate the responses to the questions as described at the end of the sample program.

Additional Applications

Although this system was designed for the learning specialist or professional, it can serve another purpose as well. A parent, for example, concerned about a child who is not achieving good grades in school observes troubling behavior patterns but is not sure what they mean. The parent might suspect the child has some sort of learning problem or disability but wants more information before seeking help. A parent may simply feel uninformed about the subject matter and would like to gain some vital information on this topic. The better informed one is before seeking professional help, the better equipped one is for making wise selective decisions. A modified system could provide assessment and information rather than diagnosis. It could then be used to determine if there is a need to seek help for a learning problem or disability. The methodology could serve as a model for other kinds of informative self-test systems as well.

Of course a system designed for at-home use would not include standardized testing because parents or people using it for self-education are not familiar with, nor are they trained in, this area. The system would contain questions pertaining to observed behaviors, background information, and some educational issues. It could include the following modified topics and subtopics that were used for LES.

A. Biological and physical
    A-1 Hereditary factors
B. Psychological and social
    B-1 Self-confidence
    B-2 Attention span
    B-3 Social awareness
C. Educational
    C-1 Academic achievement
    C-2 Language and thought development

The following is the taxonomy of facts and their weighting factors for the modified system:

A. Biological and physical
    A-1 Hereditary factors
        A-1.1 Parents with learning disabilities (1)
        A-1.2 Sibling (not a twin) with learning disability (1)
        A-1.3 Twin with learning disability (1)
        A-1.4 Chromosome anomalies or hereditary disorder in family (1)

The facts associated with the next subtopics are different from LES. They pertain more to behaviors that parents observe about their children.

B. Psychological and social
 B-1 Self-confidence
   B-1.1 Exhibits defeatism (1)
   B-1.2 Lacks motivation (1)
   B-1.3 Behaves sluggishly or apathetically (1)
   B-1.4 Downgrades self continuously (1)
 B-2 Attention span
   B-2.1 Appears restless and distracted (1)
   B-2.2 Daydreams excessively (1)
   B-2.3 Responds impulsively (1)
   B-2.4 Relies on others continuously for help with school work (1)
   B-2.5 Hands in assignments late (1)
 B-3 Social awareness
   B-3.1 Appears inept in social situations (1)
   B-3.2 Behaves excessively (loud, comical, aggressive) (1)
   B-3.3 Withdraws from social encounters (1)
   B-3.4 Disorganized about personal belongings and appearance (1)
C. Educational
 C-1 Academic achievement
   C-1.1 Has low school achievement in reading pronunciation of words or paragraphs (1)
   C-1.2 Has low school achievement in reading comprehension (1)
   C-1.3 Has low school achievement in arithmetic (1)
   C-1.4 Has poor handwriting (1)
   C-1.5 Has difficulty with expressive writing skills in school (1)
 C-2 Language and thought development
   C-2.1 Does not speak fluently (1)
   C-2.2 Has difficulty explaining self in full sentences (1)
   C-2.3 Has difficulty understanding what is said in order to follow directions (1)
   C-2.4 Has difficulty linking words with the objects the words refer to (1)
   Has poor memory for
   C-2.5 Remembering numbers (1)
   C-2.6 Remembering names (1)
   C-2.7 Recalling information in sequence presented (1)
   C-2.8 Remembering months of the year (1)
   C-2.9 Remembering days of the week (1)

A sample of how the program works follows. The answers are indicated after the question marks. Notice that the questions are phrased somewhat differently than in the previous section, although some of the content overlaps. The format for using the sum weighting factors and decision levels is the same. The educational section is last (in the previous section it was first) because the emphasis of this assessment is not on standardized testing but on a generalized study of observed behaviors.

Name of child?	Steven Jones
Age?	9 years, 2 months
Grade?	4th
Date of assessment?	June 17, 1985

A. Biological and physical
  A-1 Hereditary factors
    A-1.1 Does either parent have a learning disability? No
    A-1.2 Is there a sibling not a twin with a learning disability? No
    A-1.3 Is there a twin with a learning disability? No
    A-1.4 Are there any chromosome anomalies or hereditary disorders in family? No
        Sum weighting factor = 0
        Decision level = 1
B. Psychological and social
  B-1 Self-confidence
    Does your child
    B-1.1 Exhibit defeatism? Yes
    B-1.2 Lack motivation? Yes
    B-1.3 Behave sluggishly or apathetically? Yes
    B-1.4 Downgrade self continuously? Yes
        Sum weighting factor = 4
        Decision level = 3
  B-2 Attention span:
    B-2.1 Is your child restless and easily distractible? No
    B-2.2 Does your child daydream excessively? No
    B-2.3 Does your child respond impulsively? Yes
    B-2.4 Does your child rely continuously on school help from others? Yes
    B-2.5 Does your child hand in school assignments late? Yes
        Sum weighting factor = 3
        Decision level = 3
  B-3 Social awareness
    Does your child
    B-3.1 Appear inept in social situations? No
    B-3.2 Behave excessively? No
    B-3.3 Withdraw from social encounters? Yes
    B-3.4 Exhibit disorganization about personal belongings or appearances? Yes
        Sum weighting factor = 2
        Decision level = 3
C. Educational
  C-1 Academic achievement
    Does school report your child has low achievement in
    C-1.1 Reading pronunciation? Yes
    C-1.2 Reading comprehension? Yes

C-1.3   Arithmetic?   Yes
C-1.4   Handwriting?   No
C-1.5   Expressive writing skills?   Yes
Sum weighting factor = 4
Decision level = 2

C-2   Language and thought development
Does your child
C-2.1   Have difficulty speaking fluently and clearly?   No
C-2.2   Have limited vocabulary?   No
C-2.3   Have difficulty explaining self in full sentences?   No
C-2.4   Have difficulty understanding what is said in order to follow directions?   No
C-2.5   Have difficulty remembering numbers?   No
C-2.6   Have difficulty remembering names?   No
C-2.7   Have difficulty recalling information in sequence?   No
C-2.8   Have difficulty recalling months of the year?   No
C-2.9   Have difficulty recalling days of the week?   No
Sum weighting factor = 0
Decision level = 3

Summary of evaluation:
Names of subtopics that equal or exceed decision levels:
Self-confidence
Attention span
Academic achievement
Total number of subtopics that equal or exceed decision levels:
A score of 5 or 6 indicates that there is evidence of a learning problem or learning disability, and professional help should be sought.
A score of 3 or 4 indicates that there is little evidence of a learning problem, but professional help might be sought temporarily.
A score of 1 or 2 indicates that there is no problem indicated here that requires professional help.
Steven Jones displays a problem in three subtopics and therefore shows evidence of a learning problem that requires professional help.

It should be noted that these decision levels are not absolute. They are, in reality, hypothetical examples of how they may be used to assess learning problems. As the use of expert systems in education is new and experimental, decision levels are open to further research and discussion.

If you compare the evaluations of Sara Green and Steven Jones, you will observe that both exhibit some serious indication that a learning problem or disability exists. However, a look at the names of the subtopics shows that although both exhibit problems, Sara displays strong symptoms educationally and biologically but very little psychologically. Steven Jones displays strong symptoms psychologically along with academic underachievement. Thus the organization of facts into subtopics enables the professional evaluator or the parent to pinpoint the specific problem areas. The number of subtopics that equal or exceed the decision level indicates the extent or the severity of the problem.

Summary

This chapter has described the use of an expert system to evaluate the extent of an educational problem. Educational problems are of particular interest at this time because many American adults and children lack elementary skills. Discussion of how the current conventional methods of educational assessment can be transferred to an expert system has now been introduced. Topics, subtopics, and a list of facts comprise the basic structure. A format for arriving at sum weighting factors and comparing them with decision levels was established. The next step was verification of the data. The use of an expert system to provide a method of evaluation for the professional educational evaluator was extended to use by parents who are concerned about their children's levels of achievement. Programming examples were provided.

Programming Applications

The LES program, Listing 10-1, is provided so that you can study the concepts of this chapter with your own computer. The program is written in C.

Program Explanation

The program is divided into four segments which are

1. The initialization section in which weighting factors are supplied, comments 20 and 25
2. The acquisition of personal data, comments 60 through 85
3. The data to be used in making the evaluation, comments 100 through 240
4. The inference mechanism for making the evaluation, comments 5015 through 5140

You are encouraged to modify any of the first three sections as a means of constructing an individual evaluation system.

Program Listing

Listing 10-1 is followed by sample runs.

Listing 10-1 Learning evaluation expert system.

```
/************** learning evaluation (expert) system *************/

#include <stdio.h>

char a[11][2] /* answer array */, d[21][26] /* deficiency array */;
char np[21] /* name of person */,ne[21] /* evaluator's name */, k[26];

int w[101] /* weighting factor array */;
int dm,dd,dy /* evaluation date-month,day,year */;
int gm,gy /* grade level-month,year */, ay,am /* person's age-year,month */;
int dl /* decision level */,dp,ty,tm,se tb,y,m,i,wp,s;

void inference(void);

void inference() {
/***** inference mechanism ********/
/**** comment 5015 ****/
/* is test score above or below grade?.. below grade if tb=1 */
tb=0;
y=gy-ty;
m=gm-tm;
if(y>0) tb=1;
if((y==0) && (m>0)) tb=1;
if(tb == 1) printf("** TEST SCORE BELOW AVERAGE\n");
/************************************/
/* if answers produce a sum weighting factor at least equal to
   the decision level the there is a problem */
/* initialize sum weighting factor */
s=0;
/* add all weighting factors corresponding to a 'y' */
for(i=1;i<se+1;i++)
 if(strcmp(a[i],"Y")==0) {
  s=w[wp]+s;
  wp=wp+1;
 }
printf("** SUM WEIGHTING FACTOR IS %d \n",s);
/************************************/
/* is decision level reached */
if(s>=dl) {
printf("** DECISION LEVEL IS REACHED\n");
strcpy(d[dp],k);
dp++;
}
/************************************/
/* inconsistency determination-decision level reached but test scores
   above average */
if((s>=dl) && (tb==0)) printf("** DEFICIENCY REACHED/GOOD SCORE\n");
if((s<dl) && (tb==1)) printf("** DEFICIENCY NOT REACHED;BAD SCORE\n");
/************** comment 5140 **************/
}

main() {
/*********** comment 20 and 25 *************/
for(i=1;i<101;i++) w[i]=1;
for(i=1;i<21;i++) strcpy(d[i],"");
dp=1 /* deficiency pointer */;
wp=1 /* weighting factor pointer */;
/************** personal data ********************/
/********* comment 60 ***********/
printf("NAME OF PERSON TO BE EVALUATED? ");
gets(np);
printf("AGE OF PERSON TO BE EVALUATED YEAR-MONTH? ");
scanf("%d,%d",&ay,&am);
printf("PERSONS SCHOOL GRADE LEVEL (IF APPLICABLE) YEAR-MONTH? ");
scanf("%d,%d",&gy,&gm);
printf("DATE OF EVALUATION MONTH-DAY-YEAR? ");
scanf("%d,%d,%d",&dm,&dd,&dy);
fflush(stdin);
printf("NAME OF EVALUATOR? ");
gets(np);
```

Listing 10-1 *(Continued)*

```
/********** comment 85 **********/
/***************data acquisition section *************/
/*****************reading pronunciation section ********/
/********** comment 100 *********/
printf("ENTER READING PRONUNCIATION GRADE TEST SCORE..YEAR-MONTH? ");
scanf("%d,%d",&ty,&tm);
printf("ENTER DECISION LEVEL? ");
scanf("%d",&dl);
printf("* IS PERSON UNABLE TO:\n");
printf("RECOGNIZE LETTERS OF THE ALPHABET? ");
fflush(stdin);
gets(a[1]);
printf("PRONOUNCE WORDS WITHOUT REVERSING OR OMITTING LETTERS? ");
gets(a[2]);
printf("KNOW WHERE TO PLACE THE ACCENT? ");
gets(a[3]);
printf("BREAK DIFFICULT WORDS INT PROPER SYLLABLE DIVISION? ");
gets(a[4]);
printf("RETAIN/EVOKE SOUND EQUIVALENT OF LETTERS IN WORDS? ");
gets(a[5]);
printf("** READING PRONUNCIATION **\n");
/** go to inference mechanism..determine if decision level is exceeded
    ..verify the data as compared to the test score */
strcpy(k,"READING PRONUNCIATION");
se=5;
inference();
printf("\n");
/************reading comprehension section *************/
printf("ENTER READING COMPREHENSION GRADE TEST SCORE..YEAR-MONTH? ");
scanf("%d,%d",&ty,&tm);
printf("ENTER DECISION LEVEL? ");
scanf("%d",&dl);
printf("* IS PERSON UNABLE TO: \nRETAIN FACTS? ");
fflush(stdin);
gets(a[1]);
printf("DRAW INFERENCES? ");
gets(a[2]);
printf("HANDLE DIFFICULT VOCABULARY? ");
gets(a[3]);
printf("HANDLE CONCEPTS PRESENTED? ");
gets(a[4]);
strcpy(k,"READING COMPREHENSION");
se=4;
inference();
/* number of questions */
/************ comment 240 ***********/
/*****************************************/
printf("DEFFICIENT RESPONSES\n");
for(i=1;i<21;i++)
 if(strcmp(d[i],"") != 0) printf("%s\n",d[i]);
/* end of run */
}
```

Sample Runs

```
NAME OF PERSON TO BE EVALUATED ? SARA GREEN
AGE OF PERSON TO BE EVALUATED YEAR-MONTH ? 12,8
PERSONS SCHOOL GRADE LEVEL (IF APPLICABLE) YEAR-MONTH ? 7,10
DATE OF EVALUATION MONTH-DAY-YEAR ? 6,7,1985
NAME OF EVALUATOR ? DIANE DRANG
ENTER READING PRONUNCIATION GRADE TEST SCORE..YEAR-MONTH ? 5,8
ENTER DECISION LEVEL? 2
* IS PERSON UNABLE TO:
RECOGNIZE LETTERS OF THE ALPHABET? N
PRONOUNCE WORDS WITHOUT REVERSING OR OMITTING LETTERS? Y
KNOW WHERE TO PLACE THE ACCENT? Y
BREAK DIFFICULT WORDS INTO PROPER SYLLABLE DIVISION? Y
RETAIN/EVOKE SOUND EQUIVALENT OF LETTERS IN WORDS? Y
** READING PRONUNCIATION **
** TEST SCORE BELOW AVERAGE
** SUM WEIGHTING FACTOR IS  4
** DECISION LEVEL IS REACHED

ENTER READING COMPREHENSION GRADE TEST SCORE..YEAR-MONTH ? 4,8
ENTER DECISION LEVEL? 1
* IS PERSON UNABLE TO:
RETAIN FACTS? N
DRAW INFERENCES? Y
HANDLE DIFFICULT VOCABULARY? N
HANDLE CONCEPTS PRESENTED? Y
** TEST SCORE BELOW AVERAGE
** SUM WEIGHTING FACTOR IS  2
** DECISION LEVEL IS REACHED
DEFICIENT RESPONSES
READING PRONUNCIATION
READING COMPREHENSION
```

The sample run for Sara Green was taken directly from this chapter.

```
NAME OF PERSON TO BE EVALUATED ? JOHN SMITH
AGE OF PERSON TO BE EVALUATED YEAR-MONTH ? 12,8
PERSONS SCHOOL GRADE LEVEL (IF APPLICABLE) YEAR-MONTH ? 7,10
DATE OF EVALUATION MONTH-DAY-YEAR ? 6,7,1985
NAME OF EVALUATOR ? DIANE DRANG
ENTER READING PRONUNCIATION GRADE TEST SCORE..YEAR-MONTH ? 7,11
ENTER DECISION LEVEL? 2
* IS PERSON UNABLE TO:
RECOGNIZE LETTERS OF THE ALPHABET? N
PRONOUNCE WORDS WITHOUT REVERSING OR OMITTING LETTERS? Y
KNOW WHERE TO PLACE THE ACCENT? Y
BREAK DIFFICULT WORDS INTO PROPER SYLLABLE DIVISION? Y
RETAIN/EVOKE SOUND EQUIVALENT OF LETTERS IN WORDS? Y
** READING PRONUNCIATION **
** SUM WEIGHTING FACTOR IS  4
** DECISION LEVEL IS REACHED
** DEFICIENCY REACHED/GOOD SCORE
ENTER READING COMPREHENSION GRADE TEST SCORE..YEAR-MONTH ? 4,8
ENTER DECISION LEVEL? 1
* IS PERSON UNABLE TO:
RETAIN FACTS? N
```

```
DRAW INFERENCES? Y
HANDLE DIFFICULT VOCABULARY? N
HANDLE CONCEPTS PRESENTED? Y
** TEST SCORE BELOW AVERAGE
** SUM WEIGHTING FACTOR IS  2
** DECISION LEVEL IS REACHED
DEFICIENT RESPONSES
READING PRONUNCIATION
READING COMPREHENSION
```

Notice that under reading pronunciation the printed output "Deficiency Reached/Good Score" means that although the decision level indicated a deficiency, the test score exceeded grade level. This constitutes a contradiction and therefore instructs the user to re-examine the answers and results.

Advanced Programming Techniques for Powerful Systems

Section 4 discusses the concepts of object-oriented programming and how it is used in the design of expert systems. In order to further clarify the concepts, a program is provided which will allow you to set up your own system. If you wish to expand your conceptual understanding, you can use the subroutines provided in the program to develop more sophisticated systems.

11

Fundamentals of Object-Oriented Programming

Imagine that you have a box that has a lot of pigeon holes—like an old-fashioned box for hand-sorting mail. Each hole contains a piece of information written on a piece of paper. A hole labeled "union activities" contains the latest information concerning arbitration and grievances of the union members; a hole labeled "pensions" describes options for investing money in company-sponsored financial plans, and so on. Such a box that has a lot of holes or spaces for inserting, removing, and changing information is called a structure. A structure gathers together many pieces of information into a fixed pattern.

How is a structure built and the labeling of the holes determined? As an example, suppose someone of high authority, such as the president of a company, wishes to define and categorize all the information needed to run the business. This individual might create a plan for building the actual structure and deciding how many holes are needed and what they should be called according to the size and nature of the company. The plan would then be given to a carpenter who actually builds the structure to the plan's specifications.

Structures are also used to gather and sort information in artificial intelligence programs. In AI terminology, the holes in the box are called "slots" and the labels on the holes are called "attributes." The pieces of information placed in the slots are called "values." When values are placed into the slots, the actual "object" comes into being.

For example, suppose many people constantly want to reserve a conference room. In order to accommodate all these people, we must have a formal procedure for reserving the room. We must build a conference room structure. One of the slots of the structure must have the attribute "time the conference room is needed." After all, we cannot schedule two conferences in the same room at the same time. Another slot must have as an attribute "the person's name who is reserving the conference room," and so on, for all the pertinent attributes of this structure. When someone wishes to actually reserve a room, the values (time and name) needed to construct an object from the conference room structure would be provided.

Let's review these definitions:

1. Structure—a plan for constructing an object

2. Object—a structure that contains information

3. Slot—a place to store information

4. Attribute—a labeled slot

5. Value—information associated with an attribute and placed in a labeled slot

Let's consider the conference room example in more detail. Suppose a company has a number of very busy conference rooms and is in need of a system for assigning time in each of the rooms. The structure the company would use is a general form that employees must fill out when they need the use of a conference room. We'll call this structure the conference room form. By filling out the form, a specific instance of the structure is created, which is called an object. In this case, the object will contain a person's name and all the other items that were filled in to complete the form. During the course of a single day there may be more than one conference; each individual conference represents a separate object. Let's say it again to be sure it's absolutely clear: A structure defines attributes that are important in doing something, and an object is a specific instance of that structure.

The conference room structure should allow any employee to reserve a room and also provide enough information so that all other employees can know what is going on in the room at any time. A typical conference room structure might look like this:

1. Conference room number

2. Subject of discussion

3. Speaker's name

4. Start-time of conference

5. End-time of conference

There are five attributes that we have chosen in the conference room structure for this example. Assume there are 12 different conference rooms in the company's office building. An employee who wishes to use a conference room fills out a form that contains all the attributes of the conference room structure and provides all the required information. That conference room is now reserved for that time. An example of a conference room object that was created by filling out the form would be

1. 10   (conference room number)
2. Employee overtime rules   (subject of discussion)
3. Daniel Drang   (speaker's name)
4. 10:00   (start-time of conference)
5. 11:00   (end-time of conference)

The object's first value, 10, corresponds to the attribute "conference room number," and the second value, employee overtime rules, corresponds to the attribute "subject of the discussion." The other values also correspond to the attributes of the structure.

In both small and large companies, there are many different activities going on at all times. Each of these activities might require employees to follow a specific procedure for engaging in that activity. The procedure may in fact be as simple as a checklist. Airplane mechanics have checklists of items they must verify as working before a plane can take off. These checklists are all derived from a structure. For example, the mechanic has to determine that the plane has enough fuel and that the tires have enough air in them. Airlines have many things to do; therefore they may have many forms, each of which is a specific structure for doing something. Each structure must have an identification number, or name, so that a form for that structure can be requested and located. The name of the mechanic's checklist structure may be called "preparation for take-off." This immediately tells us something important about some needed structure properties, which are

1. Name, so that the structure can be referred to
2. Attributes, which define the structure's contents

Let's continue with the mechanic's work. After obtaining a form of the structure preparation for take-off, the mechanic goes through the checklist, fills it out, signs the form, and hands it in, thereby creating an object from the form. This object is given an identification number (which is really its name). Since there may be many of these forms filled out in a single day—at least one for each plane taking off—this particular form can be retrieved at a later time by knowing its name (identification number).

From this discussion we can conclude that an object must have the following properties:

1. Structure name, so that we know the meaning of the rules given to the objects

2. Object name, so that it can be referred to

3. Attributes, which define its items of importance

4. Values, which are pieces of information corresponding to the attributes

Another thing that must accompany a structure and its objects is a set of "procedures." For example, what is the procedure to be followed if a tire is flat? Do we fix it with all the passengers still on the plane? Are there any procedures for dealing with a leaky fuel line? Procedures are therefore an integral part of a structure.

Some procedures must be carried out before other procedures. For example, before checking various gauges on a plane, the plane's electrical power must be turned on. Therefore, we must have a procedure for turning on the power before we follow the gauge-checking procedure. The before procedure, which is not directly referred to but still must be carried out, is called a "before demon." (Procedures that exist but are not invoked directly by the user are referred to as demons.) Similarly, there might be procedures that have to be invoked after a main procedure is completed. These procedures are also not directly referred to but must be done. They are called "after demons." An example of an after demon would be a procedure for filing the preparation for take-off form after all the gauges have been checked.

Procedures can be stated directly in the structure or made known to the user of the structure in other ways. In the mechanic example, a portion of the checklist might look like this:

1. Read fuel gauge and record it.

2. If fuel gauge is less than 2000 gallons, invoke procedure on form 34555.

3. Check tire pressure and record it.

4. If tire pressure is less than . . . , invoke procedure on form 34556.

Slots 2 and 4 are references to procedures for handling certain occurrences. But the actual methods for reading the fuel gauge and checking tire pressure are part of the mechanic's training and are contained perhaps in separate forms with which the mechanic is already familiar. They are not detailed in this checklist.

Creating a Structure

Each of the properties that we described for structures and objects must be available to the programmer for constructing an object-oriented system. In review, these properties are

1. The ability to create a structure
2. The ability to create objects from that structure
3. The ability to create procedures for doing things with objects

As we discussed earlier, a structure must have a name, so that it can be referred to, and attributes, which describe the structure's makeup. By giving names to structures, the user can easily refer to a required structure by name, assign values to its attributes, and thereby create an object. This is just what mechanics might do when they go to the room where all the forms are kept: request the needed form by name, fill in the blanks, and in the process create an object.

To create an object-oriented program, we must have a procedure for creating a structure and for specifying each of the attributes. Here is the format that we will use to describe how a structure subroutine is created in a computer program. The actual C instructions are shown in Listing 11-1 at the end of the chapter.

```
CREATE-STRUCTURE (SNAME = name of the structure
                   NATTR = number of attributes for this
                           structure
            ATTR   = first attribute name
            ATTR   = second attribute name
              .
              .
              .
            ATTR    = last attribute name)
```

To illustrate how a structure is created, let's consider the following conference room structure:

1. Conference room number   (ROOM)
2. Subject of discussion   (SUBJECT)
3. Speaker's name   (SPEAKER)
4. Start-time of conference   (START)
5. End-time of conference   (END)

In order to make our discussion of the conference room structure easier to follow, we have abbreviated the attributes as shown in the list in parentheses following each one. The conference room structure has five attributes whose abbreviated names are ROOM, SUBJECT, SPEAKER, START, and END. Since the conference room structure must have a name, we'll call it CONF. Whenever we refer to CONF in our program, the system will understand that we mean the conference room structure together with the five attributes associated with it. The way in which these things are put together is

```
CREATE-STRUCTURE(SNAME = CONF, NATTR = 5, ATTR =
          ROOM, ATTR = SUBJECT, ATTR =
          SPEAKER, ATTR = START, ATTR = END)
```

Using the conference room structure, let's now consider the CREATE-STRUCTURE subroutine. As you can see, each attribute is preceded by a keyword. This tells the object-oriented system which attribute is being passed to it. The keyword SNAME = tells the system to use the name following this keyword as the name of the structure. In this case, it is CONF. The keyword NATTR = tells the system what the number of attributes it will get follows. In this case it is five. The keyword ATTR = tells the system to accept the following name as the name of the attribute. In this case there are five ATTR keywords, one for each attribute. The object-oriented system now knows the form of the conference room structure.

Creating an Object

Whenever we want to create an object of a structure, all we have to do is tell the system the name of the structure and then provide the values that should be given to each attribute. This is like applying for a job, getting a form to fill out, and then detailing your previous job history on the form. You have in essence requested a structure (the job application form) and given the attributes values (name, address, previous employment, etc.), thereby creating an object. The form you filled out is filed by your name (object name) for future reference. Let's see how this is done by the programmer. The general format for creating an object subroutine is

```
CREATE-OBJECT(SNAME  = name of structure from which object is
                        derived
              ONAME  = name of this particular object
              ATTRI1 = attribute's value
              ATTRI2 = attribute's value


              ATTRIn = attribute's value)
```

SNAME = is followed by the structure name, ONAME = is followed by the object name, and ATTRI1 = is followed by the value you have given to that particular attribute. There can be one of these for each attribute defined in the structure. If you leave out an attribute name, the object will have a space in that attribute's location when the object is created. We can provide this value at a later time, just as you might leave blank spaces on a form and come back and fill them in later.

As an example, let's assume that Susan Bard needs conference room number 10 for 1 hour begin ˙ ˌg at 10 A.M. to discuss employee overtime rules. She will create an object and give it a name that is not already used—such as TEN1- -as follows:

```
CREATE-OBJECT (SNAME = CONF, ONAME = TEN1, ROOM =
              10, SUBJECT = EMPLOYEE OVERTIME RULES,
              SPEAKER = Susan Bard, START = 10:00, END
              = 11:00)
```

By referring to the object by the object name, TEN1, the object can be accessed.

What we have done up to this point is develop a general form (structure specification) for the CREATE-STRUCTURE subroutine and one object of this form (the object being an instance of a structure), also part of the CREATE-OBJECT subroutine.

Overview of Objects and Their Operations

What we have done in creating a specific structure and objects conforming to that particular structure is in reality create a database. The objects are records in the database, and the structure specifies the format of a record and its components. (In database terminology, records consist of fields, which we have chosen to call attributes.) Some of the things we normally do with a database are

1. Place and modify values in the fields (or attributes) of each record (or object).
2. Get statistics from the database, such as the number of conferences going on at a given time.
3. Provide procedures for operations on one or more fields (attributes) of a record (object).
4. Be able to view the database as is.

Operations on Objects

Before we discuss some of the operations we can apply to objects, let's create two more objects so that we can facilitate our explanation:

CREATE-OBJECT (SNAME = CONF, ONAME = TEN2, ROOM =
10, SUBJECT = PAY RAISES, SPEAKER = Marc
Stone, START = 13:00, END = 14:00)

CREATE-OBJECT (SNAME = CONF, ONAME = ELE1, ROOM =
11, SUBJECT = SALES PROJECTIONS,
SPEAKER = Andy Rome, START = 10:00, END
= 12:00)

You should be able to read these objects easily by now: Marc Stone has
reserved conference room 10 from 1 to 2 P.M. (equivalent to 13:00 and
14:00) to discuss pay raises (object name TEN2), and Andy Rome has
reserved conference room 11 from 10:00 to 12:00 to discuss sales projections (object name ELE1).

Viewing Objects and Structures

Sometimes we would just like to view the structures and objects to find
out which ones are in the system at a given time. This is done by
sitting down at the console and typing certain commands. To list all
objects, you would call up a subroutine named, for example, LIST-
ALL-OBJECT-NAMES. In our example, the computer would respond
with

```
TEN1
TEN2
ELE1
```

To get a listing of all structure names, we could call up subroutine
LIST-ALL-STRUCTURE-NAMES. We have only created one structure so far, so the computer will respond with

```
CONF
```

We can list all the values of the attributes of a specific object by going
to the LIST-OBJECT subroutine. For our example, if we wanted to
view the object ELE1, we would enter the following responses to program queries:

```
LIST-OBJECT, SNAME=CONF, ONAME=ELE1
```

and would obtain

```
ROOM=11
SUBJECT=SALES PROJECTIONS
SPEAKER=Andy Rome
START=10:00
END=12:00
```

Object Operations

In addition to creating objects, we might also have occasion to remove them. For example, when Andy Rome's sales projections meeting is over in conference room 11, we would want to eliminate that object from our database because he finished using the room. We do that with a REMOVE subroutine. We would remove object ELE1 and then verify the removal of ELE1 with subroutine LIST-ALL-OBJECT-NAMES. We would get as a response

```
TEN1
TEN2
```

ELE1, as desired, is missing from the list.

There are times when we will want to change the value of an attribute in an object. A SEND subroutine can be used to insert a value in an object's attribute. In our example, the following responses to program queries will change the starting time (START) for object TEN1 from 10:00 to 9:00:

```
SEND (SNAME=CONF, ONAME=TEN1, START=9:00)
```

If we now ran the LIST-OBJECT subroutine, we would get

```
ROOM=10
SUBJECT=EMPLOYEE OVERTIME RULES
SPEAKER=Susan Bard
START=9:00
END=11:00
```

Notice that the starting time, as we wanted, has been changed from 10:00 to 9:00.

The last subroutine we will discuss allows us to copy the value of an object's attribute into a variable. Once the value is in the form of a variable, a whole set of operations can be performed on the variable. To do this, we use the COPY subroutine. Let's take the SPEAKER attribute of TEN2 as an example. We could use the subroutine to copy SPEAKER to the variable y and then use the C command

```
printf("%S",y);
```

and we will get

```
Marc Stone
```

If, for example, we wished to write a report for management on conference room activities, we can do it by merely "copying" and "printing" the values of the attributes into a report.

Let's review what we have learned:

1. We can create a structure via CREATE-STRUCTURE.
2. We can create objects of the structure via CREATE-OBJECT.
3. We can change an object's attribute via SEND.
4. We can obtain the value of an object's attribute via COPY.
5. We can remove an object from the database via REMOVE.
6. We can view structures and objects via LIST-ALL-STRUCTURE-NAMES, LIST-OBJECT, and LIST-ALL-OBJECTS.

Invoking Procedures

When we discussed the plane mechanic's checklist in relation to the tire pressure, we said a procedure would be invoked to reinflate the tire if the pressure was too low. The procedure might simply be to attach an air hose to the tire. In any event, the mechanic would know what the procedure is for doing that. Let's examine what we are saying on a more general level:

1. We have a procedure for checking a slot of an object for a specific value (in our example, it was a minimum tire pressure).
2. If the value exceeded some boundary condition, we invoked a procedure to deal with it (in our example, it was a procedure for reinflating the tire if the pressure was too low).

Let's examine one more example to make sure the concept of procedures is clear. In our conference room example, we described how the SEND subroutine was used to change the START time of Susan Bard's conference from 10:00 to 9:00 A.M. What would have happened if someone else had scheduled a conference in that same room between the hours of 9:00 and 10:00 A.M.? If we allowed the change to take place without any further actions, two groups would have arrived at the conference room at 9. What should have happened is this: When Susan changed the conference room time, a procedure should automatically have been invoked to check the conference room number and starting and ending times of all objects with the same conference room number in order to see if there was a conflict. If there was, Susan could then have been notified, allowing her to make appropriate arrangements.

On the other hand, if Susan simply wanted to change the title of her discussion (attribute SUBJECT) there would be no need to invoke a procedure because the change has no effect on other objects. The essential procedure philosophy is

> When certain attributes are modified, procedures may be invoked to see if any action should be taken.

A Method for Invoking Procedures

When we discussed operations on objects, we showed how a value is inserted in the slot of an object by the SEND subroutine. As we will see in the programming considerations section of this chapter, the SEND subroutine is composed of a series of instructions that locates an object of a structure and then stores a value into an attribute slot of the object. For example:

```
SEND (SNAME = CONF, ONAME = TEN1, START = 9:00)
```

will create a set of instructions that will first search the computer's memory for the location of the structure CONF and object within the structure called TEN1. Then, the value 9:00 would be inserted into the slot assigned to the attribute START. The question is, How is the procedure invoked? The answer is that an indication must be provided to the SEND subroutine that when a specific attribute has a value assigned to it, a procedure must automatically be invoked. Since it is the SEND subroutine that is changing the value, it is therefore logical for the SEND subroutine to be connected to the invoking of a procedure.

What we must do is find a way of telling the SEND subroutine that the attribute whose value is changing should invoke a procedure. For example, when we change the start-time attribute of TEN1, we want to invoke a procedure to tell us when a conflict arises. Changing the title of the attribute SUBJECT, on the other hand, should *not* invoke a procedure.

Well, the answer is very simple. When, in defining a structure, we come upon an attribute that should invoke a procedure, we do the following:

1. Precede the name of the attribute with an asterisk.
2. When the SEND subroutine "sees" this attribute, it knows a procedure should be invoked because of the asterisk.
3. The procedure name should be the very next attribute.

For example, we want to invoke a procedure if either the start- or end-time of a conference is changed. This procedure would ensure that there is no conflict when employees sign up to use the rooms. The way we accomplish all this is via the CREATE-STRUCTURE subroutine, which contains the following:

CREATE-STRUCTURE (SNAME = CONF, NATTR = 7, ATTR = ROOM, ATTR = SUBJECT, ATTR = SPEAKER, ATTR = *START, ATTR = PRO-CEDURE, ATTR = *END, ATTR = PRO-CEDURE)

Note the asterisk before the START and END attributes. Following these asterisked attributes are two additional attributes with the keyword PROCEDURE (also note that the total number of attributes have been increased to seven—NATTR = 7—as a result). These procedure slots will be used, when creating an object of the structure CONF, to specify the procedure to be invoked when the SEND subroutine changes the START or END value. Let's see how this works. The CONF object created for Susan Bard would look like this:

CREATE-OBJECT (SNAME = CONF, ONAME = TEN1, ROOM = 10, SUBJECT = EMPLOYEE OVERTIME RULES, SPEAKER = Susan Bard, START = 10:00, PRO-CEDURE = name of procedure, END = 11:00, PROCEDURE = name of procedure)

If we were implementing the CREATE-OBJECT subroutine in BASIC, we would use a number in place of "name of procedure." (In other languages, such as LISP, we could use a symbolic name such as START-PROC.) The number in BASIC would be used to identify the statement number of the procedure. Now when we view the object with the LIST-OBJECT subroutine, this is where we stand:

```
ROOM=10
SUBJECT=EMPLOYEE OVERTIME RULES
SPEAKER=Susan Bard
*START=10:00
PROCEDURE=1
*END=11:00
PROCEDURE=1
```

The PROCEDURE = 1 signifies that the same procedure is used when the SEND subroutine changes either the START or END time. If Susan now wanted to change the starting time, she would do so with the SEND subroutine. It would invoke procedure 1. This procedure would check all objects with the attribute value ROOM = 10 to see if there is an overlap with another conference being held in the same room. The sequence of events taken by the SEND subroutine to accomplish all this is

1. Find the location in computer memory where the structure is located. It is the structure that tells us if an asterisk precedes an attribute name.
2. Scan the structure's attributes for the name of the attribute whose value is changing.
3. If there is an asterisk preceding the name, get ready to invoke a procedure.
4. Now that we know if an object's attribute invokes a procedure, we can locate the object in memory.
5. Next, we invoke the procedure of the attribute that is changed if there is an asterisk preceding it. If there is no asterisk, simply change the value.

The ability to use the SEND subroutine in conjunction with the procedure invocation is one of the most important features of object-oriented programming. Since different objects have different tasks, it is this feature that allows objects with varied responsibilities to communicate with each other via a method of sending messages. This procedure is initially set up when the system is created. For example, if the procedure invoked by a conference room time change detected a time overlap with another conference for the same room causing a conflict for both conference room space and speaker time, the SEND subroutine would direct a message to a speaker object. This message would invoke another procedure that would cause a message to be triggered at the terminal, which would then inform the speaker of the conflict overlap. Now that we have journeyed through object-oriented programming, put down your pencil and paper and run the program in Listing 11-1. It will solidify all the concepts you have learned.

Programming Applications

The purpose of this portion of the chapter is to provide a set of subroutines, written in C, for doing object-oriented programming. You can use these subroutines to set up your own object-oriented system. The program is divided into two parts. One part contains the object-oriented procedures. The other part is an application program designed to acquaint you with the methodology for using these procedures. The application part is divided into eight object-oriented operations, each having a similar design in the way it interacts with the subroutines. Understanding how one works should give you a clue as to how all the operations work. Each of the eight operations can be selected by a menu. Let's see how the program works in creating a structure.

Programming Explanation

The first thing we must do is enter the object command at the console. At comment 1, the program will create the structure-object array FO, which will contain the structure definitions and the objects. Then comments 2 through 55 will cause the following menu to appear on the screen:

```
ENTER A NUMBER TO DO ONE OF THE FOLLOWING
1-CREATE A STRUCTURE
2-CREATE AN OBJECT
3-NAME OF ALL STRUCTURES
4-NAME OF ALL OBJECTS
5-VIEW A STRUCTURE
6-VIEW AN OBJECT
7-SEND A VALUE TO AN OBJECT
8-COPY A VALUE TO Z FROM AN OBJECT'S ATTRIBUTE
9-EXIT
? 1
```

In our sample runs, the user response appears after the question mark. When the user entered a 1 at the console, the program executed comment 60, causing transfer of control to the subroutine at comment 100. Comments 105 and 110 were then executed, resulting in the following screen-user dialogue:

```
ENTER STRUCTURE NAME ? CONF
ENTER NUMBER OF ATTRIBUTES ? 5
```

This resulted in the execution of comment 115 to assign 5 to N and 7 to E. The FOR loop at comments 120 through 135 caused the following screen-user dialogue:

```
ATTRIBUTE  1 -? ROOM
ATTRIBUTE  2 -? SUBJECT
ATTRIBUTE  3 -? SPEAKER
ATTRIBUTE  4 -? START
ATTRIBUTE  5 -? END
```

The last seven user responses are stored in the temporary array T. The structure-creating subroutine was then entered indirectly via comment 145, which transferred control to the subroutine at comment 3000. The program as written can only contain two structures in FO. Of course, it can be modified to contain more. One structure can start at FO[1] and the other at FO[101]. The structure locations are assigned

in the order of creation, with the first at FO[1]. The CREATE STRUC-
TURE subroutine located at comments 3000 through 3080 determines
in which half of FO to store the structure definition contained in the
temporary array T. The return from the subroutine is to comment 150,
which then displays the menu on the screen, allowing the user to select
other options.

The other menu selections work in a very similar way, making it
easy to follow their program sequences.

Program Listing

Listing 11-1 is followed by a sequence of sample runs that correspond
to the conference room discussion.

Listing 11-1 Object-oriented programming.

```
/************** object oriented programming ************/
/* structure array */

#include <stdio.h>

/********* comment 1 **********/
char fo[201][26], t[10][26], zstring[26], ch0[26], ch1[26];

int i,e,k,z,l,num,p,a,an,y,n;

void create_structure(void);
void create_a_structure(void);
void create_object_calling_sequence(void);
void create_an_object(void);
void print_structure_attributes(void);
void view_a_structure(void);
void find_attribute_number(void);
void point_to_object(void);
void view_object(void);
void view_an_object(void);
void print_objects_names(void);
void name_of_objects(void);
void prnt_name_of_struct(void);
void point_to_attribute(void);
void user_routine(void);
void send_value(void);
void send_value_to_object(void);
void cpy_att(void);
void cpy_val_fr_objects_att(void);

main() {
strcpy(ch0,"0"); /* initialize a variable to = value of 0 */
for(i=1;i<201;i++) strcpy(fo[i],"");
for(i=1;i<5;i++) strcpy(t[i],"");
do {
/************* comment 2 **********/
printf("ENTER A NUMBER TO DO ONE OF THE FOLLOWING\n");
printf("1-CREATE A STRUCTURE\n");
printf("2-CREATE AN OBJECT\n");
printf("3-NAME OF ALL STRUCTURES\n");
printf("4-NAME OF ALL OBJECTS\n");
printf("5-VIEW A STRUCTURE\n");
printf("6-VIEW AN OBJECT\n");
printf("7-SEND A VALUE TO AN OBJECT\n");
printf("8-COPY A VALUE TO Z$ FROM AN OBJECT'S ATTRIBUTE\n");
printf("9-EXIT\n");
printf("? ");
/********* comment 55 **********/
scanf("%d",&num);
fflush(stdin);
switch (num) {
/********* comment 60 **********/
case 1: create_a_structure(); break;
case 2: create_an_object(); break;
case 3: prt_name_of_struct(); break;
case 4: name_of_objects(); break;
case 5: view_a_structure(); break;
case 6: view_an_object(); break;
case 7: send_value_to_object(); break;
case 8: cpy_val_fr_objects_att(); break;
case 9: break;
}
printf("\n");
}
while(num != 9);
}
```

```c
void create_a_structure() {
/********* comment 105 *********/
printf("ENTER STRUCTURE NAME? ");
gets(t[1]);
printf("ENTER NUMBER OF ATTRIBUTES? ");
/********* comment 110 **********/
gets(t[2]);
/********* comment 115 **********/
strcpy(ch1,t[2]);
n=ch1[0]-ch0[0];
e=3+n-1;
/********* comment 210 ***********/
for(i=3;i<e+1;i++) {
 printf("ATTRIBUTE %d-? ",i-2);
 gets(t[i]); }
/********* comment 135 & 145 ***********/
create_structure();
/********* comment 150 ************/
}


void create_object_calling_sequence() {
/* structure name t[1]
   object name t[2]
   number of values of attributes t[3]
   value of attribute 1 t[4]
   value of attribute n t[n+3] */
/* point to the structure */
z=1;
if(strcmp(t[1],fo[101]) == 0) z=101;
/* last location in that structure space */
e=z+99;
i=z;
/* find 1st free object space */
while((i<=e) && (strcmp(fo[i],"") != 0)) i++;
l=i /* store object here */;
strcpy(fo[l],t[2]); /* store object name */
l=l+1;
/* get number of attributes */
strcpy(ch1,t[3]);
n=ch1[0]-ch0[0];
/* store number */
strcpy(fo[l],t[3]);
l=l+1;
e=l+n-1; /* last attribute location */
k=4; /* first attribute location */
for(i=l;i<(e+1);i++) {
 strcpy(fo[i],t[k]);
 k=k+1; }
}


void create_an_object () {
printf("ENTER STRUCTURE NAME? ");
gets(t[1]);
printf("ENTER OBJECTS NAME? ");
gets(t[2]);
printf("ENTER NUMBER OF ATTRIBUTES? ");
gets(t[3]);
strcpy(ch1,t[3]);
n=ch1[0]-ch0[0];
e=4+n-1;
for(i=4;i<e+1;i++) {
 printf("ATTRIBUTE %d-? ",i-3); gets(t[i]); }
create_object_calling_sequence();
}


void name_of_objects() {
printf("ENTER STRUCTURE NAME? ");
gets(t[i]);
print_objects_names();
}
```

Listing 11-1 *(Continued)*

```
void view_a_structure() {
printf("ENTER A STRUCTURE NAME? ");
gets(t[1]);
print_structure_attributes();
}

void view_object() {
/* structure name t[1] */
/* object name t[2] */
/* point to an object. z is the value of the pointer. n is the
   number of attributes in the object */
point_to_object();
printf("OBJECT IS %s\n",fo[z]);
z++;
printf("NUMBER OF ATTRIBUTES IS %s\n",fo[z]);
z++;
e=z+n-1;
p=1;
for(i=z;i<e+1;i++) { printf("ATTRIBUTE NUMBER %d IS %s\n",p,fo[i]);
  p++; }
}

void view_an_object() {
printf("ENTER A STRUCTURE NAME? ");
gets(t[1]);
printf("ENTER AN OBJECT NAME? ");
gets(t[2]);
view_object();
}

void send_value() {
/*********** comment 5040 **********/
/* send a value to an objects attribute */
/* structure name t[1] */
/* objects name t[2] */
/* attribute name t[3] */
/* value t[4] */
point_to_attribute();
/* store value into attribute, if no asterisk "*" a=0 */
if(a != 0) {
/* an asterisk call user written routine */
 z++;
 strcpy(ch1,fo[z]);
 n=ch1[0]-ch0[0];
 /************* comment 5050 ************/
 switch (n) {
 case 1: user_routine();
         break;
 }
 /* point to the attribute again */
 z=z-1;
 strcpy(fo[z],t[4]);
 }
else {
/* no asterisk */
 z++;
 strcpy(fo[z],t[4]);
 }
}

void send_value_to_object() {
printf("ENTER A STRUCTURE NAME? ");
gets(t[1]);
printf("ENTER AN OBJECT NAME? ");
gets(t[2]);
printf("ENTER ATTRIBUTE NAME? ");
gets(t[3]);
printf("ENTER VALUE? ");
gets(t[4]);
/* send a value to an objects attribute */
send_value();
}
```

```c
void cpy_val_fr_objects_att() {
/* copy a value to z from an objects attribute */
printf("ENTER A STRUCTURE NAME? "); gets(t[1]);
printf("ENTER AN OBJECT NAME? "); gets(t[2]);
printf("ENTER AN ATTRIBUTE NAME? "); gets(t[3]);
cpy_att(); /* copy an objects attribute to z */
printf("ATTRIBUTE VALUE IS %s\n",zstring);
}

void cpy_att() {
/* copy an object's attribute to z */
/* structure name t[1] */
/* object name t[2] */
/* attribute name t[3] */
/* value z */
/* point to an object's attribute (z) */
point_to_attribute();
strcpy(zstring,fo[z]);
/* an asterisk call user written routine */
/* point to the attribute again */
if(a != 0) strcpy(zstring,fo[z]);
 else {
 /* no asterisk */
 z++;
 strcpy(zstring,fo[z]); }
}

void create_structure() {
/* structure name t[1]
   number of attributes t[2]
   attribute 1  an * means a name then a routine number follows t[3]
   attribute n t[n+2] */
/* search for the structure name either the top or bottom half
   then store the structure arguments in that location */
/* point to lower half */
y=1;
if(strcmp(fo[1],"") != 0) y=101 /* point to top half bottom not empty */;
strcpy(ch1,t[2]);
n=ch1[0]-ch0[0];
/* number of elements in structure is number arg+2 */
n=n+2;
for(z=1;z<n+1;z++) {
 strcpy(fo[y],t[z]);
 y++; }
/****** comment 3080 *******/
}

void print_structure_attributes() {
/* structure name t[1] */
/* point to structure */
z=1;
if(strcmp(t[1],fo[101]) == 0) z=101;
printf("STRUCTURE IS %s\n",t[1]);
z=z+1;
printf("NUMBER OF ATTRIBUTES ARE %s\n",fo[z]);
strcpy(ch1,fo[z]);
n=ch1[0]-ch0[0];
z=z+1;
e=z+n-1;
/* attribute number */
k=1;
for(i=z;i<e+1;i++) {
 printf("ATTRIBUTE NUMBER %d is %s\n",k,fo[i]);
 k=k+1; }
}
```

Listing 11-1 (*Continued*)

```
void find_attribute_number() {
/* find the attribute number of an attribute in an object */
/* z=attribute number, a=0 if no *, a=1 if *             */
/* structure name t[1] */
/* attribute name t[3] */
z=1; /* point to the structure */
if(strcmp(t[1],fo[101]) == 0) z=101;
z=z+2;
n=1;
/* start the search */
while(strcmp(t[3],fo[z]) != 0) {
/* try again */
 z=z+1;
 n=n+1; }
/* does attribute have an *    */
a=0;
z=z-1;
/* point to asterisk location */
if(strcmp(fo[z],"*") == 0) a=1;
z=n+1;
}

void point_to_object() {
/* structure name t[1] */
/* object name t[2] */
/* point to the structure */
z=1;
if(strcmp(t[1],fo[101]) == 0) z=101;
/* number of structure attributes */
z=z+1;
strcpy(ch1,fo[z]);
n=ch1[0]-ch0[0];
z=z+n+1; /* 1st object in structure */
/* is this object location blank */
/* blank space search for 1st non-blank object space */
while(strcmp(fo[z],"") == 0) z=z+1;
z=z+1;
/* get the number of object attributes */
strcpy(ch1,fo[z]);
n=ch1[0]-ch0[0];
/* reset pointer to object name */
z=z-1;
/* is this the object */
while(strcmp(t[2],fo[z]) != 0) /* next object */ z=z+n+2;
/* z is the location of the object */
}

void print_objects_names() {
/* structure name t[1] */
/* point to the structure */
z=1;
if(strcmp(t[1],fo[101]) == 0) z=101;
/* end of structure array */
e=z+99;
z++;
/* number of structure attributes */
strcpy(ch1,fo[z]);
n=ch1[0]-ch0[0];
/* first object */
z=z-1;
i=z;
while(i<=e) {
 if(strcmp(fo[i],"") != 0) printf("OBJECT NAME=%s\n",fo[i]);
 i=i+n+2; }
}

prt_name_of_struct() {
printf("STRUCTURE\n");
printf("%s\n",fo[1]);
printf("%s\n",fo[101]);
}
```

```
void point_to_attribute() {
/* structure name t[1] */
/* object's name t[2] */
/* attributes name t[3] */
/* find an attribute number of the attribute (z), if attribute=* a=1 */
find_attribute_number();
an=z;
/* point to an object */
point_to_object();
/* point to the attribute */
z=z+an-1;
}

void user_routine() {
printf("**** USER ROUTINE ****%s\n",fo[z]);
}
```

Sample Runs

Sample runs for each menu item in Listing 11-1 are shown below. Remember, the user responses follow the question marks.

```
ENTER A NUMBER TO DO ONE OF THE FOLLOWING
1-CREATE A STRUCTURE
2-CREATE AN OBJECT
3-NAME OF ALL STRUCTURES
4-NAME OF ALL OBJECTS
5-VIEW A STRUCTURE
6-VIEW AN OBJECT
7-SEND A VALUE TO AN OBJECT
8-COPY A VALUE TO Z$ FROM AN OBJECT'S ATTRIBUTE
9-EXIT
? 1
ENTER STRUCTURE NAME ? CONF
ENTER NUMBER OF ATTRIBUTES ? 5
ATTRIBUTE  1 -? ROOM
ATTRIBUTE  2 -? SUBJECT
ATTRIBUTE  3 -? SPEAKER
ATTRIBUTE  4 -? START
ATTRIBUTE  5 -? END

ENTER A NUMBER TO DO ONE OF THE FOLLOWING
1-CREATE A STRUCTURE
2-CREATE AN OBJECT
3-NAME OF ALL STRUCTURES
4-NAME OF ALL OBJECTS
5-VIEW A STRUCTURE
6-VIEW AN OBJECT
7-SEND A VALUE TO AN OBJECT
8-COPY A VALUE TO Z$ FROM AN OBJECT'S ATTRIBUTE
9-EXIT
? 3
STRUCTURES
CONF

ENTER A NUMBER TO DO ONE OF THE FOLLOWING
1-CREATE A STRUCTURE
2-CREATE AN OBJECT
3-NAME OF ALL STRUCTURES
4-NAME OF ALL OBJECTS
```

```
5-VIEW A STRUCTURE
6-VIEW AN OBJECT
7-SEND A VALUE TO AN OBJECT
8-COPY A VALUE TO Z$ FROM AN OBJECT'S ATTRIBUTE
9-EXIT
? 5
ENTER A STRUCTURE NAME ? CONF
STRUCTURE IS CONF
NUMBER OF ATTRIBUTES ARE 5
ATTRIBUTE NUMBER  1 IS ROOM
ATTRIBUTE NUMBER  2 IS SUBJECT
ATTRIBUTE NUMBER  3 IS SPEAKER
ATTRIBUTE NUMBER  4 IS START
ATTRIBUTE NUMBER  5 IS END

ENTER A NUMBER TO DO ONE OF THE FOLLOWING
1-CREATE A STRUCTURE
2-CREATE AN OBJECT
3-NAME OF ALL STRUCTURES
4-NAME OF ALL OBJECTS
5-VIEW A STRUCTURE
6-VIEW AN OBJECT
7-SEND A VALUE TO AN OBJECT
8-COPY A VALUE TO Z$ FROM AN OBJECT'S ATTRIBUTE
9-EXIT
? 2
ENTER STRUCTURE NAME ? CONF
ENTER OBJECTS NAME ? TEN1
ENTER NUMBER OF ATTRIBUTES ? 5
ATTRIBUTE  1 -? 10
ATTRIBUTE  2 -? EMPLOYEE OVERTIME RULES
ATTRIBUTE  3 -? SUSAN BARD
ATTRIBUTE  4 -? 10:00
ATTRIBUTE  5 -? 11:00

ENTER A NUMBER TO DO ONE OF THE FOLLOWING
1-CREATE A STRUCTURE
2-CREATE AN OBJECT
3-NAME OF ALL STRUCTURES
4-NAME OF ALL OBJECTS
5-VIEW A STRUCTURE
6-VIEW AN OBJECT
7-SEND A VALUE TO AN OBJECT
8-COPY A VALUE TO Z$ FROM AN OBJECT'S ATTRIBUTE
9-EXIT
? 2
ENTER STRUCTURE NAME ? CONF
ENTER OBJECTS NAME ? TEN2
ENTER NUMBER OF ATTRIBUTES ? 5
ATTRIBUTE  1 -? 10
ATTRIBUTE  2 -? PAY RAISES
ATTRIBUTE  3 -? MARC STONE
ATTRIBUTE  4 -? 13:00
ATTRIBUTE  5 -? 14:00

ENTER A NUMBER TO DO ONE OF THE FOLLOWING
1-CREATE A STRUCTURE
2-CREATE AN OBJECT
3-NAME OF ALL STRUCTURES
4-NAME OF ALL OBJECTS
5-VIEW A STRUCTURE
6-VIEW AN OBJECT
```

```
7-SEND A VALUE TO AN OBJECT
8-COPY A VALUE TO Z$ FROM AN OBJECT'S ATTRIBUTE
9-EXIT
? 2
ENTER STRUCTURE NAME ? CONF
ENTER OBJECTS NAME ? ELE1
ENTER NUMBER OF ATTRIBUTES ? 5
ATTRIBUTE  1 -? 11
ATTRIBUTE  2 -? SALES PROJECTIONS
ATTRIBUTE  3 -? ANDY ROME
ATTRIBUTE  4 -? 10:00
ATTRIBUTE  5 -? 11:00

ENTER A NUMBER TO DO ONE OF THE FOLLOWING
1-CREATE A STRUCTURE
2-CREATE AN OBJECT
3-NAME OF ALL STRUCTURES
3-NAME OF ALL STRUCTURES
4-NAME OF ALL OBJECTS
5-VIEW A STRUCTURE
6-VIEW AN OBJECT
7-SEND A VALUE TO AN OBJECT
8-COPY A VALUE TO Z$ FROM AN OBJECT'S ATTRIBUTE
9-EXIT
? 4
ENTER STRUCTURE NAME ? CONF
OBJECT NAME-TEN1
OBJECT NAME-TEN2
OBJECT NAME-ELE1

ENTER A NUMBER TO DO ONE OF THE FOLLOWING
1-CREATE A STRUCTURE
2-CREATE AN OBJECT
2-CREATE AN OBJECT
3-NAME OF ALL STRUCTURES
4-NAME OF ALL OBJECTS
5-VIEW A STRUCTURE
6-VIEW AN OBJECT
7-SEND A VALUE TO AN OBJECT
8-COPY A VALUE TO Z$ FROM AN OBJECT'S ATTRIBUTE
9-EXIT
? 6
ENTER A STRUCTURE NAME ? CONF
ENTER AN OBJECT NAME ? TEN2
OBJECT IS TEN2
NUMBER OF ATTRIBUTES IS 5
ATTRIBUTE NUMBER  1 IS 10
ATTRIBUTE NUMBER  2 IS PAY RAISES
ATTRIBUTE NUMBER  3 IS MARC STONE
ATTRIBUTE NUMBER  4 IS 13:00
ATTRIBUTE NUMBER  5 IS 14:00

ENTER A NUMBER TO DO ONE OF THE FOLLOWING
1-CREATE A STRUCTURE
2-CREATE AN OBJECT
3-NAME OF ALL STRUCTURES
4-NAME OF ALL OBJECTS
5-VIEW A STRUCTURE
6-VIEW AN OBJECT
7-SEND A VALUE TO AN OBJECT
8-COPY A VALUE TO Z$ FROM AN OBJECT'S ATTRIBUTE
9-EXIT
```

```
? 6
ENTER A STRUCTURE NAME ? CONF
ENTER AN OBJECT NAME ? TEN1
OBJECT IS TEN1
NUMBER OF ATTRIBUTES IS 5
ATTRIBUTE NUMBER  1 IS 10
ATTRIBUTE NUMBER  2 IS EMPLOYEE OVERTIME RULES
ATTRIBUTE NUMBER  3 IS SUSAN BARD
ATTRIBUTE NUMBER  4 IS 10:00
ATTRIBUTE NUMBER  5 IS 11:00

ENTER A NUMBER TO DO ONE OF THE FOLLOWING
1-CREATE A STRUCTURE
2-CREATE AN OBJECT
3-NAME OF ALL STRUCTURES
4-NAME OF ALL OBJECTS
5-VIEW A STRUCTURE
6-VIEW AN OBJECT
7-SEND A VALUE TO AN OBJECT
8-COPY A VALUE TO Z$ FROM AN OBJECT'S ATTRIBUTE
9-EXIT
? 7
ENTER A STRUCTURE NAME ? CONF
ENTER AN OBJECT NAME ? TEN1
ENTER ATTRIBUTE NAME ? START
ENTER VALUE ? 09:00

ENTER A NUMBER TO DO ONE OF THE FOLLOWING
1-CREATE A STRUCTURE
2-CREATE AN OBJECT
3-NAME OF ALL STRUCTURES
4-NAME OF ALL OBJECTS
5-VIEW A STRUCTURE
6-VIEW AN OBJECT
7-SEND A VALUE TO AN OBJECT
8-COPY A VALUE TO Z$ FROM AN OBJECT'S ATTRIBUTE
9-EXIT
? 6
ENTER A STRUCTURE NAME ? CONF
ENTER AN OBJECT NAME ? TEN1
OBJECT IS TEN1
NUMBER OF ATTRIBUTES IS 5
ATTRIBUTE NUMBER  1 IS 10
ATTRIBUTE NUMBER  2 IS EMPLOYEE OVERTIME RULES
ATTRIBUTE NUMbER  3 IS SUSAN BARD
ATTRIBUTE NUMBER  4 IS 09:00
ATTRIBUTE NUMBER  5 IS 11:00
```

We will now create a new conference room structure. This time we will include procedures with the start- and end-time attributes.

```
ENTER A NUMBER TO DO ONE OF THE FOLLOWING
1-CREATE A STRUCTURE
2-CREATE AN OBJECT
3-NAME OF ALL STRUCTURES
4-NAME OF ALL OBJECTS
5-VIEW A STRUCTURE
6-VIEW AN OBJECT
7-SEND A VALUE TO AN OBJECT
```

```
8-COPY A VALUE TO Z$ FROM AN OBJECT'S ATTRIBUTE
9-EXIT
? 1
ENTER STRUCTURE NAME ? CONF1
ENTER NUMBER OF ATTRIBUTES ? 7
ATTRIBUTE  1 -? ROOM
ATTRIBUTE  2 -? SUBJECT
ATTRIBUTE  3 -? SPEAKER
ATTRIBUTE  4 -? *
ATTRIBUTE  5 -? START
ATTRIBUTE  6 -? *
ATTRIBUTE  7 -? END

ENTER A NUMBER TO DO ONE OF THE FOLLOWING
1-CREATE A STRUCTURE
2-CREATE AN OBJECT
3-NAME OF ALL STRUCTURES
4-NAME OF ALL OBJECTS
5-VIEW A STRUCTURE
6-VIEW AN OBJECT
7-SEND A VALUE TO AN OBJECT
8-COPY A VALUE TO Z$ FROM AN OBJECT'S ATTRIBUTE
9-EXIT
? 2
ENTER STRUCTURE NAME ? CONF1
ENTER OBJECTS NAME ? TEN1
ENTER NUMBER OF ATTRIBUTES ? 7
ATTRIBUTE  1 -? 10
ATTRIBUTE  2 -? EMPLOYEE OVERTIME RULES
ATTRIBUTE  3 -? SUSAN BARD
ATTRIBUTE  4 -? 10:00
ATTRIBUTE  5 -? 1
ATTRIBUTE  6 -? 11:00
ATTRIBUTE  7 -? 1

ENTER A NUMBER TO DO ONE OF THE FOLLOWING
1-CREATE A STRUCTURE
2-CREATE AN OBJECT
3-NAME OF ALL STRUCTURES
4-NAME OF ALL OBJECTS
5-VIEW A STRUCTURE
6-VIEW AN OBJECT
7-SEND A VALUE TO AN OBJECT
8-COPY A VALUE TO Z$ FROM AN OBJECT'S ATTRIBUTE
9-EXIT
? 8
ENTER A STRUCTURE NAME ? CONF1
ENTER AN OBJECT NAME ? TEN1
ENTER ATTRIBUTE NAME ? START
ATTRIBUTE VALUE IS 10:00

ENTER A NUMBER TO DO ONE OF THE FOLLOWING
1-CREATE A STRUCTURE
2-CREATE AN OBJECT
3-NAME OF ALL STRUCTURES
4-NAME OF ALL OBJECTS
5-VIEW A STRUCTURE
6-VIEW AN OBJECT
7-SEND A VALUE TO AN OBJECT
8-COPY A VALUE TO Z$ FROM AN OBJECT'S ATTRIBUTE
9-EXIT
? 7
ENTER A STRUCTURE NAME ? CONF1
```

```
ENTER AN OBJECT NAME ? TEN1
ENTER ATTRIBUTE NAME ? START
ENTER VALUE ? 08:00
***** USER ROUTINE **** 1
```

The SEND subroutine was used to change the value of the START attribute. The START attribute is preceded by an asterisk in the structure CONF1. This means that the number 1 in the fifth attribute that follows the START attribute of the object TEN1 will direct us to a subroutine that is invoked. This is done in the program's SEND sequence at comment numbers 5040 through 5055. Comment 5050, the CASE statement, will enter a user-written subroutine at comment 10000. This will cause the ****USER ROUTINE**** message to be printed.

```
ENTER ATTRIBUTE NAME ? START
ATTRIBUTE VALUE IS 10:00
ENTER A NUMBER TO DO ONE OF THE FOLLOWING
1-CREATE A STRUCTURE
2-CREATE AN OBJECT
3-NAME OF ALL STRUCTURES
4-NAME OF ALL OBJECTS
5-VIEW A STRUCTURE
6-VIEW AN OBJECT
7-SEND A VALUE TO AN OBJECT
8-COPY A VALUE TO Z$ FROM AN OBJECT'S ATTRIBUTE
9-EXIT
? 6
ENTER A STRUCTURE NAME ? CONF1
ENTER AN OBJECT NAME ? TEN1
OBJECT IS TEN1
NUMBER OF ATTRIBUTES IS 7
ATTRIBUTE NUMBER   1 IS 10
ATTRIBUTE NUMBER   2 IS EMPLOYEE OVERTIME RULES
ATTRIBUTE NUMBER   3 IS SUSAN BARD
ATTRIBUTE NUMBER   4 IS 08:00
ATTRIBUTE NUMBER   5 IS 1
ATTRIBUTE NUMBER   6 IS 11:00
ATTRIBUTE NUMBER   7 IS 1
```

Exercise

You can include a REMOVE OBJECT option in the menu using the DELETE AN OBJECT subroutine at comments 4600 through 4645.

12

Object-Oriented Programming: An Engineering Example

Now that you have a clear picture of the fundamentals of object-oriented programming, you are ready to consider an engineering example. Although the topic is somewhat complex, we will make the explanations simple enough for you to follow easily. By the time we're finished, you will be able to apply object-oriented programming to sampling data in electronic systems. This chapter will also set the stage for your understanding of object-oriented expert systems.

Analog-to-Digital Conversion

We all know, from using ordinary household appliances, that the ac voltage in a wall socket reaches 120 volts at a frequency of 60 cycles. What does this mean? Figure 12-1 should help make the matter clear. AC stands for "alternating current," which means that the current reverses its direction at regular intervals. In our example, the current moves from $+120$ volts to -120 volts and back again, moving toward 0 volts in between. Each cycle takes $1/60$ of a second, so that after 60 cycles, 1 second has elapsed. That is what is meant by a frequency of 60 cycles. As the voltage goes between $+120$ volts and -120 volts, it takes on a continuous set of values; that is, at one moment in time it is 36 volts, at another it is 112, and so on. This is known as an "analog" representation because the voltage can be represented by directly measurable quantities that visually reflect the movement of the current.

In order to perform any kind of analysis of the voltage in a computer, it must be presented to the "input channel." This is the place where everything outside a computer enters for analysis. Since a computer is an electrical device, the input channel can only interpret voltage levels. All the information in the world outside, therefore, must somehow be converted to a voltage before it is presented to the input channel. Once this is accomplished, and the information passes into the computer, the voltage's value is placed in a memory location so that it can be processed by a program.

However, life at the input channel is not so simple. Before any value can be input into the computer, its voltage must be presented in a binary digital format. What does this mean?

The basic unit of computer memory is a "bit," which is short for *binary digit*. A bit consists of either a 0 or a 1. (This system is a base 2 representation, as opposed to the base 10 representation upon which our standard counting system is founded. In base 2, the number 1 is written as 001, 2 is 010, 3 is 011, 4 is 100, and so on.) One bit represents a single line of voltage, which can take on only one of two voltage values. Every computer's basic circuitry is designed to work with two different voltage levels which can be represented by a 0 or 1.

A larger unit of computer memory is the "byte," which is an 8-bit number. The binary digital number representation of 1 volt is 0000 0001. The value of +9 volts is represented as 0000 1001. (An easy way to count in base 2 is to begin at the right. The first digit on the right has a weight of 1, the second a weight of 2, the third 4, then 8, 16, 32, 64, and 128. By simply adding up all the weights in the positions that contain 1s, you can figure out what number is represented. In this last example, 0000 1001, by adding the weight for the first digit from the right—1—to the weight of the fourth—8—we get the number 9.)

Many naturally occurring things that we may wish to analyze can be represented by an analog voltage. The continuously varying voltage in

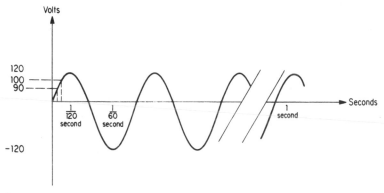

Figure 12-1 120 volts at 60 cycles.

a wall socket is one example; the oscillating picture of a heartbeat on a cardiac monitor is another. In order to analyze these analog voltages in a computer, we must ask the question: What is the methodology for converting an analog voltage to a binary digital representation?

The answer is to use a simple piece of hardware called an analog-to-digital converter, or ADC. The ADC automatically does the conversion by accepting analog voltages as its input and producing binary numbers as output. An example of how this is done is shown in Figure 12-2.

Before the ADC performs the conversion, the computer must somehow *instruct* the ADC to do it. This is accomplished by a signal that is sent by the computer to the ADC on the "convert" line, as shown in the figure. After the conversion takes place, the computer is ready to analyze the input.

For example, suppose we are analyzing the ac voltage supplied by your local power company. Let's assume that the people who run the utility are worried that the voltage may fall to unacceptably low levels, causing a brownout, or shoot up to unacceptably high voltages, ruining equipment and appliances. A picture of the ac voltage is shown in Figure 12-3. The graph shows how the voltage starts at 0 volts and passed through other voltages as it approaches 120; then it decreases, passing below 0. The cycle is repeated every 1/60 of a second.

The figure illustrates how the computer sent out convert signals at two different parts of the cycle. The first signal was sent to the ADC when the voltage value was at 30 volts and was converted to binary digital form as 0001 1110. The second convert signal, at 60 volts, resulted in the conversion to 0011 1100 by the ADC. To put it simply, the ADC takes *one* voltage line and converts it to *eight* binary voltage lines, which we refer to as a byte.

Let's review:

1. An ADC is a device that converts analog voltages to a binary digital representation.

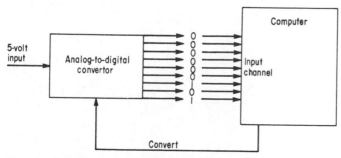

Figure 12-2 Analog to digital conversion input channel.

2. A computer can only process binary digital representations.

3. A convert line into the ADC allows the computer to control exactly when the voltage at the ADC should be converted.

An Engineering System Using Object-Oriented Programming

Now that you have a basic understanding of analog voltage, binary digital representation, and analog-to-digital conversion, you are ready to tackle an engineering problem.

The voltage supplied by a power company is going to a power supply which is supplying three pieces of sensitive electronic equipment. We want to devise a system that will prevent this sensitive equipment from becoming overloaded. If the power supply voltage exceeds 124 volts, the computer is to energize a circuit breaker that will remove the voltage from the sensitive equipment. A system that can do this is shown in Figure 12-4.

If the voltage exceeds 124 volts, the computer's input/output channel will recognize this event with the help of the ADC and will cause the circuit breaker to open, thereby removing the excess voltage and protecting the sensitive electronic equipment. We need to design an object-oriented system with a structure, objects, and procedures for monitoring the voltage.

Structure

Although Figure 12-4 looks complicated, we can create a structure that will make it quite simple. The structure must contain all the

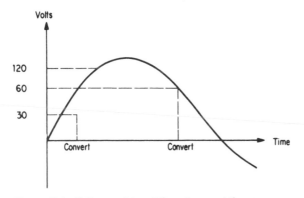

Figure 12-3   Voltages at two different convert times.

attributes that will enable us to represent the entire problem. The task at hand is to

1. Convert the voltage appearing at the sensitive equipment to binary representation and compare this voltage with a maximum acceptable limit. For example, we can tolerate a maximum of 124 volts (0111 1100).

2. If the voltage exceeds 124 volts, we want the circuit breaker to open.

3. The conversion should be done at a regular, safe time interval. For example, if we allow the time between conversions to be 60 seconds, what might happen? Let's say that at the last conversion the voltage was 123 volts, which is safe. But 20 seconds later the voltage rises to 125 volts, which is unsafe. Since we are not even looking at the voltage for another 40 seconds, the computer would never "see" the 125 volts and the equipment would be ruined. A conversion time of 2 seconds, however, *would* detect 125 volts, assuming a gradual transmission of voltage, and provides enough time to open the circuit breaker.

The structure for this problem should have the following attributes:

1. The voltage at which the circuit breaker is to be opened (VOLTAGE)

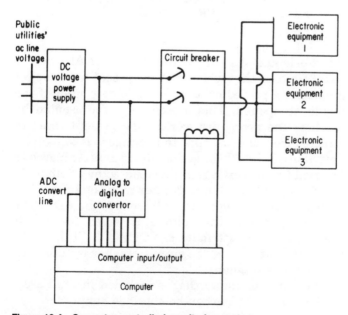

Figure 12-4   Computer controlled monitoring system.

2. The time interval for converting the voltage (CONVERT)

3. The last time we converted the voltage (LAST)

4. The present time (PRESENT)

5. The procedure for determining if we must open the circuit breaker (BREAKER)

The CREATE-STRUCTURE subroutine will create the structure. We will call the structure SENSOR because it is designed to sense excessive voltages. The sensor structure, using the format we introduced in Chapter 12, would look as follows:

CREATE-STRUCTURE (SNAME = SENSOR, NATTR = 5, ATTR = VOLTAGE, ATTR = CONVERT, ATTR = LAST, ATTR = *PRESENT, ATTR = PROCEDURE)

Note the asterisk at the attribute PRESENT. This will cause a procedure to be invoked if a SEND subroutine changes the value of the attribute PRESENT. The object is created as follows:

CREATE-OBJECT (SNAME = SENSOR, ONAME = EQUIPMENT, VOLTAGE = 124, CONVERT = 2, LAST = 0, PRESENT = 0, PROCEDURE = name of the procedure)

How does the object-oriented system use the structure? Attribute 4 represents the present time, so that when the time is sent to the object via the SEND subroutine, a procedure is invoked to determine if the circuit breaker should be opened. This procedure is represented by attribute 5. This is how the procedure works. The present time, in attribute 4, is subtracted from the *last* time the voltage was converted, as represented by attribute 3, LAST. This time interval is compared to the desired time interval for converting, as represented by attribute 2, CONVERT. If the difference is equal to or greater than the time interval for converting, then a convert signal must be sent to the ADC. The converted voltage is compared to the voltage at which the circuit breaker is to be opened, which is attribute 1, VOLTAGE. If this voltage exceeds the VOLTAGE attribute, the circuit breaker is automatically opened to protect the equipment.

Since TIME is a standard command that is included in the Pascal computer language, the present time can be obtained simply via

Y = TIME

We can then send the time value to the object with the following responses to system questions:

```
SEND (SNAME=SENSOR, ONAME=EQUIPMENT, PRESENT=Y)
```

This will invoke the routine specified in the object for checking the power supply voltage using the ADC.

Real-Time Data Acquisition

The system we have just described, which depends upon conversion of voltages and possible subsequent action, is referred to as operating in "real time." This means that something is done at specific instances of time, which in our system was the conversion of voltages every 2 seconds. The term "real-time data acquisition" means that data is acquired at precise moments in time and processed right away. Our system is therefore a real-time data acquisition system that uses object-oriented programming.

Process Control

We can use the same methods to monitor and control all kinds of processes, from plastics manufacture to egg laying to maintaining the temperature in a nuclear reactor. In these applications, we would include programs or devices that convert pressures or locations on a conveyer belt or temperatures into analog voltages. These voltages are fed in turn into an ADC so they can be processed by the computer. The computer can then make decisions that will control the pressures and temperatures or simply alert the user that not enough eggs are being laid in a given time interval. Such systems are known as "process control systems."

Programming Applications

The object-oriented program, Listing 11-1, was modified to reflect the engineering example of checking a voltage. The time at which the voltage is checked is simulated in a subroutine starting at statement 9000. A FOR loop is used as a pseudotime interval. The SEND subroutine via SEND_VALUE causes the invocation of a procedure, located at statement 10000, which checks a pseudovoltage via the RANDOM statement.

Program Listing

Listing 12-1 is followed by a sample run.

Listing 12-1   Engineering object-oriented programming.

```
/************** object oriented programming ************/
#include <stdio.h>
#include <stdlib.h>

/* structure array */
/********* comment 1 *********/
char fo[201][26], t[10][26], zstring[26], ch0[26], ch1[26];

float qq;

int qa,qb,i,e,k,z,l,num,p,a,an,y,n;

void create_structure(void);
void create_a_structure(void);
void create_object_calling_sequence(void);
void create_an_object(void);
void print_structure_attributes(void);
void view_a_structure(void);
void find_attribute_number(void);
void point_to_object(void);
void view_object(void);
void view_an_object(void);
void print_objects_names(void);
void name_of_objects(void);
void prnt_name_of_struct(void);
void point_to_attribute(void);
void user_routine(void);
void send_value(void);
void send_value_to_object(void);
void cpy_att(void);
void cpy_val_fr_objects_att(void);
void pseudo_voltage_checker(void);

main() {
srand(1); /* seed random number generator */
strcpy(ch0,"0"); /* initialize a variable to = value of 0 */
for(i=1;i<201;i++) strcpy(fo[i],"");
for(i=1;i<5;i++) strcpy(t[i],"");
do {
/************* comment 2 *********/
printf("ENTER A NUMBER TO DO ONE OF THE FOLLOWING\n");
printf("1-CREATE A STRUCTURE\n");
printf("2-CREATE AN OBJECT\n");
printf("3-NAME OF ALL STRUCTURES\n");
printf("4-NAME OF ALL OBJECTS\n");
printf("5-VIEW A STRUCTURE\n");
printf("6-VIEW AN OBJECT\n");
printf("7-SEND A VALUE TO AN OBJECT\n");
printf("8-COPY A VALUE TO Z$ FROM AN OBJECT'S ATTRIBUTE\n");
printf("9-PSEUDO VOLTAGE CHECKER\n");
printf("? ");
scanf("%d",&num);
fflush(stdin);
switch (num) {
/********* comment 60 *********/
case 1: create_a_structure(); break;
case 2: create_an_object(); break;
case 3: prt_name_of_struct(); break;
case 4: name_of_objects(); break;
case 5: view_a_structure(); break;
case 6: view_an_object(); break;
case 7: send_value_to_object(); break;
case 8: cpy_val_fr_objects_att(); break;
case 9: pseudo_voltage_checker(); break;
}
printf("\n");
}
while(num != 9);
}
```

```
void create_a_structure() {
printf("ENTER STRUCTURE NAME? ");
gets(t[1]);
printf("ENTER NUMBER OF ATTRIBUTES? ");
gets(t[2]);
strcpy(ch1,t[2]);
n=ch1[0]-ch0[0];
e=3+n-1;
for(i=3;i<e+1;i++) {
 printf("ATTRIBUTE %d-? ",i-2);
 gets(t[i]); }
create_structure();
}

void create_object_calling_sequence() {
/* structure name t[1]
   object name t[2]
   number of values of attributes t[3]
   value of attribute 1 t[4]
   value of attribute n t[n+3] */
/* point to the structure */
z=1;
if(strcmp(t[1],fo[101]) == 0) z=101;
/* last location in that structure space */
e=z+99;
i=z;
/* find 1st free object space */
while((i<=e) && (strcmp(fo[i],"") != 0)) i++;
l=i /* store object here */;
strcpy(fo[l],t[2]); /* store object name */
l=l+1;
/* get number of attributes */
strcpy(ch1,t[3]);
n=ch1[0]-ch0[0];
/* store number */
strcpy(fo[l],t[3]);
l=l+1;
e=l+n-1; /* last attribute location */
k=4; /* first attribute location */
for(i=l;i<(e+1);i++) {
 strcpy(fo[i],t[k]);
 k=k+1; }
}

void create_an_object () {
printf("ENTER STRUCTURE NAME? ");
gets(t[1]);
printf("ENTER OBJECTS NAME? ");
gets(t[2]);
printf("ENTER NUMBER OF ATTRIBUTES? ");
gets(t[3]);
strcpy(ch1,t[3]);
n=ch1[0]-ch0[0];
e=4+n-1;
for(i=4;i<e+1;i++) {
 printf("ATTRIBUTE %d-? ",i-3); gets(t[i]); }
create_object_calling_sequence();
}

void name_of_objects() {
printf("ENTER STRUCTURE NAME? ");
gets(t[i]);
print_objects_names();
}

void view_a_structure() {
printf("ENTER A STRUCTURE NAME? ");
gets(t[1]);
print_structure_attributes();
}
```

Listing 12-1 *(Continued)*

```
void view_object() {
/* structure name t[1] */
/* object name t[2] */
/* point to an object. z is the value of the pointer. n is the
    number of attributes in the object */
point_to_object();
printf("OBJECT IS %s\n",fo[z]);
z++;
printf("NUMBER OF ATTRIBUTES IS %s\n",fo[z]);
z++;
e=z+n-1;
p=1;
for(i=z;i<e+1;i++) { printf("ATTRIBUTE NUMBER %d IS %s\n",p,fo[i]);
  p++; }
}

void view_an_object() {
printf("ENTER A STRUCTURE NAME? ");
gets(t[1]);
printf("ENTER AN OBJECT NAME? ");
gets(t[2]);
view_object();
}

void send_value() {
/*********** comment 5040 **********/
/* send a value to an objects attribute */
/* structure name t[1] */
/* objects name t[2] */
/* attribute name t[3] */
/* value t[4] */
point_to_attribute();
/* store value into attribute, if no asterisk "*" a=0 */
if(a != 0) {
/* an asterisk call user written routine */
 z++;
 strcpy(ch1,fo[z]);
 n=ch1[0]-ch0[0];
 /************ comment 5050 ***********/
 switch (n) {
 case 1: user_routine();
           break;
 }
 /* point to the attribute again */
 z=z-1;
 strcpy(fo[z],t[4]);
 }
else {
/* no asterisk */
 z++;
 strcpy(fo[z],t[4]);
 }
}

void send_value_to_object() {
printf("ENTER A STRUCTURE NAME? ");
gets(t[1]);
printf("ENTER AN OBJECT NAME? ");
gets(t[2]);
printf("ENTER ATTRIBUTE NAME? ");
gets(t[3]);
printf("ENTER VALUE? ");
gets(t[4]);
/* send a value to an objects attribute */
send_value();
}

void cpy_val_fr_objects_att() {
/* copy a value to z from an objects attribute */
printf("ENTER A STRUCTURE NAME? "); gets(t[1]);
printf("ENTER AN OBJECT NAME? "); gets(t[2]);
printf("ENTER AN ATTRIBUTE NAME? "); gets(t[3]);
cpy_att(); /* copy an objects attribute to z */
printf("ATTRIBUTE VALUE IS %s\n",zstring);
}
```

```
void cpy_att() {
/* copy an object's attribute to z */
/* structure name t[1] */
/* object name t[2] */
/* attribute name t[3] */
/* value z */
/* point to an object's attribute (z) */
point_to_attribute();
strcpy(zstring,fo[z]);
/* an asterisk call user written routine */
/* point to the attribute again */
if(a != 0) strcpy(zstring,fo[z]);
 else {
 /* no asterisk */
 z++;
 strcpy(zstring,fo[z]); }
 }

void create_structure() {
/* structure name t[1]
    number of attributes t[2]
    attribute 1  an * means a name then a routine number follows t[3]
    attribute n t[n+2] */
/* search for the structure name either the top or bottom half
    then store the structure arguments in that location */
/* point to lower half */
y=1;
if(strcmp(fo[1],"") != 0) y=101 /* point to top half bottom not empty */;
strcpy(ch1,t[2]);
n=ch1[0]-ch0[0];
/* number of elements in structure is number arg+2 */
n=n+2;
for(z=1;z<n+1;z++) {
 strcpy(fo[y],t[z]);
 y++; }
 }

void print_structure_attributes() {
/* structure name t[1] */
/* point to structure */
z=1;
if(strcmp(t[1],fo[101]) == 0) z=101;
printf("STRUCTURE IS %s\n",t[1]);
z=z+1;
printf("NUMBER OF ATTRIBUTES ARE %s\n",fo[z]);
strcpy(ch1,fo[z]);
n=ch1[0]-ch0[0];
z=z+1;
e=z+n-1;
/* attribute number */
k=1;
for(i=z;i<e+1;i++) {
 printf("ATTRIBUTE NUMBER %d is %s\n",k,fo[i]);
 k=k+1; }
 }

 void find_attribute_number() {
 /* find the attribute number of an attribute in an object */
 /* z=attribute number, a=0 if no *, a=1 if *          */
 /* structure name t[1] */
 /* attribute name t[3] */
 z=1; /* point to the structure */
 if(strcmp(t[1],fo[101]) == 0) z=101;
 z=z+2;
 n=1;
 /* start the search */
 while(strcmp(t[3],fo[z]) != 0) {
 /* try again */
  z=z+1;
  n=n+1; }
```

Listing 12-1 *(Continued)*

```
/* does attribute have an *    */
a=0;
z=z-1;
/* point to asterisk location */
if(strcmp(fo[z],"*") == 0) a=1;
z=n+1;
}

void point_to_object() {
/* structure name t[1] */
/* object name t[2] */
/* point to the structure */
z=1;
if(strcmp(t[1],fo[101]) == 0) z=101;
/* number of structure attributes */
z=z+1;
strcpy(ch1,fo[z]);
n=ch1[0]-ch0[0];
z=z+n+1; /* 1st object in structure */
/* is this object location blank */
/* blank space search for 1st non-blank object space */
while(strcmp(fo[z],"") == 0) z=z+1;
z=z+1;
/* get the number of object attributes */
strcpy(ch1,fo[z]);
n=ch1[0]-ch0[0];
/* reset pointer to object name */
z=z-1;
/* is this the object */
while(strcmp(t[2],fo[z]) != 0) /* next object */ z=z+n+2;
/* z is the location of the object */
}

void print_objects_names() {
/* structure name t[1] */
/* point to the structure */
z=1;
if(strcmp(t[1],fo[101]) == 0) z=101;
/* end of structure array */
e=z+99;
z++;
/* number of structure attributes */
strcpy(ch1,fo[z]);
n=ch1[0]-ch0[0];
/* first object */
z=z-1;
i=z;
while(i<=e) {
 if(strcmp(fo[i],"") != 0) printf("OBJECT NAME-%s\n",fo[i]);
 i=i+n+2; }
}

prt_name_of_struct() {
printf("STRUCTURE\n");
printf("%s\n",fo[1]);
printf("%s\n",fo[101]);
}

void point_to_attribute() {
/* structure name t[1] */
/* object's name t[2] */
/* attributes name t[3] */
/* find an attribute number of the attribute (z), if attribute=* a=1 */
find_attribute_number();
an=z;
/* point to an object */
point_to_object();
/* point to the attribute */
z=z+an-1;
}
```

```
void user_routine() {
/************* comment 10000 **************/
qq=rand();
qq=qq/32767;
if(qq > 0.7) printf("VOLTAGE TOO HIGH= %f\n",qq);
}

void pseudo_voltage_checker() {
/* the pseudo voltage via 'rand' is checked at the
   pseudo time intervals via 'for' loop */
   /************* comment 9000 *************/
strcpy(t[1],"VOLTAGE");
strcpy(t[2],"EQUIP");
strcpy(t[3],"TIME");
strcpy(t[4],"5");
for(qa=1;qa<31;qa++) {
 send_value();
 /* pseudo time delay */
 for(qb=1;qb<1000;qb++) { }
 }
 }
```

Sample Run

```
ENTER A NUMBER TO DO ONE OF THE FOLLOWING
1-CREATE A STRUCTURE
2-CREATE AN OBJECT
3-NAME OF ALL STRUCTURES
4-NAME OF ALL OBJECTS
5-VIEW A STRUCTURE
6-VIEW AN OBJECT
7-SEND A VALUE TO AN OBJECT
8-COPY A VALUE TO Z$ FROM AN OBJECT'S ATTRIBUTE
9-PSEUDO VOLTAGE CHECKER
? 1
ENTER STRUCTURE NAME ? VOLTAGE
ENTER NUMBER OF ATTRIBUTES ? 2
ATTRIBUTE  1 -? *
ATTRIBUTE  2 -? TIME

ENTER A NUMBER TO DO ONE OF THE FOLLOWING
1-CREATE A STRUCTURE
2-CREATE AN OBJECT
3-NAME OF ALL STRUCTURES
4-NAME OF ALL OBJECTS
5-VIEW A STRUCTURE
6-VIEW AN OBJECT
7-SEND A VALUE TO AN OBJECT
8-COPY A VALUE TO Z$ FROM AN OBJECT'S ATTRIBUTE
9-PSEUDO VOLTAGE CHECKER
? 2
ENTER STRUCTURE NAME ? VOLTAGE
ENTER OBJECTS NAME ? EQUIP
ENTER NUMBER OF ATTRIBUTES ? 2
ATTRIBUTE  1 -? 9:00
ATTRIBUTE  2 -? 1
```

```
ENTER A NUMBER TO DO ONE OF THE FOLLOWING
1-CREATE A STRUCTURE
2-CREATE AN OBJECT
3-NAME OF ALL STRUCTURES
4-NAME OF ALL OBJECTS
5-VIEW A STRUCTURE
6-VIEW AN OBJECT
7-SEND A VALUE TO AN OBJECT
8-COPY A VALUE TO Z$ FROM AN OBJECT'S ATTRIBUTE
9-PSEUDO VOLTAGE CHECKER
? 9
VOLTAGE TOO HIGH=   0.808740
VOLTAGE TOO HIGH=   0.895962
VOLTAGE TOO HIGH=   0.822840
VOLTAGE TOO HIGH=   0.746605
VOLTAGE TOO HIGH=   0.858943
VOLTAGE TOO HIGH=   0.710501
VOLTAGE TOO HIGH=   0.988525
```

13

Object-Oriented Expert Systems

Now that you understand objects and how to write programs using them, let's see how we can use them in an expert system. As an example, we will design an expert system that can predict when a town that is located along a river should be evacuated because there is a danger of flooding. The system will use a rule-based structure that utilizes objects. As we've said before, don't worry that the subject matter may sound complicated; we will lead you carefully through every step in the design of the flood-warning system.

Designing the Structure

Since our problem deals with flood warning, the first thing we must do in designing the structure is to identify those things that must be considered to warn the people in a town of possible flooding. These things are the attributes of the structure. We will consider four crucial attributes and define the attributes' values in fuzzy terms such as high, hot, etc. The attribute names, with explanation of their meaning are

1. WATER-LEVEL This is the water level of the river near the town. If it is high, there is danger of flooding. If it is low, it can absorb runoff of a heavy rain or swiftly melting snow.

2. RAIN This is the weather forecast in terms of rain. If it is heavy and the water level is high, there is a chance of flooding. If no rain is forecast, then rain cannot contribute to a flood.

3. TEMPERATURE If the weather forecast is for a hot day and there is a lot of snow in the mountains surrounding the river and the water level is high, there is a danger of flooding.

4. SNOW   The level of snow in the mountain. Melting snow can cause run-off into the river and increase the danger of flooding. A low level of snow contributes very little to danger of flooding no matter what the rain or temperature.

We can create the FLOOD structure via the Create-Structure subroutine, as follows:

CREATE-STRUCTURE (SNAME = FLOOD, NATTR = 4, ATTR = WATER-LEVEL, ATTR = RAIN, ATTR = TEMPERATURE, ATTR = SNOW)

Creating an Object

Remember, an object is an instance on a particular day, one in April 1985. We were working in the weather laboratory and decided to create objects to represent the weather status of our two towns, River City and Redwood City. Using the flood structure, we can create objects to represent the two towns at different locations along a river. We will name the objects according to the names of the towns. Let's call the towns and their objects names RIVER-CITY and REDWOOD-CITY. The created objects are

CREATE-OBJECT (SNAME = FLOOD, ONAME = RIVER-CITY, WATER-LEVEL = HIGH RAIN = HEAVY RAIN, TEMPERATURE = HOT, SNOW = A LOT)

This object's name is RIVER-CITY. Today, the water level is high, the rain in the area is heavy, the temperature is hot, and there is a lot of snow in the mountains. The other object created is

CREATE-OBJECT (SNAME = FLOOD, ONAME = REDWOOD-CITY, WATER-LEVEL = LOW RAIN = NO RAIN, TEMPERATURE = WARM, SNOW = A LOT)

This object is REDWOOD-CITY. Today, the water level is low, there is no rain, it is warm, and there is a lot of snow in the mountains.

Building the Knowledge Base

As we have done previously, we will first represent the knowledge base by a decision tree and then convert this tree into a set of IF-THEN rules. The decision tree is shown in Figure 13-1.

Remember how we convert the decision tree to a set of rules? By following every path that leads to a conclusion. In this example there is

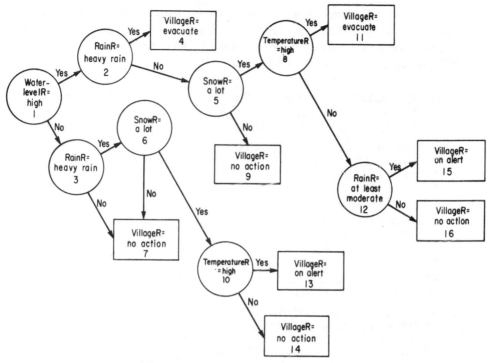

Figure 13-1   Decision tree for a flood alert system.

one conclusion, which is whether or not an evacuation should take place.

Writing the Rules

The following nine paths can be drawn from the tree:

1. 1, 2, 4
2. 1, 2, 5, 8, 11
3. 1, 2, 5, 8, 12, 15 ·
4. 1, 2, 5, 8, 12, 16
5. 1, 2, 5, 9
6. 1, 3, 6, 10, 13
7. 1, 3, 6, 10, 14
8. 1, 3, 6, 7
9. 1, 3, 7

From these paths we can write the corresponding rules for the knowledge base. Notice that we've added an R onto the end of the names of the following rule variables; we don't want to confuse a variable name with its corresponding attribute name.

1 IF WATER-LEVELR = HIGH AND
   RAINR = HEAVY RAIN
   THEN VILLAGER = EVACUATE

2 IF WATER-LEVELR = HIGH AND
   RAINR = NOT HEAVY RAIN AND
   SNOWR = A LOT AND
   TEMPERATURER = HIGH
   THEN VILLAGER = EVACUATE

3 IF WATER-LEVELR = HIGH AND
   RAINR = NOT HEAVY RAIN AND
   SNOWR = A LOT AND
   TEMPERATURER = NOT HIGH AND
   RAINR = AT LEAST MODERATE
   THEN VILLAGER = ON ALERT

4 IF WATER-LEVELR = HIGH AND
   RAINR = NOT HEAVY RAIN AND
   SNOWR = A LOT AND
   TEMPERATURER = NOT HIGH AND
   RAINR = LESS THAN MODERATE
   THEN VILLAGER = NO ACTION

5 IF WATER-LEVELR = HIGH AND
   RAINR = NOT HEAVY RAIN AND
   SNOWR = NOT A LOT
   THEN VILLAGER = NO ACTION

6 IF WATER-LEVELR = NOT HIGH AND
   RAINR = HEAVY RAIN AND
   SNOWR = A LOT AND
   TEMPERATURER = HIGH
   THEN VILLAGER = ON ALERT

7 IF WATER-LEVELR = NOT HIGH AND
   RAINR = HEAVY RAIN AND
   SNOWR = A LOT AND
   TEMPERATURER = NOT HIGH
   THEN VILLAGER = NO ACTION

8 IF WATER-LEVELR = NOT HIGH AND
   RAINR = HEAVY RAIN AND
   SNOWR = NOT A LOT
   THEN VILLAGER = NO ACTION

9 IF WATER-LEVELR = NOT HIGH AND
   RAINR = NOT HEAVY RAIN
   THEN VILLAGER = NO ACTION

Using the Knowledge Base

In order to see how the rules use the objects, let us first rewrite the objects as follows:

Name of attributes	River City	Redwood City
WATER-LEVEL	HIGH	LOW
RAIN	HEAVY RAIN	NO RAIN
TEMPERATURE	HOT	WARM
SNOW	A LOT	A LOT

Let's take rule 1 as an example and see how it uses objects:

1   IF WATER-LEVELR = HIGH AND
    RAINR = HEAVY RAIN
    THEN VILLAGER = EVACUATE

Assume we wish to know whether River City should be evacuated. We would instantiate WATER-LEVELR, and we have to instantiate all the condition variables (water level and rain). The way a variable is instantiated with the value in an object is via the COPY subroutine. If we provide the COPY subroutine with the structure name, object name, and the attribute of that object, it will reach into the object's attribute, take the value, and place it with the variable, shown here on the left side of the copy expression. For example, the COPY subroutine would do the following:

WATER-LEVELR = COPY (SNAME = FLOOD, ONAME = RIVER-CITY, WATER-LEVEL)

(WATER-LEVEL is the name of the attribute, not the name of the variable WATER-LEVELR.)

What this subroutine does is find the object, RIVER-CITY, obtain the value in the attribute WATER-LEVEL, which in this case is HIGH, and pass it to the variable called WATER-LEVELR.

Returning to the first condition clause of rule 1, we see that it is satisfied because it says, "IF WATER-LEVELR IS HIGH." We must now see if the second condition clause, which is RAINR = HEAVY RAIN, is also true. We do this by using the COPY subroutine again:

RAINR = COPY (SNAME = FLOOD, ONAME = RIVER-CITY, RAIN)

Since the RAIN attribute for RIVER-CITY is HEAVY RAIN, the COPY subroutine will cause RAINR to get the value HEAVY RAIN.

The THEN part of the rule will be invoked since both clauses of the

IF part are true. We must then evacuate the town. We could do the same thing, of course, for Redwood City. What these copy subroutines do is to transfer a factual situation about these towns, one day in April, into the rule variables so the reference technique can be applied to see if a flood warning is warranted.

Backward or Forward Chaining

The only difference between executing a backward or forward chaining operation on objects as opposed to executing them on just variables is the way we access the attributes in the objects. That is, we use the SEND and COPY subroutines for setting or obtaining values of objects. All the other features are the same, allowing us to follow the explanations of the chapters describing backward and forward chaining for objects as well.

Briefly, when would we choose a backward chaining technique and when would we instead opt for forward chaining? As you've probably guessed already, this system would make the best use of a forward chaining technique because it is intended to predict the outcome (conclusion) from various factors (conditions). The conditions are, it is raining, the snow is low, etc. In terms of the system, that means we search the IF parts of the rules for conditions that will lead to the invoking of the THEN parts.

Don't count backward chaining out of this problem, though. It could be very useful in the aftermath of a flood in trying to determine the causes once the flood has occurred. This is the conclusion. In order to determine the condition that caused it, we would invoke backward chaining. The situation is very much like a criminal case or a mechanical problem in your car or any other backward chaining example we have previously discussed. In other words, once a particular situation exists, the task is to look for causes. In the backward chaining system, the rules are scanned for THEN parts that match the actual event—in this case, a flood—and the IF parts are then instantiated to see if the circumstances in the rule fit the actual occurrence.

Finding the causes of previous floods through backward chaining would be a very good way of setting up a flood-warning system based on forward chaining—once the factors that caused the flood are known, they can be carefully monitored to avoid a future disaster. Backward chaining discovers, forward chaining predicts.

Advanced Knowledge Representation for Smart Systems

Section 5 contains a potpourri of topics that briefly describe additional artificial intelligence representations, dealing with uncertainty and an introduction to automated learning. It is chock-full of examples and programs that will enhance your understanding of the topics.

14

Semantic Nets

In this chapter we will give you an introductory understanding of some other important artificial intelligence concepts used in expert systems. Semantic nets are graphical representations of knowledge. Like a decision tree, they consist of nodes that are represented by circles, and arcs that are represented by lines with arrows. The nodes contain pieces of information and the arcs show the relationship between them.

A semantic net illustrating a knowledge base for some form of bird and plane is shown in Figure 14-1. Every arc indicates some relationship between items contained in the nodes. For example, as you can see from the figure, the relationship between the node "gasoline" and the node "engine" is that the engine "uses" gasoline, as indicated on the arc.

Structure and Objects of Semantic Nets

One of the ways we can use a semantic net is to create objects. Let's see how this works with the semantic net shown in Figure 14-1. First, we will concentrate on developing a structure for a bird. The objects of the structure, BIRD, that is, specific instances of the structure, are identified by the "is a" relationship. These are FALCON and EAGLE, meaning falcon is a bird, and eagle is a bird. Other arc relationships will provide us with the attributes of BIRD. From the "has" relationship, we see three of the attributes, which are WINGS, FEATHERS, and BEAK; in other words, BIRD has all of these, as shown in the semantic net. From the "does" relationship, we see an attribute, namely FLY; that is, a bird does fly, and from the "uses" relationship, we get the attribute AERODYNAMIC PRINCIPLES; the bird uses aerodynamic principles. From these attributes we can now create the STRUCTURE, BIRD:

CREATE-STRUCTURE (SNAME = BIRD, NATTR = 5, ATTR =
                  BEAK, ATTR = FEATHERS, ATTR =
                  WINGS, ATR = FLY, ATTR = AERODY-
                  NAMIC PRINCIPLES)

Using the structure, we can now create the objects EAGLE and FAL-CON. For example, the object EAGLE is created by

CREATE-OBJECT (SNAME = BIRD, ONAME = EAGLE, BEAK =
               LONG, FEATHERS = LIGHT, WINGS = WIDE,
               FLY = HIGH, AERODYNAMIC PRINCIPLES =
               GLIDING)

We could now use the objects to create a knowledge base that can help us to answer specific questions about the objects.

Rule-Based System Using Semantic Nets

From the semantic net we can also set up a knowledge base that would enable us to identify whether a flying object is a bird or plane. The

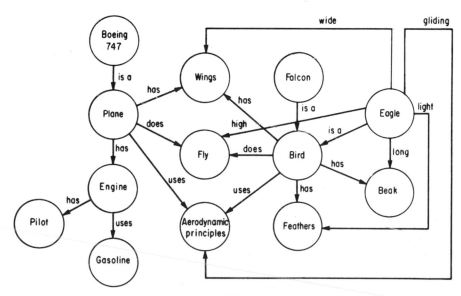

Figure 14-1   Semantic net showing relationships between parts of a bird and a plane.

following are some of the rules that can be part of the bird-plane knowledge base:

```
IF OBJECT-ATTRIBUTE = BEAK
THEN FLYING OBJECT = BIRD

IF OBJECT-ATTRIBUTE = WINGS
THEN FLYING-OBJECT = BIRD OR
     FLYING-OBJECT = PLANE

IF OBJECT-ATTRIBUTE = FALCON OR
   OBJECT-ATTRIBUTE = EAGLE
THEN FLYING-OBJECT = BIRD

IF OBJECT-ATTRIBUTE = FEATHERS AND
   OBJECT-ATTRIBUTE = BEAK AND
   OBJECT-ATTRIBUTE = WINGS
THEN FLYING-OBJECT = BIRD

IF FLYING-OBJECT = BIRD
THEN OBJECT-ATTRIBUTE = FEATHERS
```

Here is a summary of some of the principles of semantic nets:

1. Semantic nets describe relationships between things that are represented by nodes.

2. The nodes are circles that have names.

3. The relationships between nodes are represented by arcs that connect the circles.

4. A semantic net can be used to generate structures and objects.

5. A semantic net can be used to generate rules for a knowledge base.

Programming Applications

Let's examine a program written in C, Listing 14-1, which manipulates the semantic net shown in Figure 14-2. This semantic net is a subset of the one we used to describe the concepts.

Program Explanation

Listing 14-1 is divided into three functional parts. Each part performs an operation that allows you to view a particular aspect of the semantic net. For example, we can obtain a list of all node pairs for a particular relationship. The "is a" relationship has node pairs FALCON-BIRD and EAGLE-BIRD. Each operation is simply understood by tracing through at most 15 C statements. The semantic net is defined

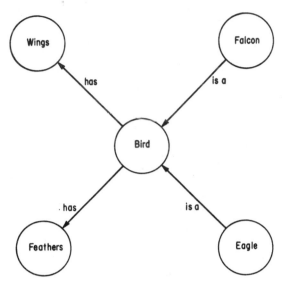

Figure 14-2   A semantic net.

within two arrays. One array contains the names of the nodes and is symbolically represented as N. The other array is a two-dimensional array and contains the arc relationship names. This is symbolically represented as R. We have given values to these two arrays in comment numbers 70 and 75 to correspond to Figure 14-3. We can alternately represent the semantic net with the N and R array values as shown in the matrix of Figure 14-3.

	1. Bird	2. Falcon	3. Eagle	4. Wings	5. Feathers
1. Bird				Has	Has
2. Falcon	Is a				
3. Eagle	Is a				
4. Wings					
5. Feathers					

Figure 14-3   Relationship matrix R.

The semantic net program, Listing 14-1, offers the following options
that are defined in comments 300 through 365:

```
ENTER A NUMBER CORRESPONDING TO ONE OF THE FOLLOWING
1-OBTAIN ALL RELATIONSHIP NODES FOR A PARTICULAR NODE
  AND A PARTICULAR RELATIONSHIP
2-OBTAIN A LIST OF ALL NAMES WITH THEIR RELATIONSHIP FOR A
  PARTICULAR NODE
3-OBTAIN ALL NODE PAIRS CORRESPONDING TO A PARTICULAR RELATIONSHIP
4-EXIT
?
```

The statements implementing these options are located in comment
numbers 1000, 1100, and 1200, respectively.

Program Listing

Listing 14-1 is followed by a set of sample runs.

Listing 14-1   Semantic nets.

```
#include <stdio.h>

/* relationship array. this is the matrix that holds the arc's name */
char r[11][11][6];
/* name array. this tells us the name of each node */
char n[11][11];
/* node string */
char nn[11];
/* relationship string */
char rn[6];

int num,i,j;

main() {
/* initialize relationship array and name array */
for(i=1;i<11;i++)
 for(j=1;j<11;j++) {
  strcpy(r[i][j],"");
  strcpy(n[i],"");
 }
/* this section sets values for the name array and the relationship
   array. the values are assigned but the programmer can remove
   them and use input statements to assign values in general */
/**************** semantic net ***************/
/********** comment 70 ************/
strcpy(n[1],"BIRD");
strcpy(n[2],"FALCON");
strcpy(n[3],"EAGLE");
strcpy(n[4],"WINGS");
strcpy(n[5],"FEATHERS");
/********** comment 75 ************/
strcpy(r[2][1],"IS A");
strcpy(r[3][1],"IS A");
strcpy(r[1][4],"HAS");
strcpy(r[1][5],"HAS");
/************************************/
num=0;
while(num != 4) {
 printf("\n");
/********** comment 300 ***********/
printf("ENTER A NUMBER CORRESPONDING TO ONE OF THE FOLLOWING\n");
printf("1-OBTAIN ALL RELATIONSHIP NODES FOR A PARTICULAR NODE\n");
printf("  AND A PARTICULAR RELATIONSHIP\n");
printf("2-OBTAIN A LIST OF ALL NAMES WITH THEIR RELATIONSHIP FOR A\n");
printf("  PARTICULAR NODE\n");
printf("3-OBTAIN ALL NODE PAIRS CORRESPONDING TO A PARTICULAR RELATIONSHIP\n");
printf("4-EXIT\n? ");
/********** comment 365 ************/
scanf("%d",&num);
fflush(stdin);
switch (num) {
/********** comment 1000 ************/
/* obtain all relationship nodes for a particular node
   and a particular relationship */
 case 1: printf("ENTER NODE NAME YOU ARE INTERESTED IN? ");
         gets(nn);
         printf("ENTER RELATIONSHIP NAME YOU ARE INTERESTED IN? ");
         gets(rn);
         i=1;
         while((i < 10) && (strcmp(nn,n[i]) != 0)) i++;
/* for this node number (i) in the relationship matrix find
   those names (j) that contain the relationship (rn) */
         for(j=1;j<10;j++)
           if(strcmp(r[i][j],rn) == 0) printf("%s\n",n[j]);
          break;
```

```
/*********** comment 1100 *********/
/* obtain a list together with all their relationships for
   a particular node */
 case 2: printf("ENTER NAME OF NODE? ");
         gets(nn);
/* find row in relationship matrix containing the name */
         i=1;
         while((i<=10) && (strcmp(nn,n[i]) != 0)) i++;
         j=1;
/* print all relationships and their corresponding nodes */
         while(j<=10) {
           if(strcmp(r[i][j],"") != 0) printf("%s    %s\n",n[j],r[i][j]);
           j++; }
         break;
/*********** comment 1200 ***********/
/* obtain all node pairs corresponding to a particular relationships */
   case 3: printf("ENTER RELATIONSHIP NAME? ");
         gets(rn);
         for(i=1;i<11;i++)
          for(j=1;j<11;j++)
           if(strcmp(r[i][j],rn) == 0) printf("%s    %s\n",n[i],n[j]);
         break;
   case 4: /* exit */;
 }
}
}
```

Sample Runs

```
ENTER A NUMBER CORRESPONDING TO ONE OF THE FOLLOWING
1-OBTAIN ALL RELATIONSHIP NODES FOR A PARTICULAR NODE
  AND A PARTICULAR RELATIONSHIP
2-OBTAIN A LIST OF ALL NAMES WITH THEIR RELATIONSHIP FOR A
  PARTICULAR NODE
3-OBTAIN ALL NODE PAIRS CORRESPONDING TO A PARTICULAR RELATIONSHIP
4-EXIT
? 1
ENTER NODE NAME YOU ARE INTERESTED IN? BIRD
ENTER RELATIONSHIP NAME YOU ARE INTERESTED IN? HAS
WINGS
FEATHERS

ENTER A NUMBER CORRESPONDING TO ONE OF THE FOLLOWING
1-OBTAIN ALL RELATIONSHIP NODES FOR A PARTICULAR NODE
  AND A PARTICULAR RELATIONSHIP
2-OBTAIN A LIST OF ALL NAMES WITH THEIR RELATIONSHIP FOR A
  PARTICULAR NODE
3-OBTAIN ALL NODE PAIRS CORRESPONDING TO A PARTICULAR RELATIONSHIP
4-EXIT
? 1
ENTER NODE NAME YOU ARE INTERESTED IN? EAGLE
ENTER RELATIONSHIP NAME YOU ARE INTERESTED IN? IS A
BIRD
```

```
ENTER A NUMBER CORRESPONDING TO ONE OF THE FOLLOWING
1-OBTAIN ALL RELATIONSHIP NODES FOR A PARTICULAR NODE
   AND A PARTICULAR RELATIONSHIP
2-OBTAIN A LIST OF ALL NAMES WITH THEIR RELATIONSHIP FOR A
   PARTICULAR NODE
3-OBTAIN ALL NODE PAIRS CORRESPONDING TO A PARTICULAR RELATIONSHIP
4-EXIT
? 2
ENTER NAME OF NODE? BIRD
WINGS  HAS
FEATHERS  HAS
```

In this run it is important to note that a relationship is only valid for arcs *leaving a node*. The two "is a" arcs entering the BIRD node are considered relationships of the FALCON and EAGLE, respectively.

```
ENTER A NUMBER CORRESPONDING TO ONE OF THE FOLLOWING
1-OBTAIN ALL RELATIONSHIP NODES FOR A PARTICULAR NODE
   AND A PARTICULAR RELATIONSHIP
2-OBTAIN A LIST OF ALL NAMES WITH THEIR RELATIONSHIP FOR A
   PARTICULAR NODE
3-OBTAIN ALL NODE PAIRS CORRESPONDING TO A PARTICULAR RELATIONSHIP
4-EXIT
? 3
ENTER THE RELATIONSHIP NAME? HAS
BIRD  WINGS
BIRD  FEATHERS
```

Certainty Factors

Certainty Factors (CF) are used in the mathematical field called fuzzy logic. Since heuristics are based on expert rules that are learned from experience, we may not always be completely certain that an IF-THEN rule is correct. Nor can the user of an expert system be certain that the value he or she provides when instantiating a variable is a hundred percent correct. For example, the rule

```
IF INTEREST RATES = FALL AND TAXES = DECREASED
THEN STOCK MARKET = RISE
```

may not work all the time. Therefore, we may assign to the rule a CF, which is a value that approximates the degree to which we *think* the rule is correct. Values of CF range between −1 and +1. A CF of a negative number indicates a predominance of opposing evidence for the rule being correct. A positive CF indicates a predominance of confirming evidence for the rule being correct. Therefore, a CF of +1 indicates absolute certainty that the rule is correct, while a CF of −1 indicates absolute certainty that the rule is incorrect. Of course, if we had a CF that equaled −1, we would not even consider stating the rule.

Assume we assign a CF of 0.9 to the stock market rule. Also, assume that we are not really sure that interest rates are falling and assign a CF of 0.6 to that clause. Assume further that changes in the tax laws will include some increases as well as some reductions. But on the average we *think* the taxes will be reduced with a CF of 0.8. We can then represent the rule as

```
IF INTEREST RATES = FALL (CF = 0.6) AND
TAXES = REDUCED (CF = 0.8)
THEN STOCK MARKET = RISE (Rule CF = 0.9)
```

We can calculate the CF that the stock market is rising by multiplying the minimum of the clauses connected by AND in the IF part by the CF of the rule. In our example this works out to be

(Minimum (0.6, 0.8)) * 0.9 = 0.6 * 0.9 = 0.54

We therefore have a 0.54 certainty that the stock market will rise.

If we have another rule that also tells us the stock market will rise but uses a different set of conditions to arrive at the answer, we will take the highest, or maximum, CF of the two answers. Don't worry if this sounds complicated; you will soon see an example of how this works.

We will first summarize the rules for you, then work out a general example:

1. From a rule, take the minimum CF of clauses connected by AND.
2. If there are OR connections in the rule, take the maximum CF value of all the AND clauses that are connected by ORs.
3. Multiply the final CF of the clauses by the CF of the rule.
4. If there is more than one rule leading to the same conclusion, take as the final CF the maximum CF values of all those rules.

Consider the following two rules. They both lead to the same conclusion, which is C.

```
IF A (CF = 0.3) AND B (CF = 0.6)
THEN C (CF = 0.5)
IF D (CF = 0.4) AND E (CF = 0.7)
THEN C (CF = 0.9)
```

The CF of C is the higher of the CFs of the two rules, as follows:

Maximum ((minimum (0.3, 0.6) * 0.5),
(minimum (0.4, 0.7) * 0.9))
= maximum ((0.3 * 0.5), (0.4 * 0.9))
= maximum (0.15, 0.36)
= 0.36

Another example, this time using the logical operator OR is

```
IF A (CF = 0.3) AND
   B (CF = 0.6) OR
   D (CF = 0.5)
THEN C (CF = 0.4)
```

The CF for C is

Maximum (minimum (0.3, 0.6), 0.5) * 0.4
= maximum (0.3, 0.5) * 0.4
= 0.5 * 0.4 = 0.2

Certainty Level Restrictions

In many cases certainty levels are given. What this means is that an inference is valid only if the CF exceeds this level. If the CF is below this level, a search through the knowledge base continues until an inference exceeds the level. The way the certainty level is calculated is as follows. Assume that the CF for a particular inference is 0.4. We place 0.4 for that inference into a CF accumulator. We compare the CF accumulator with the certainty level (assume it to be 0.8). The accumulated value is less than the level and therefore the knowledge base search proceeds. The next time the same inference is encountered in the knowledge base search we multiply the CF for this new inference by 1 minus the value in the CF accumulator and add the result to the CF accumulator. The 1 in the equation comes from the absolute certainty value = 1. We now compare the CF accumulator with the certainty level. If greater, we have our answer. If not, we continue the search. The equation is

Accumulated CF = old accumulated CF + (1 − old accumulated CF) * CF of the rule

For example:

Certainty level   =   0.8
Rule   =   if A then B (assume CF = 0.6)
Accumulated CF   =   0.6
New rule   =   if C then B (assume CF = 0.7)
Accumulated CF   =   0.6 + (1 − 0.6) × 0.7
                  =   0.88 (exceeds certainty level; stop)

Programming Applications

Let's examine a program written in C, Listing 15-1, which allows us to apply the certainty factor concepts we have just discussed.

Program Explanation

The rule used to illustrate the certainty factors concepts is shown in Listing 15-1 in the comments 20 and 60 and executed in comments 400 and 430. Each rule has a sequence of locations assigned to it in the CF array, with one CF location for each condition variable. Since the rule has three condition variables, A, B, and C, we can assign CF[1], CF[2], and CF[3] to these variables. The user is asked to enter a value for A, B, and C along with certainty factors for each variable in comments 320, 340, and 360. If the user enters a certainty factor for any of the variables, this certainty factor replaces a default certainty factor value in the CF array which is assigned to that variable as shown in comments 330, 350, and 370. Default certainty factor values are contained in the default array. Each value of the default array is initially set to a 1 as shown in comments 150 through 170. The knowledge engineer can override these values as shown in comment 190. The default values are then transferred to the CF array in comments 230 through 250. The user can replace the default values, as previously described, in comments 320 through 370. We then calculate the certainty of the result in comments 450 through 500.

Program Listing

Listing 15-1 is followed by a set of sample runs.

Listing 15-1   Certainty factors.

```
#include <stdio.h>

/*********** comment 20 *************/
/* consider the following rule
   if    a=2   (cf=.6) and
         b=3   (cf=.3) and
         c=5   (cf=1.0)
   then d=5    (cf=.4)
   alongside, in parenthesis, each clause is the certainty factor.
   the cf numbers are the default numbers that the writer of the rule has
   in the clause itself. these numbers are considered default values. the
   user can override these default values with his or hers own cf values. */
   /******** comment 60 **************/

float cf[101] /* confidence factor array */, dval[101] /* default array */;
float a,b,c,c1,fcf,x;

int d,ex,i;

main() {
for(i=1;i<101;i++) dval[i]=1; /* initialize d array, a cf=1 */
/*********** comment 170 ***********/
/********** default values ***********/
/*********** comment 190 ***********/
dval[1]=0.6;
dval[2]=0.3;
/* the default values are transferred to the confidence factor array
   at the start of the program */
/*********** comment 230 ***********/
for(i=1;i<101;i++) cf[i]=dval[i];
/*********** comment 250 ***********/
/********* instantiate the variables ********/
printf("ENTER ONE VALUE FOR INSTANTIATING A VARIABLE FOLLOWED BY \n");
printf("A COMMA, THEN OPTIONALLY FOLLOWED BY A CERTAINTY FACTOR \n");
printf("(CF) VALUE. IF YOU DO NOT PROVIDE A CF ENTER A '0' AND \n");
printf("THEN THE DEFAULT VALUE WILL BE USED \n");
/* rule 1 will use the first 3 cf elements */
printf("VARIABLE A IS ? ");
/*********** comment 320 ***********/
scanf("%f,%f",&a,&c1);
fflush(stdin);
/*********** comment 330 ***********/
if(c1 != 0) cf[1]=c1;
printf("VARIABLE B IS ? ");
/*********** comment 340 ***********/
scanf("%f,%f",&b,&c1);
fflush(stdin);
/*********** comment 350 ***********/
if(c1 != 0) cf[2]=c1;
printf("VARIABLE C IS ? ");
/*********** comment 360 ***********/
scanf("%f,%f",&c,&c1);
fflush(stdin);
/*********** comment 370 ***********/
if(c1 != 0) cf[3]=c1;
/* execute flag if ex=1 then execute the then part and cf */
ex=0;
if((a==2.0) && (b==3.0) && (c==5.0)) ex=1;
if(ex != 0) {
/*********** comment 400 ***********/
/* execute rule */
 d=5;
 printf("RULE EXECUTED D=%d\n",d);
/*********** comment 450 *********/
 x=cf[1];
/*********** comment 430 *********/
/* calculate cf for rule */
/* cf=(minimum c[1],c[2],c[3]) * .4 */
 printf("CF[1]= %f  CF[2]= %f  CF[3]= %f\n",cf[1],cf[2],cf[3]);
 if(cf[2]<x) x=cf[2];
 if(cf[3]<x) x=cf[3];
 fcf=x * 0.4;
 printf("CF IS %f",fcf); }
 else printf("**** RULE DID NOT FIRE");
/*********** comment 500 ********/
}
```

Sample Runs

```
ENTER ONE VALUE FOR INSTANTIATING A VARIABLE FOLLOWED BY A COMMA
THEN OPTIONALLY FOLLOWED BY A CERTAINTY FACTOR (CF) VALUE. IF
YOU DO NOT PROVIDE A CF, ENTER A 0 AND THEN THE DEFAULT VALUE
WILL BE USED
VARIABLE A IS ? 2,0
VARIABLE B IS ? 3,0
VARIABLE C IS ? 5,0
RULE EXECUTED D= 5
CF(1) = .6  CF(2) = .3  CF(3) = 1
CF IS .12
Break in 500
Ok
ENTER ONE VALUE FOR INSTANTIATING A VARIABLE FOLLOWED BY A COMMA
THEN OPTIONALLY FOLLOWED BY A CERTAINTY FACTOR (CF) VALUE. IF
YOU DO NOT PROVIDE A CF, ENTER A 0 AND THEN THE DEFAULT VALUE
WILL BE USED
VARIABLE A IS ? 2,.4
VARIABLE B IS ? 3,.6
VARIABLE C IS ? 5,0
RULE EXECUTED D= 5
CF(1) = .4  CF(2) = .6  CF(3) = .6
CF IS .16

ENTER ONE VALUE FOR INSTANTIATING A VARIABLE FOLLOWED BY A COMMA
THEN OPTIONALLY FOLLOWED BY A CERTAINTY FACTOR (CF) VALUE. IF
YOU DO NOT PROVIDE A CF, ENTER A 0 AND THEN THE DEFAULT VALUE
WILL BE USED
VARIABLE A IS ? 2,0
VARIABLE B IS ? 4,0
VARIABLE C IS ? 3,0
**** RULE DID NOT FIRE
```

16

Automated Learning

There are many ways a person can learn. One way is being told a fact directly, another is learning by example. If we tell a child that he may get burned by touching a hot stove, the child may not automatically infer that by touching *anything* hot he will get burned. Another way of teaching a child not to touch a hot stove is to tell him that the general rule that touching anything hot will cause a burn.

Whatever method is used to learn something, an individual may modify what was previously thought to be as a result of the newly acquired knowledge. For example, if a child didn't already infer that anything hot may burn her and then puts her hand in hot water, she may finally get the point. This modification process occurs via something known as "feedback." A diagram of this feedback structure is shown in Figure 16-1. The feedback path and an input experience both contribute to the learning process by referring to knowledge that has already been learned. A person's knowledge can thereby be modified by each learning experience.

We do the same with a "learning" computer program. We first develop an algorithm for storing a set of facts and making inferences. The conclusions are mixed in the feedback portion of the program with new inputs to modify the facts. A learning system example which we will consider will operate on the following premise:

> The learning system will only modify what it has learned if what has been learned is now thought to be wrong.

The premise is similar to what human beings do automatically. After all, isn't it true that people usually don't modify their thinking unless they know or sense that it is wrong?

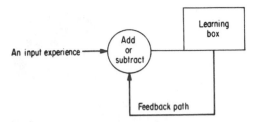

Figure 16-1   Learning mechanism.

Example of a Learning System

Let us consider a system that must learn to tell the difference between a car and tank. A few features that differentiate between a car and tank are shown in Figure 16-2. We can read the diagram in the figure as

The tank has a cannon and a hatch.

The car has a door and wheels.

Both the tank and car have a body.

The computer learning program that we will present can only learn to tell the difference between two objects, but the principles can be expanded to consider more than two objects.

The program has three lists: list 1 to hold the attributes of the car it will learn about; list 2 to hold the attributes of the tank it will learn

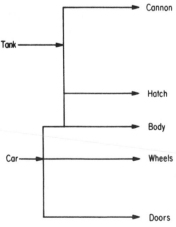

Figure 16-2   Differentiating features.

about; and the common list to contain those attributes that are common to both.

Note that the two objects could have been almost anything, such as rain or no rain in a weather forecasting system. The program functions in the same way no matter what objects are being compared.

The learning program will first ask the user to name the two objects. The names of the objects are entered by the following computer interaction:

```
ENTER OBJECT 1 NAME ?  CAR
ENTER OBJECT 2 NAME ?  TANK
```

The program will then assume you are observing one of the objects and are ready to enter its attributes. It will do this by the following dialogue:

```
INPUT ANY OBJECT'S ATTRIBUTES—WHEN FINISHED TYPE RETURN
ENTER ATTRIBUTE 1 ?  CANNON
ENTER ATTRIBUTE 2 ?  HATCH
ENTER ATTRIBUTE 3 ?  BODY
ENTER ATTRIBUTE 4 ?  ENTER key
```

The program will first compare the attributes entered at the computer console with the attributes in list 1, the car list. Since initially there are no attributes in that list because the program hasn't learned anything yet about a car, a score of 0 is given, indicating that no attributes match. For the same reason list 2, the tank list, produces a score of 0. Whenever there is a tie score, the computer program will guess that the attributes belong to the name assigned to list 1. In the learning system the user responds no to the question because it is really a tank that was described, not a car. Since the guess is wrong, the feedback mechanism goes into action. We have just told the system that the input attributes do not apply to a car, so no attributes can be placed on the car list, which is list 1. No attributes can be placed on the common list, either, so the three attributes are placed on list 2, the tank list. If there *had* been any attributes entered that matched attributes on list 1, they would have been removed and placed in the common list. This is done automatically because the system assumed that an attribute belonging to both objects belongs on the common list.

After all these maneuvers are complete, the three lists look like this:

List 1 (car)	List 2 (tank)	List 3 (common)
	CANNON	
	HATCH	
	BODY	

Why not design the system to place the attributes in the right list in the first place and avoid all these maneuvers? Of course that could be done, but that's the difference between being told something and learning it for oneself. This way, our system thinks like a person, not like a machine, and has to figure out where to put the attributes.

We now enter another set of attributes, for the object car:

```
INPUT ANY OBJECT'S ATTRIBUTES-WHEN FINISHED TYPE RETURN
ENTER ATTRIBUTE 1 ?  DOORS
ENTER ATTRIBUTE 2 ?  WHEELS
ENTER ATTRIBUTE 3 ?  BODY
ENTER ATTRIBUTE 4 ?  ENTER key
```

The program will first compare the attributes entered with the attributes in list 1, the car list. Since there is still nothing on the car list, it will still have a score of 0. But, when compared to list 2, the tank list, we see there is one match, namely, the attribute BODY. This gives the tank list a score of 1 and therefore leads the program to guess tank. The user will respond to the system question:

```
IS THE SYSTEM A TANK ?  NO
```

We have another wrong guess, and again the feedback mechanism is called into play. The system attempts to see if any of these attributes—DOORS, WHEELS, BODY—are on the tank list. Since there is one—the BODY attribute—the program will place it on list 3, the common list (since it is not already there). It has again assumed that any attribute belonging to both objects should be on the common list. Now the input list, less any attributes moved to the common list, is placed on list 1, the car list. The lists now look like this:

List 1 (car)	List 2 (tank)	List 3 (common)
DOOR	CANNON	BODY
WHEELS	HATCH	

If we now provide another set of inputs, the program will be able to guess correctly. The system has "learned," via input attributes and feedback, the difference between a car and tank. Let's summarize how this was done:

1. The system only alters itself when it makes a wrong guess. This is its feedback mechanism.

2. The system compares the input attributes with attributes for the items it is trying to identify and chooses the most likely. This is done via a score and is called its inference mechanism.

Programming Applications

Let's examine a program, written in C, which applies the LEARNING concepts of this chapter.

Program Explanation

In Listing 16-1 the three arrays, list 1 (L1), list 2 (L2), and the common list (LC), are initialized to "empty" in comments 30 through 50. The objects are named in comments 60 and 70. The user describes the attributes of an unnamed object in comments 90 through 130. The learning program attempts to identify the object belonging to those attributes in comments 180 through 220. It does this by developing a score. The score is developed by comparing the attributes that have been input with those assigned to each object. The object with the highest score is guessed as the object with the attributes supplied by the user. This is done in comment 240. In case of tie, object 1 is guessed. If the guess is correct, the attributes that are not already in the list of the object or the common list are entered into the list of the object. But first we move attributes from the other list into the common list as shown in comments 330 through 410 for object 1 and 780 through 860 for object 2. The rest of the operation occurs in comments 420 through 560 for object 1 and 920 through 990 for object 2.

Program Listing

Listing 16-1 is followed by sample runs.

Listing 16-1 Learning program.

```
#include <stdio.h>

/* program to guess object from the attributes
   initialization section for
   list of object 1 (01)
   list of object 2 (02)
   list of object common (1c)
   temporary attribute buffer t */

char lc[11][11], o1[11][11], o2[11][11], t[12][11], yorn[11];
char ob1[11], ob2[11];

int blank,i,k,l,s1,s2;

void print_lists();

main() {
for(i=1;i<11;i++) {
/******** comment 30 *******/
 strcpy(o1[i],"");
 strcpy(o2[i],"");
 strcpy(lc[i],"");
/********* comment 50 *******/ }
printf("ENTER OBJECT 1 NAME? ");
/******** comment 60 ********/
gets(ob1);
printf("ENTER OBJECT 2 NAME? ");
/******* comment 70 **********/
gets(ob2);
b80: printf("INPUT ANY OBJECT'S ATTRIBUTES-WHEN FINISHED TYPE RETURN\n");
/******** comment 90 *********/
for(i=1;i<12;i++) strcpy(t[i],"");
blank=0;
i=1;
while(blank==0 && i<=11) {
 printf("ENTER ATTRIBUTE %d ? ",i);
 gets(t[i]);
 if(strcmp(t[i],"") == 0) blank=1;
  else i++; }
/********* comment 130 ***********/
/* number of attributes is one less since a null was included */
l=i-1;
/* compare the attributes to object list 1 and 2
   initially set score for object 1 and object 2 to 0 */
/********* comment 180 *********/
s1=0;
s2=0;
for(i=1;i<l+1;i++)
 for(k=1;k<11;k++) {
  if(strcmp(o1[k],t[i]) == 0) s1++;
  if(strcmp(o2[k],t[i]) == 0) s2++;
 }
/******** comment 220 **********/
/* guess object 2 only if score 2 is greater than score 1 */
/******** comment 240 ***********/
if(s1 >= s2) {
 printf("OBJECT IS %s\n",ob1);
 printf("IS THAT CORRECT...Y OR N? ");
 gets(yorn);
 if(strcmp(yorn,"N") != 0) {
/* place each attribute of the temporary attribute buffer that is not
   in the common list and not in the object list 1...into list 1 move
   the attributes from list 2 into the common list that are equal to
   both i.e., common */
/******** comment 330 **********/
b330: for(i=1;i<l+1;i++)
       for(k=1;k<11;k++)
        if(strcmp(t[i],o2[k]) == 0)
         /* move the attribute from list 2 to the common list */
         for(l=1;l<11;l++)
          if(strcmp(lc[l],"") == 0) {
           strcpy(lc[l],o2[k]);
           strcpy(o2[k],"");
           strcpy(t[i],""); }
```

```
/******** comment 410 *********/
        for(i=1;i<1+1;i++) {
        /* temporary buffer pointer */
/******** comment 420 **********/
        /* common list pointer and object 1 list pointer */
            k=1;
            while(strcmp(t[i],lc[k]) != 0 && strcmp(t[i],o1[k]) != 0 && k<=10)
            k++;
            if(k > 10) {
            /* place variable into list 1 which is not in the lists
               search for the 1st empty space and place it there */
            k=1;
            while(strcmp(o1[k],"") && k<=10) k++;
            if(strcmp(t[i],"") != 0)
              if(strcmp(o1[k],"") == 0) strcpy(o1[k],t[i]); }
            } /* next attribute */
        print_lists(); /* print all lists */
        goto b80; /* anymore attributes */
/******** comment 560 *********/
    }
    }
    else {
    printf("OBJECT IS %s\n",ob2);
    printf("IS THAT CORRECT...Y OR N? ");
    gets(yorn);
    if(strcmp(yorn,"N") == 0) goto b330; }
/* place each attribute of the temporary attribute buffer
   that is not in the common list and not in the object
   list 2...into list 2. move that attributes from list 1
   into the common list that are equal to both i.e., common */
/******** comment 780 ***********/
    for(i=1;i<1+1;i++)
     for(k=1;k<11;k++)
      if(strcmp(t[i],o1[k]) == 0)
      /* move that attribute from list 1 to the common list */
       for(l=1;l<11;l++)
        if(strcmp(lc[l],"") == 0) {
         strcpy(lc[l],o1[k]);
         strcpy(o1[k],"");
         strcpy(t[i],""); }
/******** comment 860 *********/
    for(i=1;i<1+1;i++) {
    /* temporary buffer pointer */
/******** comment 920 *******/
    /* common list pointer and object 2 list */
    k=1;
    while(strcmp(t[i],lc[k]) != 0 && strcmp(t[i],o2[k]) != 0 && k<=10) {
     /* is it the common list */
     /* is it in object 2 list */
     k++; }
    if(k>10) {
     /* place variable into list 2 which is not in the above lists
        search for the first empty space and place it there */
     k=1;
     while(strcmp(o2[k],"") != 0 && k<=10) k++;
      if(strcmp(t[i],"") != 0)
       if(strcmp(o2[k],"") == 0) strcpy(o2[k],t[i]); }
     /* next attribute */
     }
     /******* comment 990 ***********/
     print_lists();
     /* anymore attributes */
     goto b80;
}

void print_lists() {
/* routine to print all lists */
printf("%s\t%s\tCOMMON LIST\n",ob1,ob2);
for(i=1;i<11;i++) printf("%s\t%s\t%s\n",o1[i],o2[i],lc[i]);
}
```

Sample Run

```
ENTER OBJECT 1 NAME ? CAR
ENTER OBJECT 2 NAME ? TANK
INPUT ANY OBJECT'S ATTRIBUTES-WHEN FINISHED TYPE RETURN
ENTER ATTRIBUTE 1 ? CANNON
ENTER ATTRIBUTE 2 ? HATCH
ENTER ATTRIBUTE 3 ? BODY
ENTER ATTRIBUTE 4 ?
OBJECT IS A CAR
IS THAT CORRECT...Y or N ? N
CAR     TANK       COMMON LIST
        CANNON
        HATCH
        BODY

INPUT ANY OBJECT'S ATTRIBUTES-WHEN FINISHED TYPE RETURN
ENTER ATTRIBUTE 1 ? BODY
ENTER ATTRIBUTE 2 ? WHEELS
ENTER ATTRIBUTE 3 ? DOOR
ENTER ATTRIBUTE 4 ?
OBJECT IS A TANK
IS THAT CORRECT...Y or N ? N
CAR       TANK      COMMON LIST
WHEELS    CANNON    BODY
DOOR      HATCH
INPUT ANY OBJECT'S ATTRIBUTES-WHEN FINISHED TYPE RETURN
ENTER ATTRIBUTE 1 ? BODY
ENTER ATTRIBUTE 2 ? DOOR
ENTER ATTRIBUTE 3 ?
OBJECT IS A CAR
IS THAT CORRECT...Y or N ? Y
CAR       TANK      COMMON LIST
WHEELS    CANNON    BODY
DOOR      HATCH
```

Languages Used in
Artificial Intelligence

PROLOG and LISP are two languages that are used to implement expert systems. Both are introduced in a very simple way in this section.

Using PROLOG to Design Expert Systems

PROLOG is short for Programming in Logic. It is a computer language that was created especially for answering questions about a knowledge base that consists of rules and facts. PROLOG has backward chaining built right in and also utilizes another technique known as "backtracking." Backward chaining, as you know, is a technique in which a conclusion or consequence is assumed to be true, and then a knowledge base of rules and facts is examined to see if it supports the assumption. If the assumption turns out *not* to be correct, backtracking is used to get rid of the original assumption and replace it with a new one.

Conceptual Example

In order to understand PROLOG's concepts, let's first consider a suitable program that we will try to solve with a pencil and paper technique. The solution to this problem will demonstrate the concepts of backward chaining in conjunction with backtracking.

Consider the following rule:

> IF a male named X with mother named M is in the room AND a female named Y with mother named M is in the room,
> THEN the male X and female Y are brother and sister.

This rule presents a set of conditions for determining if a brother and a sister are in the same room. Before we can solve this problem, we need a set of supporting facts. These facts take the form of two lists: one contains all the males in the room and their mothers, and the other list contains all the females in the same room and their mothers. By comparing the two lists for a common mother's name, we can identify those males and females that have the same mother. Having satisfied this condition, we can then invoke the rule to conclude that a brother and sister are in the same room. Let's see how this is implemented.

Consider the two facts tables that we have compiled.

Male Facts List		Female Facts List	
Male	Mother	Female	Mother
Daniel	Diane	Ann	Lori
Larry	Lori	Lauren	Shirley
Michael	Bonnie	Susan	Bonnie
Peter	Jane		

By just scanning both lists, you can select the following possible brother and sister pairs:

Larry with Ann (mother Lori)

Michael with Susan (mother Bonnie)

By using a pencil and paper, we can imitate PROLOG in arriving at these answers.

First assume that the THEN part of the rule is true, then assume there actually is male X and female Y who are brother and sister. We have started backward chaining by assuming this conclusion is true. We must now try to support this conclusion by seeing if each of the rule's conditions is true. The first condition is "a male X with mother named M is in the room." This is our first goal, to find a male named X with mother M in the male facts list. This is easily satisfied with the first name on top of the list, which is

Daniel with mother Diane

The value X would be instantiated to DANIEL and the mother M would be instantiated to DIANE, as follows

X = Daniel

M = Diane

We must now satisfy the second condition, which is "a female named Y with a mother named M in the room." Since M is instantiated to DIANE, we must find a female Y with a mother named DIANE in the female facts list:

Male Facts List		Female Facts List	
Male	Mother	Female	Mother
Daniel	Diane	Ann	Lori
		Lauren	Shirley
		Susan	Bonnie

There is none. We must backtrack to the first condition again and try to find another male X and mother M that would meet the condition. This means resuming the search of the male facts list. The male after Daniel is

Larry with mother Lori

The value X would now be instantiated to LARRY and mother M to LORI:

X = LARRY
M = LORI

We must now satisfy the second condition again by finding a female Y with mother Lori in the female facts list:

Male Facts List		Female Facts List	
Male	Mother	Female	Mother
Daniel	Diane	Ann	Lori
Larry	Lori	Lauren	Shirley
		Susan	Bonnie

Scanning the female facts list, we see that the first entry, Ann, has the same mother, Lori. Therefore

Y = ANN

We can invoke the THEN part and arrive at the conclusion that

X = LARRY AND
Y = ANN

are brother and sister.

Review

Let's examine what we have done so we can solidify the concepts:

1. We took the THEN part of the rule as a conclusion and tried to see if each condition clause supported this conclusion.
2. Our first goal was to see if the first condition was true.
3. Scanning the facts list, we were able to reach our goal of making the first condition true. This dictated the values of the variables in the first condition.
4. Our next goal was to see if the second condition was true.
5. Scanning the facts list, we couldn't reach our goal.
6. We now backtracked to see if we could reach a goal of making the first condition true again with a *new* set of X and Y facts. We did.
7. With the new values of X and Y we tried to reach our goal of making the second condition true and succeeded.
8. We now had instantiated the variables in the THEN part.

Converting Rules to PROLOG

What we have done is only to imitate PROLOG. In reality PROLOG does all that searching for you using backward chaining and backtracking automatically. We are now ready to take a set of knowledge base rules and convert it to a set of PROLOG rules.

There is a one to one corespondence between the format of a PROLOG rule and the rules in the knowledge base. Consider the following knowledge base rule from the example used in Chapter 6:

```
IF DEGREE = NO
THEN POSITION = NO
```

A PROLOG rule that says exactly the same thing is:

```
position(no):-write('DEGREE'), read(DEGREE), DEGREE=no.
```

The "write" and "read" parts of the rule are methods for obtaining a value for the variable DEGREE. The phrase write('DEGREE') will cause DEGREE to be printed on the user's terminal as a prompt to the user to enter whether the applicant has a degree. The phrase read (DEGREE) will cause the value entered by the user to be assigned to DEGREE. The next phrase, DEGREE = no, is true if the user entered no. Using this rule as an example, here are some of the properties and syntax of PROLOG:

1. The entire PROLOG rule, position(no):-write('DEGREE'), read(DE-GREE), DEGREE = no, is called a "clause." In PROLOG, there are two types of clauses: rule clauses and fact clauses. (We will discuss fact clauses later.) The clause above is a rule clause.

2. The part of the PROLOG clause, which is equivalent to the THEN part of position(no), is written to the left of the :- and is called the "head" of the rule.

3. The IF part, which is write('DEGREE'), read(DEGREE), DE-GREE = no, is written to the right of the :- and is called the "body" of the clause.

4. The body contains a number of items separated by commas. Each of these items is called a goal. (The commas mean AND.) The body of our PROLOG clause can therefore be read as
    write ('DEGREE') AND
    read (DEGREE) AND
    DEGREE = no,
   where write('DEGREE'), read(DEGREE), and DEGREE = no are each goals.

5. The entire clause is ended with a period.

6. The word preceding a parenthesis is called a "predicate." The predicates in this example are position, write, and read. Predicate words always begin with lowercase letters.

7. Each word appearing within the parentheses of a predicate is called an "argument." The argument for position(no) is no and position is the predicate. Arguments can be variables as well as values. Variable words begin with capital letters; values begin with lowercase letters. The argument word no is a value since it begins with a lowercase n.

8. The symbol :- is read as IF. The PROLOG clause qualify(yes):-degree(yes) is read as "qualify is yes if degree is yes."

Let's see how the IF-THEN rules that we used in the chapter on backward chaining for the problem of whether to offer a job to an applicant are converted to PROLOG rules. The IF-THEN rules are

    10   IF DEGREE = NO
         THEN POSITION = NO

20   IF DEGREE = YES
    THEN QUALIFY = YES

30   IF DEGREE = YES AND DISCOVERY = YES
    THEN POSITION = RESEARCH

40   IF QUALIFY = YES AND AVERAGE < 3.5 AND
    EXPERIENCE > 2
    THEN POSITION = SERVICE ENGINEERING

50   IF QUALIFY = YES AND AVERAGE < 3.5 AND
    EXPERIENCE < 2
    THEN POSITION = NO

60   IF QUALIFY = YES AND AVERAGE >= 3.5
    THEN POSITION = PRODUCT ENGINEERING

The equivalent PROLOG rules are

```
/*10*/  position(no):-write('DEGREE'), read(DEGREE), DEGREE=no.
/*20*/  qualify(yes):-write('DEGREE'), read(DEGREE), DEGREE=yes.
/*30*/  position(research):-write('DEGREE'), read(DEGREE), DEGREE=yes,
        write('DISCOVERY'), read(DISCOVERY), DISCOVERY=yes.
/*40*/  position(service engineering):-qualify(yes), write('AVERAGE'),
        read(AVERAGE),AVERAGE<3.5, write('EXPERIENCE'),
        read(EXPERIENCE), EXPERIENCE>2.0.
/*50*/  position(no):-qualify(yes), write('AVERAGE'),
        read(AVERAGE),AVERAGE<3.5,write('EXPERIENCE'),
        read(EXPERIENCE), EXPERIENCE<2.0.
/*60*/  position(product engineering):-qualify(yes), write('AVERAGE'),
        read (AVERAGE),AVERAGE>=3.5.
```

The numbers to the left of the PROLOG statement are direct trans-
lations of the equivalent numbered IF-THEN rules. In PROLOG they
are enclosed between slashes and asterisks (/*10*/, /*20*/ . . . etc.) but
have no operational effect; PROLOG ignores them. These are known as
"comment statements" and appear as an aid to your understanding. In
this case, they are used to indicate which IF-THEN rules correspond to
the PROLOG statements.

Consider the "brother and sister in the same room" rule:

IF a male named X with mother M is in the room AND a female named
Y with mother M is in the room,
THEN the male and female are brother and sister.

Next we construct a knowledge base using this rule and the set of
facts of males, females, and mothers, as follows. These facts are taken
from the male and female fact lists.

```
/*1*/  brother-sister(X, Y, M):-male(X, M), female(Y, M).
/*2*/  male(daniel, diane)
/*3*/  male(larry, lori)
```

```
/*4*/  male(michael, bonnie)
/*5*/  male(peter, jane)
/*6*/  female(ann, lori)
/*7*/  female(lauren, shirley)
/*8*/  female(susan, bonnie)
```

The "brother-sister" predicate arguments stand for X = brother, Y = sister, and M = mother. The male predicate translates into "X is a male with mother M," and the female predicate, into "Y is a female with the same mother M."

Now we will show you an actual PROLOG-user dialogue to illustrate how PROLOG answers questions. When PROLOG issues a prompt, which is ?-, it allows the user to enter a question. In response to the prompt, you might enter the following question based upon our example:

```
?-brother-sister(X, Y, M)
```

PROLOG would first try to instantiate X and M in the first term of the first rule it came to which contains the goal male (X,M). The first fact in the knowledge base with male as a predicate is fact /*2*/, male(daniel,diane). PROLOG would assume, that is, instantiate, X = daniel and M = diane. It would then try to prove that the second term, female(Y,M), is true. Since M is already instantiated to diane, it would search the facts list for a fact containing the same mother, namely, female(Y, diane). Since facts /*6*/ to /*8*/ contain female as a predicate but do not contain diane in the second argument, female (Y, diane) is *not* true. Therefore, PROLOG backtracks. The system "uninstantiates" X and M and uses (X, M) to find new values for X and M. Fact /*3*/, male(larry, lori), causes PROLOG to instantiate X to larry and M to lori. PROLOG now tries to prove female(Y, lori) true. Scanning the facts, it finds /*6*/, female(ann, lori), which meets the requirements. Therefore, Y is instantiated to ann and PROLOG will print

```
?-X = larry
  Y = ann
  M = lori
```

PROLOG verifies that Larry and Ann are brother and sister because they both have Lori as their mother.

Summary

This chapter has introduced the reader to PROLOG and its two main features, backward chaining and backtracking.

Chapter

18

LISP

Introduction to LISP

LISP is short for List Processing. It is a computer language that is used in many applications of artificial intelligence. One of its major qualities is that it can manipulate lists easily. A list could be the words in a sentence, the names of people on a job, or any sequence of words arranged in any order. The parts of a list can be removed from context one at a time so that various operations can be performed on them.

In this chapter we will acquaint you with some of the fundamentals of LISP—just enough to whet your appetite to do advanced reading.

Function Evaluation

LISP evaluates functions. A function is written in prefix format, meaning that the function comes first, and is enclosed with a left parenthesis, (, and a right parenthesis,). For example, + is a function that adds numbers, which are its arguments. If the user constructs the following LISP statement

```
(+  4 2)
```

the system will respond with 6. Prefix format requires us to write the + first, followed by the arguments. Another function, −, subtracts numbers, as in the example

```
(−  5 2)
```

with the result 3. The value 3 is automatically returned by the system. In this example, the user enters

```
(+ (- 5 2) 4)
```

and LISP returns

```
7
```

The LISP system first evaluates the function within the inner parentheses

```
(- 5 2)
```

and returns 3. The system replaces the inner parentheses function with 3 and next evaluates

```
(+ 3 4)
```

and returns 7.

The multiplication and maximum functions are as follows. The user enters

```
(* 5 4)
```

and LISP returns

```
20
```

The user enters

```
(MAX 5 9 2)
```

and LISP returns

```
9
```

The important points to remember are

1. Functions are written in prefix notation.
2. Functions are enclosed in parentheses.

Lists

A list is a set of items. We call the items in the list, "members" of the list. For example, we could construct a list of all people owing us money. This list would consist of names of people such as

`'(BOB TOM MAY SUE)`

You should note that a list is enclosed in parentheses, just as a function is. Another example of a list are the items on a desk:

`'(PENCIL PEN PAPER CLOCK PAPER-CLIP)`

You will note that there can be *no* embedded blanks in a member's name. Therefore, the name PAPER-CLIP has a connecting hyphen. A space is used only to separate the names of the members of the list.

We could also have lists of numbers. These could be the number of people in each department of a company, such as

`'(20 10 30)`

We could also have a list of lists. For example, you may want a list of all people you know in three different towns:

`'((BOB LORI JANE) (TOM HARRY) (JOHN DAVID))`

Notice the two left parentheses at the start. The first one designates a list of something. Since that something is also a list, this inner list must also start with a parenthesis. In other words, the members of this list are lists.

We hope you noticed the single quotation mark at the start of each list. Let's examine why this single quotation mark must precede each list. Suppose we had the following list:

`'(GOTO YOUR HOME)`

If there was no quotation mark in front of the parenthesis, it would have all the characteristics of a function, whose concepts we just discussed. Remember, functions are written in prefix form in which the first symbol at the left parenthesis is the function name. Without the quotation mark, LISP would then interpret GOTO as a function. What the quotation mark does is tell LISP to accept whatever follows as is and not evaluate it in any way. GOTO would then be correctly interpreted as the first member of a list.

List Functions

List functions perform "operations" on lists. Some important functions are CAR, CDR, CONS, and APPEND.

CAR removes the first member of a list. The user enters

```
(CAR '(A B C))
```

and LISP returns the first member

```
A
```

In the next example, (1 2) is the first member and also happens to be a list. The user enters

```
(CAR '((1 2) A B))
```

and LISP returns

```
(1 2)
```

CDR returns the remainder of a list *after* the first member is removed. The user enters

```
(CDR '(A B C))
```

and LISP returns

```
(B C)
```

This is a list comprising every member of the original after the first member is removed. The user enters

```
(CDR '((A B) (C D)))
```

and LISP returns

```
((C D))
```

where the first member (A B) is removed, leaving the list (C D) as the only member.

CONS adds a member to the beginning of a list. The user enters

```
(CONS 'K '(J K L))
```

and LISP returns

(K J K L)

The user enters

(CONS '(A B) '(J K L))

and LISP returns

((A B) J K L)

APPEND joins two lists together, that is, makes them one list. The user enters

(APPEND '(A B) '(J K L))

and LISP returns

(A B J K L)

LISP provides many more functions that we won't discuss here; our objective is to lay the groundwork for your understanding of how LISP operates.

Predicates or Testing Functions

Remember that a conditional clause contained in the IF part of an IF-THEN rule can be either true or false. If it is true, the THEN part is invoked. If FALSE, it is not. LISP has a set of functions that perform tests and then tell us if the results of the tests are true or false. In LISP, true is designated by T and false by NIL. Functions that perform a test and return T or NIL are called "predicates."

Let's examine some predicate functions. The EQUAL predicate returns a T if its arguments are the same. For example, the user enters

(EQUAL 8 8)

and LISP returns

T

The user enters

(EQUAL 3 2)

and LISP returns

```
NIL
```

The user enters

```
(EQUAL '(1 2 A) '(1 2 A))
```

and LISP returns

```
T
```

The > symbol checks arguments to see if each succeeding argument is greater than the next one. For example, the user enters

```
(> 5 2 1)
```

and LISP returns

```
T
```

The user enters

```
(> 1 3 2)
```

and LISP returns

```
NIL
```

Now here's one

```
(> 5 4 (+ 1 2))
```

which LISP first evaluates to

```
(> 5 4 3)
```

and then returns

```
T
```

Variable Assignments

The next concept we should understand is how LISP instantiates variables. The value of a variable can be assigned by the following LISP function:

```
(SETQ X Y)
```

where X is instantiated to the value of Y. For example, the user enters

```
(SETQ X 25)
```

and LISP returns

25

The variable X will be instantiated to the value 25. Here is another example:

```
(SETQ X '(A B C))
```

will instantiate X to the list (A B C).

IF-THEN Rules through the Condition Function

The condition (COND) function allows us to test a set of conditions and then do something if a condition is T. This sounds like an IF-THEN statement because it is very close to one. As an example, consider the following:

```
(COND ((EQUAL 5 2) (SETQ X 5)))
```

The condition, or IF part, of the COND statement is (EQUAL 5 2). The THEN part is (SETQ X 5). Since (EQUAL 5 2) is a NIL because 5 does not equal 2, we cannot invoke the THEN part, which is (SETQ X 5). But consider

```
(COND ((EQUAL 3 3) (SETQ X 5)))
```

We see that (EQUAL 3 3) returns a T and therefore will cause (SETQ X 5) to be invoked, resulting in X being instantiated to 5. Let's examine two more COND statements:

```
(COND((EQUAL Y 3) (SETQ X 5)))
(COND((GREATERP 4 Z) (SETQ P 3)))
```

The first statement is translated as follows: IF Y has a value 3, THEN instantiate X to 5. The second statement says IF 4 is greater than Z, THEN instantiate P to 3.

For our examples, the COND statement consists of an IF part and a THEN part, that is

```
(COND((< IF part >)(< THEN part >)))
```

In general, the COND function can be expanded to include many IF-THEN parts.

New Functions

New functions are defined in LISP with the DEFUN function. An example of how this works is

```
(DEFUN ADD-DIF (X Y Z)
  (+ Z (- X Y)))
```

The first symbol after the DEFUN is the name of the function. In our example, the name of the function is ADD-DIF. The items in parentheses after the function name are the variables that will be used in the function evaluation part. In this case the variables are X, Y, and Z. The evaluation part is

```
(+ Z (- X Y))
```

This should look somewhat familiar because we discussed this type of example earlier in the chapter. What we do to evaluate the function is subtract Y from X and then add the result to Z. Let's see how this works. If we typed the procedure ADD-DIF with

```
(ADD-DIF 5 4 6)
```

we would get 7. The function first instantiates X to 5, Y to 4, and Z to 6 and then subtracts 4 from 5, leaving 1. We would then add 1 to 6 giving us 7.

Before we continue, let us give an example of the PRINT function. If we entered

```
(PRINT'EXAMPLE)
```

we would get the following lines from LISP

```
EXAMPLE
EXAMPLE
```

It is not necessary here to understand why EXAMPLE prints twice. The following new function

```
(DEFUN IF-THEN (X)
  (COND((EQUAL X 3)(PRINT'EXAMPLE))))
```

will cause the PRINT to take place if X equals 3. That is, the user enters

```
(IF-THEN 3)
```

and LISP returns

```
EXAMPLE
EXAMPLE
```

But if the user enters

```
(IF-THEN 4)
```

LISP returns

```
NIL
```

The reason for this is that the condition part of the COND statement is (EQUAL X 3). If this is T, the THEN part, (PRINT'EXAMPLE) is invoked. In the first example, (IF-THEN 3) results in the first part of the COND to be (EQUAL 3 3) returning a T. Therefore COND invokes the PRINT function. But the next example (IF-THEN 4) results in the first part of the COND to be (EQUAL 4 3) which returns a NIL.

Summary

Let us now summarize the important concepts.

1. We have shown you the concepts of functions and the role of parentheses in defining them.
2. We have discussed the concepts of a list.

We recommend that you try these concepts on one of the many LISP programs for your computer.

Artificial Neural Networks

Neural networks learn and provide self-improvement via internal feedback structures. They acquire knowledge that is beyond the scope of experts. Simple examples will provide you with basic concepts enabling you to design your own neural network.

19

Neural Networks Overview

Creating an artificial intelligence system that has the flexibility, creativity, and learning ability of the human biological system is a major goal in artificial intelligence research. The attempt to imitate this human process has been marked in history by periods of feverish activity, followed by waning interest, and culminating today with the most intensely directed studies ever undertaken by countries, corporations, and universities. During these periods of research, many models of our intelligent biological system have appeared. Each was designed to function the way our brain and nervous system function. The intelligent biological model that concerns this discussion is called the "artificial neural system model." This model uses a representation of a single human neuron and the interactions between neurons as its basis.

Neural Systems and Expert Systems

In classical artificial intelligence, experts are used to supplying their own tested methods and knowledge to give the computer the basis for appropriate answers for a specific domain. A system constructed by the contribution of each expert is called an "expert system." If we can't find new expertise, the domain knowledge and methods for handling this knowledge stop growing (Figure 19-1). On the other hand, a neural system learns directly by interacting with the domain. It does not need any expert knowledge about the domain. Given enough time and experience or training, the neural system will learn everything about the domain; it will be able to learn what is presently not known by any of the experts (Figure 19-2).

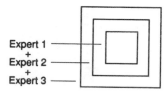

**Figure 19-1   The expert system
equals the sum of the experts.**

The Unification of Learning Theory

Since the human neural systems learn and are able to eliminate misconceptions, a goal of the artificial intelligence practitioner is to understand exactly how this is done. The understanding will lead to the implementation of an artificial neural system. The implementation leads us to the second goal of extracting domain knowledge that is beyond our present comprehension.

There are many methods we use in order to learn. These methods depend on the subject matter (domain) we are learning about. If we are learning to drive a car, we learn by being instructed. We are told to stop at a red light and proceed at a green light. If the domain is image recognition, we learn by a combination of instruction and discovery. We are told the name of a shape, but we discover its features and the differences between it and other shapes. Learning by direct instruction, learning by discovery, and other learning methods appear on the surface to be quite different from one another in their approach to learning. One of the goals of an artificial biological system is to unify these different learning approaches under one methodology.

In the Beginning

The quest to understand and simulate the human neural system began centuries ago. However, the first real model of a single nerve cell that could be simulated by computer hardware or software was developed only 45 years ago by McCulloch and Pitts. This model is appropriately known as the McCulloch-Pitts neuron and is illustrated in Figure 19-3.

**Figure 19-2   The neural system
uses a learning method to acquire
domain knowledge.**

Figure 19-3   A simple McCulloch-Pitts neuron model.

The human neuron system consists of networks of highly intercon-nected neurons, each of which performs a discrete computation at any given moment. The results of the computations are transmitted to other neurons along a neural pathway. A single neuron can send the results to as many as 10,000 other neurons as signals to the inputs of the other neurons in the form of voltages. These signals can either inhibit the other neurons from sending signals in turn or excite them into sending signals to other neurons along the pathways. The McCulloch-Pitts neu-ron accepts inhibiting input signals as negative values and excitory signals as positive values. It then sums the positive and negative values. If the sum exceeds a value called the "threshold level," the neuron can then send the signal to other neurons to which it is connected. The process of exceeding a threshold and sending a signal is called "firing."

In 1949, the neurobiologist Hebb formulated methods for determining how well one neuron is connected to another. Since the connection between neurons carries a signal, the quality of the connection becomes important: a weak connection might degrade the signal while a strong connection can enhance it. The quality of the connection is referred to as its strength, as illustrated in Figure 19-4. Hebb formulated a procedure for assigning a strength value to the connection, and in the 1980s, D. Ackley, G. Hinton, T. Senjnowski, J. Hopfield, D. Tank, and others provided further understanding of the computing method and connec-tionist methods of the neural system as learning and modifications occur.

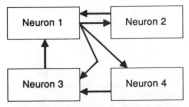

Figure 19-4   Neurons are connected to each other. Hebb formulated a method for determining the strength of the con-nection.

Design Philosophy of an Artificial Neural System

The human neural system consists of a set of input neurons (sensors), connected to a vast array of computing neurons (hidden neurons), which are in turn connected to a set of output neurons controlling the muscles (Figure 19-5). The sensors could be likened to the eyes seeing images, the ears hearing sounds, the nose smelling odors, or the skin feeling sensation. The output controls muscles that react to the sensors, and a portion of the hidden neurons could be located in the brain. Although we don't see them, there is an array of calculations being done by the hidden neurons. Similarly, an artificial neural system would have to contain electrical and mechanical sensors to provide inputs. These artificial sensors could be television cameras, microphones, or mechanical pressure sensors. The hidden neurons could be represented by McCulloch-Pitts neurons interconnected with connection strengths calculated by using Hebb's theories. The muscles could be a variety of output devices such as robot arms and feet, displays, valves, or various control devices.

Training the System

When the human neural system sees an object, some of the eye sensors are activated, as in Figure 19-6. These sensors fire, sending signals to the hidden neurons. According to Hebb's theory, neurons that fire during the same training session increase the connection strength between them. The same time the object appears, the appropriate connections have been strengthened, thus making it easier to provide information about that object. When another object appears before the same sensors, the connections for that object would initially not be strengthened. The neural system would have to be trained to recognize that object (Figure 19-7).

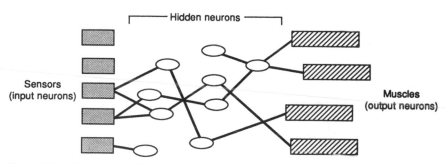

Figure 19-5   A human neural structure.

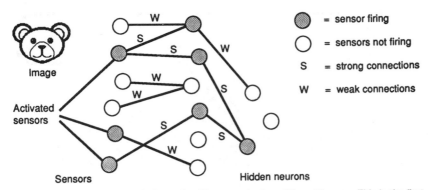

Figure 19-6   A human system being trained to recognize two different images. This is the first image.

Self-Modification

When the human neural system makes an incorrect guess, the system modifies itself so that a correct guess is made under the same circumstances the next time. The artificial neural system must do the same. Determining the methodology for effecting this is one of the major goals of artificial intelligence researchers. They must build this process into their attempts to create a model of the neural system.

To summarize: Neural systems are constructed to imitate the intelligent human biological processes of learning, self-modification, and learning by making inferences; while expert system knowledge is bounded by what is currently known about the established domain. Neural systems extract the knowledge directly from the domain during the training sessions, and this self-modification of a neuron system provides a dynamic learning experience.

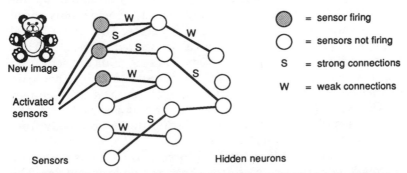

Figure 19-7   A human system being trained to recognize two different images. This is the second image.

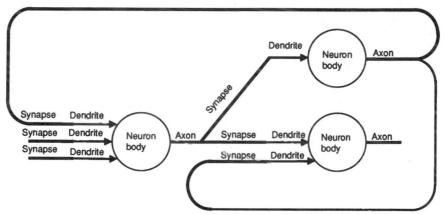

Figure 19-8 A connectionist neuron model showing neuron output, which is the axon connected to many synapses, each of which sends a signal to a neuron's input via a dendrite.

Modeling the Neural System

First, all the elements that comprise the biological neural system must be collected in a computer program for it to be properly described as possessing an artificial neural system capability. In order to accomplish this, neural biologists, mathematicians, and computer scientists conducted intensive physiological neural studies. One of the many results of these studies was the McCulloch-Pitts neural mode which can be expanded to display a set of interconnected neural models as shown in Figure 19-8.

Modeling the Single Neuron

The neuron is an electrical device that responds to electrical signals. The response can be thought of as being generated by a small computer that is part of the neuron. For our purposes, we will consider only one of the many responses that the neuron can generate. The single model consists of dendrites, the neuron body, an axon, and synapses. Dendrites carry the input signals to the neuron body. These signals are sent from sensors or are the outputs of other neurons (Figure 19-9). The dendrite signals can have positive or negative voltages; the positive voltages contribute to exciting the neuron body into sending a signal while the negative voltages will contribute to inhibiting the neuron body from sending a signal (Figure 19-10).

The neuron body is the computer that processes the signals carried by the dendrites. The actual processing can be very simple or complex. The neuron body model that we will consider sums the signals being carried

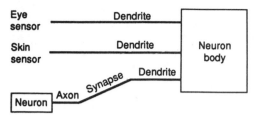

Figure 19-9   An example of a neural situation

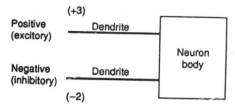

Figure 19-10   Positive signals excite the neuron to fire. Negative signals inhibit the neuron from firing.

by its dendrites and then determines its course of action, as demonstrated in Figure 19-11. If the sum exceeds the threshold level, the neuron body will fire, generating its own signal to the downstream neurons within the system; if the sum does not exceed the threshold level, the neuron body will not fire.

Bias Voltage, Axon, Synapse, and Weighting Factor

The neuron body may process specific dendrites differently than others. For example, it may add or subtract a constant voltage (called a bias) from a dendrite. Examples of a bias voltage affecting the firing of a neuron are displayed in Figure 19-12. There is one axon for each neuron (Figure 19-13). The axon carries the fired voltage from the neuron body to many connections with other neurons. These connections are the

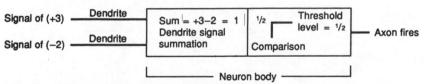

Figure 19-11   The sum of the dendrite signals equals 1, which is greater than ½, causing the neuron to fire, that is, to produce a signal on the axon.

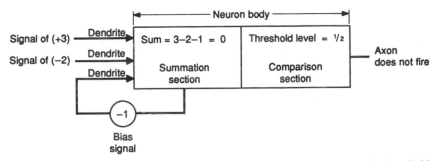

Figure 19-12 The neuron does not fire since the bias signal reduced the sum below the threshold level.

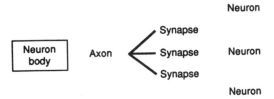

Figure 19-13 One axon sends signals to many neurons.

synapses, and there may be thousands of synapses connected to a single axon. The synapse forms a connection between the axon of one neuron with the dendrite of another. The strength of the synapse connection determines the amount of signal reaching the dendrite. The value of the strength of the synapse is called the "weighting factor." In Figure 19-14 the weighting factor of a synapse-A is a 3, and for synapse-B it is a −2. The value of the synapse strength is the weighting factor, with positive weighting factors being considered excitory and negative factors inhibitory. The weighting factors act to multiply the axon signal. The product

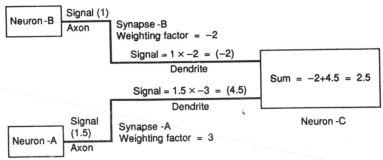

Figure 19-14 The signal to a dendrite is equal to the axon firing signal times the weighting factor of the synapse.

is passed to the connected dendrite providing the input signal to the connected neuron. The synaptic weighting factor multiplies the axon signal passing the product to the dendrite.

Summary

1. There are many neural system models presently being considered. This reflects the intense research being conducted.

2. The model selected to acquaint the reader with neural network theory is the McCulloch-Pitts model in which the neuron body reacts to simultaneous inputs from the dendrites.

3. The dendrites carry the input signal. There are many dendrites in a single neuron. Positive dendrite signals are called "excitory," and negative dendrite signals are called "inhibitory."

4. The neuron body provides a bias to one or more of its dendrites. It then sums the dendrite signals and compares the sum to a threshold level. The neuron fires if the threshold level is exceeded. There is one neuron body in a single neuron.

5. The axon carries the output signal to many neural connectors. There is only one axon in a single neuron.

6. The synapse forms the connections between neurons. The input to the synapase is an axon. The output is to a dendrite. A strong synaptic connection has a larger weighting factor than a weak one. The signal input to the synapse is multiplied by the synapse weight to form the signal sent to the dendrite.

20

Neural Networks—Software Design

Now that you have a clear picture of the neural system, you are ready to consider its software implementation. Although the topic is somewhat complex, we will make the explanation simple enough for you to follow. By the time we are finished you will be able to apply this design to a neural network system. The design will contain features which will allow the neural network to have *self-organization* capabilities. Self-organization is the ability to create a *thinking and reasoning* being with the ability to *modify* itself. The design objective is to create *human qualities in a simple electronic computational unit.*

This means the design must contain the capability to allow the system to *put its own components together* into a working structure and then *modify* the arrangement when appropriate.

We must caution you that extensive work must still be completed in this area and this chapter is just a scratch on the surface.

The Problem Statement

The first thing to do when planning a neural network is to state the problem that it is to solve. Let's consider an example in the domain of "attribute extraction and identification"; it's one we will use as the central example throughout this chapter.

The problem is to construct a neural network to associate human physical characteristics, such as height and weight, with the person these characteristics belong to. This may not seem to be a very complicated problem at first glance. But, as you will see, we will be able to use the same neural network design philosophy to solve problems in other domains such as "image recognition."

Continuing with our problem statement, Table 20.1 identifies four people together with their characteristics. The table tells us that person.1 has the following characteristics:

Mustache is yes, which equals 1 at the input.

Glasses is yes, which equals 1 at the input.

Hair color is light, which equals 0 at the input.

Weight is heavy, which equals 1 at the input.

Height is small, which equals 0 at the input.

Person.1 is identified at the output as the two-digit binary number 0 1.

Design of the Neural Network

The neural network to solve this problem will contain five inputs, one for each characteristic. Since a person is referred to by a two-digit binary number, two neurons are needed to provide the output, one for each digit. Neuron [0] will output the least significant digit and neuron [1] the most significant digit.

The configuration of the neural network will contain one level of neurons which connects to both the input and output as shown in Figure 20-1.

Initialization

As a first step we must provide initial values for the components of the neural network. There are two components we are concerned with; one is threshold and the other is the weights. In order to simplify our discussion, and without loss of generality, the threshold will be assigned a constant value of 0. Initially all weighting values will be assigned a value of 1. Compare statements 110 to 140 in Listing 20-1 with the resulting dialogue shown below:

Table 20.1   Characteristics of Four People

	Person	Person.1	Person.2	Person.3	Person.4
Input	Output	0 1	1 0	1 1	0 0
Mustache (yes=1, no=0)		1	0	1	1
Glasses (yes=1, no=0)		1	0	0	1
Hair color (dark=1, light=0)		0	0	1	1
Weight (heavy=1, light=0)		1	1	0	0
Height (tall=1, small=0)		0	1	1	0

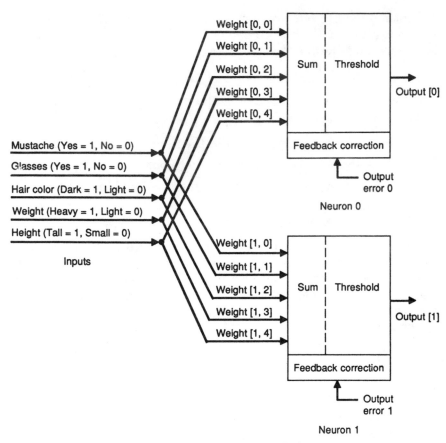

Figure 20-1 A neural network to identify the person having the inputs.

```
Enter weighting value for neuron 0 input 0? 1
Enter weighting value for neuron 0 input 1? 1
Enter weighting value for neuron 0 input 2? 1
Enter weighting value for neuron 0 input 3? 1
Enter weighting value for neuron 0 input 4? 1
Enter weighting value for neuron 1 input 0? 1
Enter weighting value for neuron 1 input 1? 1
Enter weighting value for neuron 1 input 2? 1
Enter weighting value for neuron 1 input 3? 1
Enter weighting value for neuron 1 input 4? 1
```

Training the Network

Next we must train the network to relate specific characteristic inputs to the person associated with those inputs. That is, the characteristi inputs of person.1 as seen in Table 20.1 are:

11010   (mustache, glasses, light hair, heavy, small)

Upon receiving those inputs, the network's "ideal" output would be:

01   (which is identified as person.1)

If the "actual" output is not 0 1, the network trainer will respond with:

Output.error = 1

at each neuron which is in error. For example, if the network should have identified person.1 but instead produced an output of:

11   (which is identified as person.3)

neuron [1] is in error since its output should have been 0.

This method of training is the way people learn. Examples are presented and responses made. If a response is an error, the person attempts to modify the reasoning process so as to eliminate the error. If the response is correct, nothing happens. Similarly, when an output error is presented to a neuron, it will begin self-modification by modifying its weight values to correct the error.

Let us get started with a step by step explanation of the training method used to modify the weight values.

Forward Propagation

The first phase in the training session is to apply an input and calculate the resulting output. This is called "forward propagation." It is the process of flowing from input to output.

Applying the Input

Just as an instructor plans a curriculum prior to teaching a class, planning the types and sequences of inputs should involve careful consideration.

The input is controlled by statements 160 to 190. First we input the characteristics of person.1. The dialogue is shown below:

```
**** TRAINING SESSION ****
Enter the characteristics of this person. These are the inputs to the neural
system.
Does person have a mustache..yes=1, no=0? 1
Does person have a glasses...yes=1, no=0? 1
Does person have a dark hair.yes=1, no=0? 0
```

```
Is person heavy ..............yes=1, no=0? 1
Is man tall..................yes=1, no=0? 0
```

Calculating the Sum for Each Neuron

Each input signal is multiplied by the weight value associated with the input as shown below:

```
input[0] * weight[0,0]   +
input[1] * weight[0,1]   +   →sum
                         +
```

The neuron's sum unit will then add all the products associated with each input to arrive at a sum. Each neuron in the network will calculate its own sum.

The product summation is controlled by statements 200 to 255. The dialogue is shown below:

```
**** CALCULATING THE SUM FOR EACH NEURON ****

Neuron number=0 Input number=0 Input=  1.0000000000E+00
 Weight=  1.0000000000E+00 Product contribution=  1.0000000000E+00

Neuron number=0 Input number=1 Input=  1.0000000000E+00
 Weight=  1.0000000000E+00 Product contribution=  1.0000000000E+00

Neuron number=0 Input number=2 Input=  0.0000000000E+00
 Weight=  1.0000000000E+00 Product contribution=  0.0000000000E+00

Neuron number=0 Input number=3 Input=  1.0000000000E+00
 Weight=  1.0000000000E+00 Product contribution=  1.0000000000E+00

Neuron number=0 Input number=4 Input=  0.0000000000E+00
 Weight=  1.0000000000E+00 Product contribution=  0.0000000000E+00

 SUM[0]=  3.0000000000E+00

Neuron number=1 Input number=0 Input=  1.0000000000E+00
 Weight=  1.0000000000E+00 Product contribution=  1.0000000000E+00

Neuron number=1 Input number=1 Input=  1.0000000000E+00
 Weight=  1.0000000000E+00 Product contribution=  1.0000000000E+00

Neuron number=1 Input number=2 Input=  0.0000000000E+00
 Weight=  1.0000000000E+00 Product contribution=  0.0000000000E+00

Neuron number=1 Input number=3 Input=  1.0000000000E+00
 Weight=  1.0000000000E+00 Product contribution=  1.0000000000E+00

Neuron number=1 Input number=4 Input=  0.0000000000E+00
 Weight=  1.0000000000E+00 Product contribution=  0.0000000000E+00

 SUM[1]=  3.0000000000E+00
```

Comparison with the Threshold

Each neuron has a threshold. If the sum exceeds the threshold, the neuron "fires," which is represented as a 1 at the output. If the threshold is not exceeded, the neuron does "not fire," which is represented as a 0 at the output. That is:

If sum > threshold, then fire;   then output = 1

If sum < = threshold, then not fire;   then output = 0

Threshold comparison is controlled by statements 260 to 285.

Backward Propagation

The output of each neuron is referred to as the "actual output." The "ideal output" is the output a neuron is expected to have based upon the current input or sequence of inputs. If the actual and ideal outputs are not equal, an "error" has been detected. If so, the network must "go backward" from the output toward the input, correcting the weighting values to reduce or eliminate the error. This process is known as "backward propagation."

Let us examine Backward Propagation, which is a form of feedback, in a step by step manner.

Is the Output Correct?

The first step of backward propagation is to determine if there is an output error by comparing every neuron's actual output with the ideal output. This is done in statements 290 to 320. Let's continue with our examination of backward propagation using the dialogue as shown below:

```
**** IS THE THRESHOLD EXCEEDED ****
**** IS THE OUTPUT CORRECT ****
Output neuron 0 = 1.    Is neuron output in error..yes=1, no=0? 0
Output neuron 1 = 1.    Is neuron output in error..yes=1, no=0? 1
```

Since the input is from person.1, we see from Table 20.1 that the ideal output should be output[0]=1 and output[1]=0. However, the actual output is output[0]=1 and output[1]=1. The trainer responded with an error for output [1] and no error for output[0]. The network has now been informed that "all" weight values contributing to neuron[1]'s output must be corrected to reduce or eliminate the error.

Calculating the Error

The second step is to determine the size of the error since, as you will soon see, this will affect the magnitude of the correction.

An output error will result in one of two ways. One way is when the sum exceeds the threshold, causing the neuron to fire when it shouldn't have fired, i.e., its ideal output is 0. This is what happened to output[1] in our example. The other way is for the sum not to exceed the threshold, causing the neuron not to fire when it should have fired, i.e., its ideal output is a 1. The error is directly caused by an incorrect sum.

Let us consider the case where the sum exceeded the threshold and is an error as shown below:

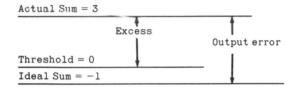

```
Actual Sum = 3
```

The actual sum exceeds the threshold by 3. The ideal sum is below the threshold and would prevent firing. A value of −1 was chosen to simplify the calculations. But, as you will see later, the value of −1 affects the rate at which the network will converge to the final weights and may be modified if the reader experiments with the network by modifying the program. The reader can change the ideal sum by modifying the 1s in statements 360 to 362.

The output error is defined as:

Output error = actual sum − ideal sum

For our example the output error[1] = 3 − (−1) = 4.

The alternate case occurs when the sum does not exceed the threshold when ideally it should have, as shown below:

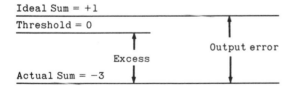

The actual sum is less than the threshold, i.e., −3. The ideal sum is arbitrarily placed at +1 for convenience of explanation. If the sum reached the ideal value, the neuron would fire and be correct. The output error is, from the output error equation, − 3 − (+1) = −4.

The output error is calculated in statements 345 to 375. The person.1 dialogue for this section is shown below:

```
**** ERROR CORRECTION—USE BACKWARD PROPAGATION ****
Error for neuron 0=   0.0000000000E+00
Error for neuron 1=   4.0000000000E+00
```

Changing the Weight Values

If the sum of a neuron is in error, we must determine the degree of responsibility that each input has in contributing to the error. The name we give this degree of responsibility is "blame." We attach a blame value to each input that may have contributed to the error. The weights for those inputs with the largest blame values will receive the largest change.

Another factor affecting the degree of weight change is the magnitude of the output error. The greater the neuron's output error, the greater each of the neuron's weights must change. Therefore, the change in a neuron's input weight values is proportional to both the neuron's output error and the input's blame value. The following equation will be used to calculate a "new weight value" at the neuron's input:

Weight.new[n,i] = weight.old[n,i]
  − (B ∗ blame[n,i] ∗ output.error[n])

Where n is the neuron number, i is the input number, and B is the "learning factor." B is one of the variables that controls the rate at which the final, corrected weight values are reached. The value of B in our example has been made a constant equal to 0.5. The reader can experiment with different values for B, which will modify the rate at which the neuron reaches its true values.

Calculating the Blame

The blame is the percentage contribution that an input to a neuron has in forming the output error. The contribution of an input to a neuron's output error is:

Contribution[n,i] = input value[n,i] ∗ weight[n,i]

The blame is therefore

Blame[n,i] = contribution[n,i] / sum[n]

Statements 380 to 450 are used to calculate the blame. Continuing with the person.1 example, the blame dialogue is shown below:

```
* BLAME OF EACH INPUT FOR CONTRIBUTION TOWARD ERROR *

Neuron number=0 Input number=0 contribution=  1.0000000000E+00
 input=  1.0000000000E+00 weight=  1.0000000000E+00
sum=  3.0000000000E+00 blame=  3.3333333333E-01

Neuron number=0 Input number=1 contribution=  1.0000000000E+00
 input=  1.0000000000E+00 weight=  1.0000000000E+00
sum=  3.0000000000E+00 blame=  3.3333333333E-01
```

```
Neuron number=0 Input number=2 contribution=   0.0000000000E+00
 input=   0.0000000000E+00 weight=   1.0000000000E+00
sum=   3.0000000000E+00 blame=   0.0000000000E+00

Neuron number=0 Input number=3 contribution=   1.0000000000E+00
 input=   1.0000000000E+00 weight=   1.0000000000E+00
sum=   3.0000000000E+00 blame=   3.3333333333E-01

Neuron number=0 Input number=4 contribution=   0.0000000000E+00
 input=   0.0000000000E+00 weight=   1.0000000000E+00
sum=   3.0000000000E+00 blame=   0.0000000000E+00

Neuron number=1 Input number=0 contribution=   1.0000000000E+00
 input=   1.0000000000E+00 weight=   1.0000000000E+00
sum=   3.0000000000E+00 blame=   3.3333333333E-01

Neuron number=1 Input number=1 contribution=   1.0000000000E+00
 input=   1.0000000000E+00 weight=   1.0000000000E+00
sum=   3.0000000000E+00 blame=   3.3333333333E-01

Neuron number=1 Input number=2 contribution=   0.0000000000E+00
 input=   0.0000000000E+00 weight=   1.0000000000E+00
sum=   3.0000000000E+00 blame=   0.0000000000E+00

Neuron number=1 Input number=3 contribution=   1.0000000000E+00
 input=   1.0000000000E+00 weight=   1.0000000000E+00
sum=   3.0000000000E+00 blame=   3.3333333333E-01

Neuron number=1 Input number=4 contribution=   0.0000000000E+00
 input=   0.0000000000E+00 weight=   1.0000000000E+00
sum=   3.0000000000E+00 blame=   0.0000000000E+00
```

Calculating the New Weight Values

The new weight values are calculated using the weight. new equation in statements 455 to 515. The dialogue is shown below:

```
**** CALCULATE A NEW CORRECTED WEIGHT ****
neuron number=0 Input number=0 blame=   3.3333333333E-01
 output error=   0.0000000000E+00
 old weight =   1.0000000000E+00  new weight=   1.0000000000E+00

neuron number=0 Input number=1 blame=   3.3333333333E-01
 output error=   0.0000000000E+00
 old weight =   1.0000000000E+00  new weight=   1.0000000000E+00

neuron number=0 Input number=2 blame=   0.0000000000E+00
 output error=   0.0000000000E+00
 old weight =   1.0000000000E+00  new weight=   1.0000000000E+00

neuron number=0 Input number=3 blame=   3.3333333333E-01
 output error=   0.0000000000E+00
 old weight =   1.0000000000E+00  new weight=   1.0000000000E+00

neuron number=0 Input number=4 blame=   3.3333333333E-01
 output error=   0.0000000000E+00
 old weight =   1.0000000000E+00  new weight=   1.0000000000E+00

neuron number=1 Input number=0 blame=   3.3333333333E-01
 output error=   4.0000000000E+00
 old weight =   1.0000000000E+00  new weight=   3.3333333333E-01

neuron number=1 Input number=1 blame=   3.3333333333E-01
 output error=   4.0000000000E+00
 old weight =   1.0000000000E+00  new weight=   3.3333333333E-01
```

```
neuron number=1 Input number=2 blame=  0.0000000000E+00
  output error=  4.0000000000E+00
  old weight =  1.0000000000E+00  new weight=  1.0000000000E+00
neuron number=1 Input number=3 blame=  3.3333333333E-01
  output error=  4.0000000000E+00
  old weight =  1.0000000000E+00  new weight=  3.3333333333E-01
neuron number=1 Input number=4 blame=  0.0000000000E+00
  output error=  4.0000000000E+00
  old weight =  1.0000000000E+00  new weight=  1.0000000000E+00
```

Is the Training Over?

After many "training cycles," you are ready to tryout the network. During tryout there is no error correction. To do this, select a sequence of inputs and record the number of output errors. If the network responds correctly a percentage of the time that meets your criteria, you have finished. If not, you must examine your training sequence or the design of the Neural Network to correct any differences.

The tryout phase is contained in statements 525 to 710.

Programming Applications

At the end of the chapter there is a program listing that will aid you in understanding the neural network concepts. Initially, run the program using only person.1 as the input. Cycle through the training session a few times until person.1 is correctly identified. During each cycle note that the error output is reduced and the new weight values for neuron[1] move in the negative direction until neuron[1] does not fire.

Experiment with the network by changing the values of B, the threshold, and the ideal outputs one at a time. Observe the results. Then experiment with other people in any combination.

Other Applications—Image Recognition

The neural model we used has application in other domains. We will discuss one more domain application, image recognition.

Pixels and Image Recognition

Each image can be divided by a pixel background. The word "pixel" is an abbreviation for a picture element. As an example, a picture of the letter P is enclosed in a background of 20 pixels as shown in Figure 20-2. Each pixel is assigned a unique number. If we think of each pixel as a neuron input, we have 20 inputs. If the domain of interest is alphabetic images, we would have 26 members, one for each letter. Twenty-six letters can be

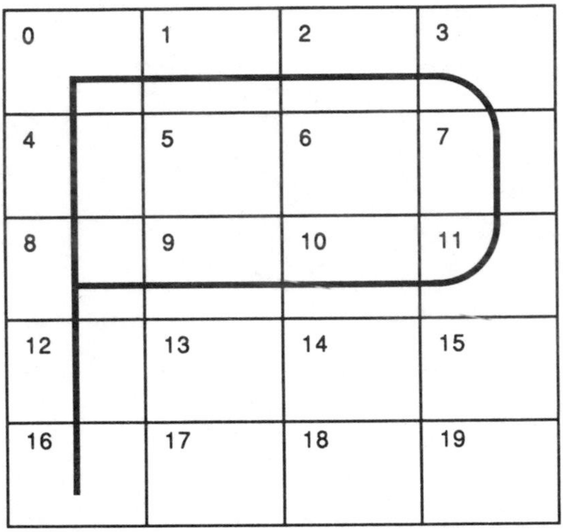

0	1	2	3
4	5	6	7
8	9	10	11
12	13	14	15
16	17	18	19

Figure 20-2   The actual sum exceeds the threshold and is in error. The ideal sum should not have exceeded the threshold.

represented by five binary digits. For example, the first letter, A, would have a representation of 00001, the second letter, B, would have a representation of 00010, and so on. The five digits of output could be represented by five neurons, one for each digit. The network program implementation would be identical to the one just considered with the exception that the number of neurons would be expanded from two to five, and the number of inputs from 5 to 20 (one for each pixel). To implement this network we would modify the following statements:

```
for neuron.num = 0 to 1
for neuron.inp = 0 to 4
```

to

```
for neuron.num = 0 to 4
for neuron.inp = 0 to 20
```

In addition we would change the input dialogue from:

```
"Does person have a . . . . "
```

to

```
"Enter for pixel number p . . . yes=1, for pixel on, no=0, for pixel off"
```

Multiple Levels of Neurons—
Hidden Neurons

You may want to experiment with more than one level of neurons. Levels of neurons not connected to inputs or outputs are referred to as "hidden" neurons. Let us analyze the multiple level neural network shown in Figure 20-3.

Forward Propagation

When networks are configured in multiple levels, we calculate the neuron outputs at each level in sequence as we move from input to output. The lowest level of neurons are level 0 neurons. At each level we would calculate the sum and make a threshold comparison in the same way we had done, using the following equations:

Sum $= \Sigma$ input $*$ weight
If sum $>$ threshold then neuron fires (=1) else (=0)

The input for each neuron is the output of the previous neuron level.

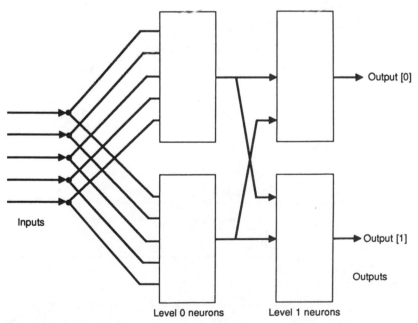

Figure 20-3   The actual sum is below the threshold and is in error. The ideal sum should have exceeded the threshold.

Backward Propagation

When an output error occurs, we must backward propagate the error in order to determine the new weights. We use the same equation as previously discussed to modify the weights, i.e.,

Weight.new = weight.old − (B * blame * output error)

At the output level we can determine if an error occurred in the same way as we previously did. That is, we know the input and therefore what the ideal output should be. During forward propagation we calculated the actual output. We can therefore calculate the output error as:

Actual Output − Ideal Output

Intermediate Error Determination

At an intermediate level we must use a different method to determine which neuron output is in error and the magnitude of the error. The diagram in Figure 20-4 will be used to explain the methodology. The network has two errors, one at neuron N2 and the other at neuron N4. Neuron N1 is connected to two of the error neurons, N2 and N4. Neuron N6 is connected to neuron N2. Using the diagram in Figure 20-4, a method will be outlined for determining the output error of intermediate neurons. Consider the following proposition:

Every neuron connected to the input of another neuron, which is in error, contributes to the error. The contribution may vary from zero to any number.

From the proposition, neurons N1 and N6 are both at fault in causing the error at neuron N2. We calculate the blame of N1 and N6 for N2's error using the following equations:

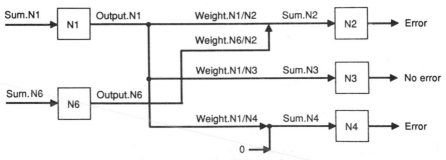

Figure 20-4   An image enclosed in an area divided into panels.

Contribution.N1 = output.N1 ∗ weight.N1/N2
Contribution.N6 = output.N6 ∗ weight.N6/N2

Sum.N2   = contribution.N1 + contribution.N6

Blame.N1 / N2 = contribution.N1 / sum.N2
Blame.N6 / N2 = contribution.N6 / sum.N2

We now calculate the blame N1 has in causing the error at N4. Since N1 is the only contributing input to N4, i.e., the other line is a 0,

Blame.N1 / N4 = 1

We calculate the average blame for neuron N1 with respect to all other neurons with output errors that N1 is connect to as

Blame.N1.AV = (blame.N1 / N2 + blame.N1 / N4)/2

The output error for N1 is

Output.error.N1 = blame.N1.AV ∗ sum.N1

The new weight values for N1 can be calculated using the standard equation:

Weight.new = weight.old − (B ∗ blame.N1.AV ∗ output error)

The following example (see also Figure 20-5) uses the above concepts:

Level 1 Calculation

B   = 1   [for simplicity assume B=1]
Out.error.N2 = 5 − (−1) = 6   [Actual − ideal]
Out.error.N4 = 9 − (−1) = 10
Blame.N1/N2 = 2/5 = .4   [(Output ∗ weight) / sum]
Blame.N6/N2 = 3/5 = .6
Blame.N1/N4 = 3/9 = .33

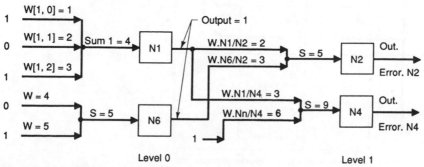

Figure 20-5   A multilevel neural network.

Wnew.N1 / N2 = 2 − 1∗.4∗6 = −.4 [W.old − B ∗ blame ∗ out.error]
Wnew.N6 / N2 = 3 − 1∗.6∗10 = −3

Level 0 Calculation

Blame.N1.AV = (blame.N1 / N2 + blame.N1 / N4) / 2
Blame.N1.AV = (.4 + .33) / 2 = .365
Out.error.N1 = Blame.N1.AV ∗ sum1 = .365 ∗ 4 = 1.46
Blame.10   = 1/4 = .25   [Input 0 of neuron N1]
Blame.11   = 0   [Input 1 of neuron N1]
Blame.12   = 3/4 = .75   [Input 2 of neuron N1]
Wnew.[1,0]   = 1 − 1 ∗ (.25) ∗ (1.46)[W.old − B ∗ blame ∗ out.error]
        = .616
Wnew.[1,1]   = 2 − 1 ∗ (0) ∗ (1.46) = 2
Wnew[1,2]   = 3 − 1 ∗ (.75) ∗ (1.46) = 1.848

In a similar way the reader can calculate the output error for N6 and new weights for the N6 inputs. The reader can also experiment with different values of "B."

Other Neural Network Configurations— Hebbian Networks

Hebb was a pioneer in explaining the modification procedures neural networks use during training. Simply stated, Hebb theorized that the

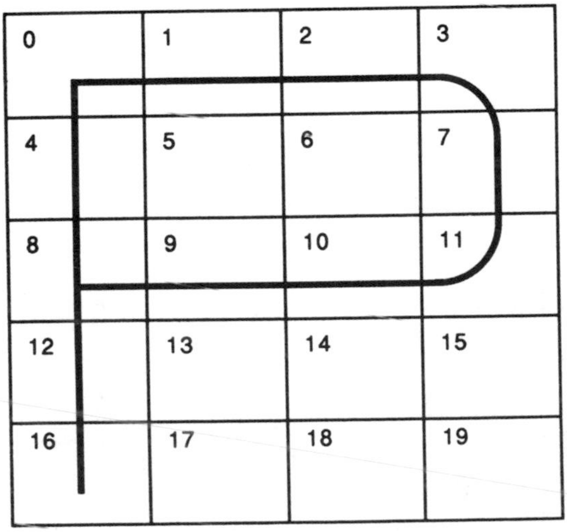

Figure 20-6 An example of using a two-level neural network.

weight values between connected neurons are strengthened if they both fire during a training cycle and are reduced if one fires and the other doesn't. Let's apply a slight modification to his theory with an example previously discussed using a different approach. The example is the recognition of the letter P as shown in Figure 20-6.

The neural network structure that is considered here has the following characteristics. Each pixel will provide a unique input to only one neuron. Every neuron provides an input to every other neuron except itself. A portion of the network is shown in Figure 20-7.

Weight Matrix

Let us represent the weights between neurons with a weight matrix as shown in Figure 20-8. The cross-hatched section represents the weight value between the output of neuron 3 to the input connection to neuron 2. Since a neuron has no connection between its own output and input, the intersection of rows and columns having the same number have no weight and are represented by a "—." In order to apply Hebb's theorem to determine the weights between neurons, the following equation suggested by J. Hopfield is used:

Weight between neuron x and neuron y = weight.old
 + (2 * f.x−1) * (2 * f.y−1)

where f.x is a 1 if neuron x fires, else it is a 0; f.y is a 1 if neuron y fires, else it is a 0; Threshold = 0, and all weights are initially 0.

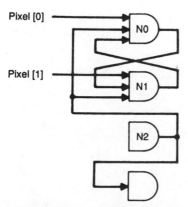

Figure 20-7   A numerical example of a multilevel neural network.

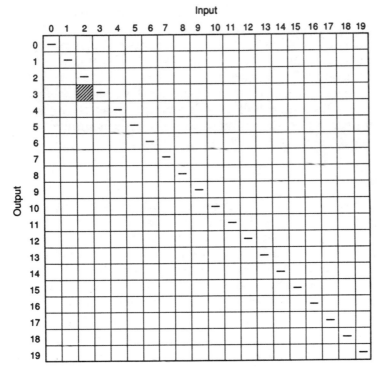

Figure 20-8   A letter P enclosed in a pixel background.

Calculating the Weights

First the sum at each neuron is calculated. As an example, sum[0] is calculated below:

Sum[0] = pixel[0] + output[1] * weight between 0 and 1 + output[2] * weight between 0 and 2 + $\cdots$ +, output[19] * weight between 0 and 19

Since P intersects pixel[0], pixel[0] = 1. All weights have been initialized to 0; therefore,

Sum[0] = 1 + 0 + 0 + $\cdots$ + 0 = 1

The reader can verify the other sum values of the following

SUM [1]=1	SUM [6]=0
SUM [2]=1	SUM [7]=1
SUM [3]=1	SUM [8]=1
SUM [4]=1	SUM [9]=1
SUM [5]=0	SUM [10]=1

SUM [11]=1 SUM [15]=0
SUM [12]=1 SUM [16]=1
SUM [13]=0 SUM [17]=0
SUM [14]=0 SUM [18]=0
SUM [19]=0

All sums exceeding a threshold of 0 will fire. Using Hopfield's weight equation, we get:

$$\text{Weight between neurons 1 and 2} = 0 + (2 * 1 - 1) * (2 * 1 - 1) = (1) * (1) = 1$$

$$\text{Weight between neurons 1 and 5} = 0 + (2 * 1 - 1) * (2 * 0 - 1) = (1) * (-1) = -1$$

$$\text{Weight between neurons 5 and 6} = 0 + (2 * 0 - 1) * (2 * 0 - 1) = (-1) * (-1) = 1$$

The reader can verify that if two neurons do the same thing, i.e., both fire or don't fire, their connecting weights are increased. On the other hand,

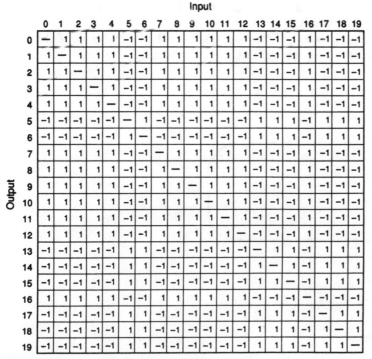

Output \ Input	0	1	2	3	4	5	6	7	8	9	10	11	12	13	14	15	16	17	18	19
0	—	1	1	1	1	−1	−1	1	1	1	1	1	1	−1	−1	−1	1	−1	−1	−1
1	1	—	1	1	1	−1	−1	1	1	1	1	1	1	−1	−1	−1	1	−1	−1	−1
2	1	1	—	1	1	−1	−1	1	1	1	1	1	1	−1	−1	−1	1	−1	−1	−1
3	1	1	1	—	1	−1	−1	1	1	1	1	1	1	−1	−1	−1	1	−1	−1	−1
4	1	1	1	1	—	−1	−1	1	1	1	1	1	1	−1	−1	−1	1	−1	−1	−1
5	−1	−1	−1	−1	−1	—	1	−1	−1	−1	−1	−1	−1	1	1	1	−1	1	1	1
6	−1	−1	−1	−1	−1	1	—	−1	−1	−1	−1	−1	−1	1	1	1	−1	1	1	1
7	1	1	1	1	1	−1	−1	—	1	1	1	1	1	−1	−1	−1	1	−1	−1	−1
8	1	1	1	1	1	−1	−1	1	—	1	1	1	1	−1	−1	−1	1	−1	−1	−1
9	1	1	1	1	1	−1	−1	1	1	—	1	1	1	−1	−1	−1	1	−1	−1	−1
10	1	1	1	1	1	−1	−1	1	1	1	—	1	1	−1	−1	−1	1	−1	−1	−1
11	1	1	1	1	1	−1	−1	1	1	1	1	—	1	−1	−1	−1	1	−1	−1	−1
12	1	1	1	1	1	−1	−1	1	1	1	1	1	—	−1	−1	−1	1	−1	−1	−1
13	−1	−1	−1	−1	−1	1	1	−1	−1	−1	−1	−1	−1	—	1	1	−1	1	1	1
14	−1	−1	−1	−1	−1	1	1	−1	−1	−1	−1	−1	−1	1	—	1	−1	1	1	1
15	−1	−1	−1	−1	−1	1	1	−1	−1	−1	−1	−1	−1	1	1	—	−1	1	1	1
16	1	1	1	1	1	−1	−1	1	1	1	1	1	1	−1	−1	−1	—	−1	−1	−1
17	−1	−1	−1	−1	−1	1	1	−1	−1	−1	−1	−1	−1	1	1	1	−1	—	1	1
18	−1	−1	−1	−1	−1	1	1	−1	−1	−1	−1	−1	−1	1	1	1	−1	1	—	1
19	−1	−1	−1	−1	−1	1	1	−1	−1	−1	−1	−1	−1	1	1	1	−1	1	1	—

Figure 20-9 New weight matrix after training.

if they do the opposite, their connecting weights are decreased. The weight matrix is changed as shown in Figure 20-9.

A Noisy Input

Let us see how noise affects our calculations by applying the noisy P, i.e., pixel[17] = 1 shown in Figure 20-10. The reader can verify that the sum's outputs are:

SUM [0]=1	SUM [10]=1
SUM [1]=1	SUM [11]=1
SUM [2]=1	SUM [12]=1
SUM [3]=1	SUM [13]=0
SUM [4]=1	SUM [14]=0
SUM [5]=0	SUM [15]=0
SUM [6]=0	SUM [16]=1
SUM [7]=1	SUM [17]=0
SUM [8]=1	SUM [18]=0
SUM [9]=1	SUM [19]=0

This is the exact neuron output given for the original P. The network filtered, i.e., removed, the slight noise at Pixel[17].

The reader is encouraged to experiment with the Hebb/Hopfield network in both training and tryout.

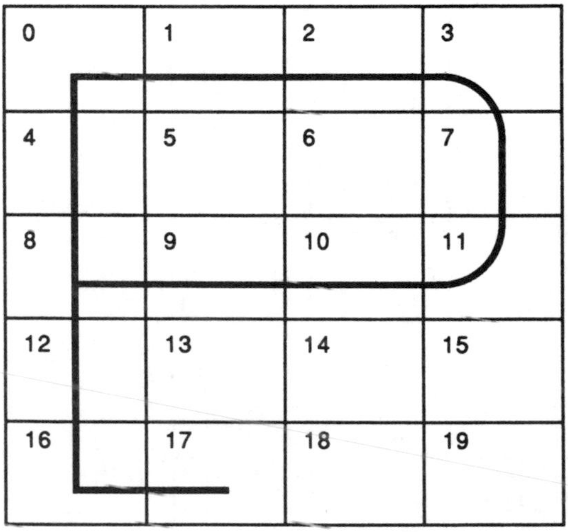

Figure 20-10   A weight matrix without values.

Summary

Let us review some important aspects of neural networks:

1. There are many configurations of neural networks. The user should select the one appropriate to the domain.
2. Although the neural network model responded to threshold logic, there are many other types the reader can consider, such as continuous nonlinear input output functions.
3. There are two phases of neural network construction.
   (a) Training, where selection of the training process is important.
   (b) Tryout, which is the determination of the networks success.

Listing 20-1 Single layer neuron example.

```
/************* single layer neuron example ***********/
/* This program is operationally the same as one written in BASIC. It */
/* will therefor have blocks of this program commented with statement */
/* numbers as a reference for the text. The text when referencing a   */
/* Variable with a ".", i.e. NEURON.NUM, will find its equvalent in   */
/* the program as NEURON_NUM. That is, the Pascal program replaces a  */
/* period with a underscore.                                          */
/* The program will halt to allow you to view the screen. When it does*/
/* enter the <return> key to continue.                                */
/********************************************************************/
#include <stdio.h>

float threshold = 0.0; /* for this example each neuron has the same */
                       /* theshold of zero. */
float b = 0.5 /* Learning Factor */, product /* input * output */;
float excess /* output error */, dv /* temporary divisor */;
float wt /* temporary weight */;
float inpt[5] /* inputs from external source */;
float weight[2][5] /* each neuron 0 & 1 has inputs 0 to 4 */;
float er[2] /* each neuron may produce an output error */;
float contribution[2][5] /* contribution=product=inpt * weight */;
float blame[2][5] /* blame=contribution/sum */;
float sum [5] /* sum of contributions */;
float outpt_er[2] /* output error of a neuron */;

int neuron_num /* number of neurons */, t, train_flag /* training flag */;
int neuron_inp /* number inputs per neuron */;
int err_flg /* output error flag */, try_out /* tryout network */;
int outpt[2] /* two output neurons */;

char cr /* character to handle <return> */;

main() {
/**** statements 110 to 140 ****/
for(neuron_num=0;neuron_num<2;neuron_num++)
 for(neuron_inp=0;neuron_inp<5;neuron_inp++) {
  printf("Enter weight value for neuron %d input %d ? ",neuron_num,neuron_inp);
  scanf("%f",&weight[neuron_num][neuron_inp]);
  fflush(stdin); }
gets(&cr);
try_out=0;
train_flag=0;
while(try_out == 0) { /* try out failed..need more training */
 while(train_flag == 0) { /* training loop continues */
  printf("**** TRAINING SESSION ****\n\n");
  printf("Enter the characteristics of this person. These are the\n");
  printf("inputs to the neural system\n");
  printf("Does person have a mustache..yes=1, no=0? ");
  scanf("%f",&inpt[0]);
  printf("Does person wear glasses.....yes=1, no=0? ");
  scanf("%f",&inpt[1]);
  printf("Does person have dark hair...yes=1, no=0? ");
  scanf("%f",&inpt[2]);
  printf("Is person heavy..............yes=1, no=0? ");
  scanf("%f",&inpt[3]);
  printf("Is person tall...............yes=1, no=0? ");
  scanf("%f",&inpt[4]);
  fflush(stdin);
  gets(&cr);
  /**** statements 200 to 255 ****/
  printf("**** CALCULATING THE SUM FOR EACH NEURON ****\n");
  for(neuron_num=0;neuron_num<2;neuron_num++) {
   sum[neuron_num]=0;
   for(neuron_inp=0;neuron_inp<5;neuron_inp++) {
    printf("\n");
    product=inpt[neuron_inp]*weight[neuron_num][neuron_inp];
    printf("Neuron number=%d   Input number=%d",neuron_num,neuron_inp);
    printf("  Input=%f\n",inpt[neuron_inp]);
    printf("  Weight=%f",weight[neuron_num][neuron_inp]);
    printf("  Product contribution=%f\n",product);
    sum[neuron_num]=sum[neuron_num] + product;
    gets(&cr); }
   printf("  SUM[%d]=%f\n",neuron_num,sum[neuron_num]); }
```

```
/**** statements 260 to 285 ****/
printf("\n");
printf("**** IS THE THRESHOLD EXCEEDED ****\n");
for(neuron_num=0;neuron_num<2;neuron_num++) {
 outpt[neuron_num]=0;
 /* if threshold exceeded, output is a one, i.e., fires */
 if(sum[neuron_num]>threshold) outpt[neuron_num]=1;
 else outpt[neuron_num]=0; }
/**** statements 290 to 320 ****/
printf("**** IS THE OUTPUT CORRECT ****\n");
err_flg=0; /* Determine if there is an output error */
for(neuron_num=0;neuron_num<2;neuron_num++) {
 printf("Output neuron %d = %d",neuron_num,outpt[neuron_num]);
 printf(".   Is neuron output in error..yes=1, no=0? ");
 scanf("%f",&er[neuron_num]);
 if(er[neuron_num] == 1) err_flg=1; }
if(err_flg == 0) printf("**** OUTPUT CORRECT ****\n");
else {
 /**** statements 345 to 375 ****/
 printf("\n**** ERROR CORRECTION—USE BACKWARD PROPAGATION ****\n");
 /* Calculate the error as sum - threshold +- 1 */
 for(neuron_num=0;neuron_num<2;neuron_num++) {
  /**** statements 360 to 362 ****/
  excess=sum[neuron_num] - threshold;
  if(er[neuron_num] == 0) excess=0;
  else if(sum[neuron_num] > threshold) excess++;
        else excess--;
  outpt_er[neuron_num]=excess; /* error output of neuron */
  printf("Error for neuron %d= %f\n",neuron_num,outpt_er[neuron_num]); }
 fflush(stdin);
 gets(&cr);
 /**** statements 380 to 450 ****/
 printf("\n");
 printf("* BLAME OF EACH INPUT FOR CONTRIBUTION TOWARD ERROR *");
 /* Contribution of an input is equal to the product of the input
    value and the weight value of the input */
    for(neuron_num=0;neuron_num<2;neuron_num++)
     for(neuron_inp=0;neuron_inp<5;neuron_inp++) {
        product=inpt[neuron_inp]*weight[neuron_num][neuron_inp];
        contribution[neuron_num][neuron_inp]=product;
        printf("\n");
        printf("Neuron number=%d  Input number=%d  ",neuron_num,neuron_inp);
        printf("Contribution=%f\n",contribution[neuron_num][neuron_inp]);
        printf(" Input=%f  Weight=",inpt[neuron_inp]);
        printf("%f\n",weight[neuron_num][neuron_inp]);
        dv=contribution[neuron_num][neuron_inp]/sum[neuron_num];
        blame[neuron_num][neuron_inp]=dv;
        printf("Sum=%f  Blame=",sum[neuron_num]);
        printf("%f\n",blame[neuron_num][neuron_inp]);
        gets(&cr); }
 /**** statements 455 to 515 ****/
 printf("\n**** CALCULATE A NEW CORRECTED WEIGHT ****");
 /* Wnew = Wold - B * Blame * Output error */
 for(neuron_num=0;neuron_num<2;neuron_num++)
  for(neuron_inp=0;neuron_inp<5;neuron_inp++) {
   product= -b*blame[neuron_num][neuron_inp]*outpt_er[neuron_num];
   printf("\nNeuron number=%d  Input number=",neuron_num);
   printf("%d",neuron_inp);
   printf("  Blame=%f\n",blame[neuron_num][neuron_inp]);
   printf("  Output error=%f\n",outpt_er[neuron_num]);
   printf("  Old weight=%f",weight[neuron_num][neuron_inp]);
   wt=weight[neuron_num][neuron_inp] + product;
   weight[neuron_num][neuron_inp]=wt;
   printf("  New weight=%f\n",weight[neuron_num][neuron_inp]);
   gets(&cr); }
} /* else */
/**** statements 525 to 710 ****/
printf("**** Is training complete...yes=1, no=0? ");
scanf("%d",&train_flag);
fflush(stdin); } /* while train_flag */
while(train_flag == 1) {
 printf("\n**** TRAINING COMPLETE — NEURAL NETWORK TRYOUT ****\n\n");
 printf("Enter the characteristics of this person. These are the\n");
 printf("inputs to the neural system\n");
```

Listing 20-1 *(Continued)*

```
printf("Does person have a mustache..yes=1, no=0? ");
scanf("%f",&inpt[0]);
printf("Does person wear glasses.....yes=1, no=0? ");
scanf("%f",&inpt[1]);
printf("Does person have dark hair...yes=1, no=0? ");
scanf("%f",&inpt[2]);
printf("Is person heavy..............yes=1, no=0? ");
scanf("%f",&inpt[3]);
printf("Is person tall...............yes=1, no=0? ");
scanf("%f",&inpt[4]);
fflush(stdin);
gets(&cr);
printf("**** CALCULATING THE SUM FOR EACH NEURON ****\n");
for(neuron_num=0;neuron_num<2;neuron_num++) {
 sum[neuron_num]=0;
 for(neuron_inp=0;neuron_inp<5;neuron_inp++); {
  product=inpt[neuron_inp]*weight[neuron_num][neuron_inp];
  printf("Neuron number=%d  Input number=%d",neuron_num,neuron_inp);
  printf("  Input=%f\n",inpt[neuron_inp]);
  printf("  Weight=%f",weight[neuron_num][neuron_inp]);
  printf("  Contribution=%f\n",product);
  sum[neuron_num]=sum[neuron_num] + product;
  gets(&cr); }}
printf("**** IS THE THRESHOLD EXCEEDED ****\n");
for(neuron_num=0;neuron_num<2;neuron_num++) {
 outpt[neuron_num]=0;
 /* If threshold is exceeded, output is a one, i.e., fires */
 if(sum[neuron_num] > threshold) outpt[neuron_num]=1;
 else outpt[neuron_num]=0;
 printf("Output neuron %d = %d\n",neuron_num,outpt[neuron_num]); }
printf("**** END OF NEURAL NETWORK TRYOUT ****\n");
printf("Do you want to end session=2, another tryout=1, ");
printf("more training=0? ");
scanf("%d",&train_flag);
fflush(stdin);
if(train_flag==2) try_out=2;
} /* while train_flag */
} /* while try_out */
}
```

Bibliography and Recommended Readings

The following is a list and description of books and articles related to the subject matter of this book. The description discusses each book and article with regard to individual subject matter.

Books

Barr, A., and E. A. Feigenbaum: *The Handbook of Artificial Intelligence Volumes I and II.* HeurisTech Press and William Kaufmann, Inc., Los Altos, CA, 1981.

Cohn, P. R. and E. A. Feigenbaum: *The Handbook of Artificial Intelligence Volume III,* HeurisTech Press and William Kaufmann, Inc., Los Altos, CA, 1982.
All topics discussed in our book are also discussed in a more mathematically rigorous way in one of the volumes of *The Handbook*.

Clocksin, W. F. and C. S. Mellish: *Programming in PROLOG,* Springer-Verlag New York, Inc., 1984.
PROLOG is discussed throughout the book. Many well-illustrated examples are used to explain the concepts. Backward chaining and backtracking are discussed in Chapter 1, "Tutorial Introduction," and Chapter 4, "Backtracking and Cuts." Natural language processing and other areas related to artificial intelligence have working examples in the later chapters.

Graham, Neil: *Artificial Intelligence—Making Machines "Think,"* TAB Books Inc., Blue Ridge Summit, PA, 1979.
Semantic nets are discussed on pages 203–205. Examples are included. Object-oriented programming is discussed under the topics "Property Lists" (pages 201–203), and "Frames" (pages 205–207). Examples are included. Natural language processing is discussed on pages 209–219.

Hayes-Roth, F., D. A. Waterman, and D. B. Lenat: *Building Expert Systems,* Addison-Wesley Publishing Co. Inc., Reading, MA, 1983.
Blackboard concept is discussed in the way it's used in two expert systems, Age and Hearsay. Fuzzy applications and certainty factors are discussed under the topic "Unreliable Data or Knowledge" (pages 93–96).

Lipschutz, S.: *Finite Mathematics,* McGraw-Hill Book Company, New York, 1966.
Use of probability and fuzzy conditions in expert systems is discussed in terms of conditional probability and Bayes theorems in Chapter 18. In addition, it covers inter-

esting concepts such as Markov chains (Chapter 20) and game theory (Chapter 25) which can be applied to expert systems engaged in winning strategies.

Naylor, Chris: *Build Your Own Expert System,* Halsted Press, a Division of John Wiley and Sons Inc., New York, 1983.
Use of probability and fuzzy conditions in expert systems is discussed in terms of probability theory in the design of expert systems. Many programming examples are included. Automated learning concepts are initially provided via a simple learning program (page 37) which is enhanced as you continue reading.

Negoita, C. N.: *Expert Systems and Fuzzy Systems,* The Benjamin/Cummings Publishing Co., Menlo Park, CA, 1985.
Certainty factors are discussed under the topic "Degrees of Belief" (pages 27–30). Use of probability and fuzzy conditions in expert systems is discussed in terms of fuzzy conditions. Linguistic variables and hedges are discussed throughout the book. Under the topic "Production Rules Can Be Derived from Verbal Models" (pages 74–77) two tables are presented which show the affects of hedges. The book contains an extensive bibliography on the subject matter.

Winston, P. H. and B. K. P. Horn: *LISP,* Addison-Wesley Publishing Co. Inc., Reading, MA, 1981.
LISP is discussed throughout the book. There is a section of the book which produces answers to all the problems. Object-oriented programming is also discussed. Chapter 5, "Properties, A-Lists, Arrays, and Access Functions," provides some basics. Chapter 22, "Frames," discusses objects, slots, inheritance, demons, and active values. Backward and forward chaining is discussed in Chapter 8, "Expert Problem Solving Using IF-THEN Rules."

Articles

The articles are listed by subject matter.

Fuzzy Logic

Zadeh, L. A.: "Making Computers Think Like People" *IEEE SPECTRUM,* vol. 21, no. 8, August 1984, pp. 26–32.

General Overview of Artificial Intelligence

Hayes-Roth, F.: "The Knowledge-Based Expert Systems: A Tutorial," *IEEE COMPUTER,* vol. 17, no. 9, September 1984, pp. 11–28.

Knowledge Representation
(Semantic Nets, PROLOG, etc.)

IEEE COMPUTER vol. 16, no. 10 October, 1983.

Object-Oriented Programming

Cox, B. J.: "Message/Object Programming: An Evolutionary Change in Programming Technology," *IEEE SOFTWARE,* vol. 1, no. 1, Jauary, 1984, pp. 51–61.
Mudge, T. N.: "Object Based Computing and the Ada Language," *IEEE COMPUTER,* vol. 18, no. 3, March 1985, pp 11–19.

References for Chapters on Expert Systems

Financial Planning

Casey, Douglas: *Crisis Investing*, Pocket Books, Simon & Schuster Publishing Co., New York, 1979.

Huang, Stanley: *Investment Analysis and Management*, Little, Brown & Co., Boston, 1981.

Weinstein, Grace W.: *The Lifetime Book of Money Management*, The New American Library, Inc., New York, 1983.

Sales

Buzzotte, V. R., R. E. Lefton, and M. Sherberg: *Effective Selling through Psychology*, Psychological Associates, 1981.

Haas, Kenneth, and J. W. Ernest: *Creative Salesmanship, Understanding Essentials*, Glencoe Publishing Co., Inc., Encino, CA, 1974.

Learning Evaluation System

Brutten, Milton, Sylvia Richardson, and Charles Mangel: *Something's Wrong with My Child*, Harcourt Brace Jovanovich, New York, 1973.

DeHirsch, Katrina: "Learning Disabilities: An Overview," *Bulletin*, N.Y. Academy of Medicine, vol. 50, no. 4, April 1974.

Green, L. J.: *Kids Who Hate School; A Survival Handbook on Learning Disabilities*, Humanics Press, Atlanta, GA, 1984.

Machalaba, Danielle, "Hidden Handicap; For Americans Unable to Read Well, Life Is a Series of Small Crises," *Wall Street Journal*, Tuesday, January 17, 1984.

Sanders, Marion: *Clinical Assessment of Learning Problems*, Allyn & Bacon, Inc., Newton, MA, 1978.

Neural Networks

Brown, Robert Jay: "An Artificial Neural Network Experiment," *Dr. Dobb's Journal*, April 1987.

Caudill, Maureen: "Neural Network Primer (many parts)," *AI Expert Magazine*, San Francisco, CA, December 1987.

Jorgensen, Chuck, and Chris Matheus: "Catching in Neural," *AI Expert Magazine*, December 1986.

Index

For your convenience, a disk containing all the programs listed in this book can be purchased for the IBM Personal Computer. Please send $10.95 to:

Intelligent Tutoring Series
P.O. Box 1600
North Massapequa, NY 11758

Allow two weeks for delivery. Please specify C version.

Also available from the authors is a tutorial disk entitled "The Intelligent Tutoring Series." For more information, write to the above address.